Crime and Crime Reduction

The problems associated with groups that commit crime are well known and notoriously complex. However, there are many questions that we still cannot answer with certainty. This book seeks to deepen understanding of the group processes involved in crime and the treatment of offenders' thoughts and behavior. Together, the chapters in this volume address the following questions:

- Are people more likely to commit crime because of the influence of their group?
- Does group membership cause people to become criminals, or does the group merely foster people's pre-existing criminal inclinations?
- How does group membership exert such a strong hold on people so that some risk imprisonment or even death, rather than relinquish their membership?

The contributors to *Crime and Crime Reduction* consider the social psychological influences of groups and specific forms of group crime such as street and prison gangs, terrorism, organized criminal networks, and group sexual offending. The book also addresses important questions about the role of groups in treating offenders, and why existing group membership should be considered when treating offenders.

Group criminal activity is a key area of study for researchers and for students of forensic psychology and criminology courses. This book will therefore be of interest to students, scholars, and law enforcement practitioners who want to understand the group processes involved in crime and its reduction.

Jane L. Wood is a Chartered Forensic Psychologist, Director of the MSc in Forensic Psychology and Senior Lecturer in Forensic Psychology at CORE-FP, School of Psychology at the University of Kent, UK.

Theresa A. Gannon is Director of the Centre for Research and Education in Forensic Psychology (CORE-FP) and Reader in Forensic Psychology at the University of Kent, UK.

Crime and Crime Reduction
The importance of group processes

**Edited by Jane L. Wood and
Theresa A. Gannon**

Routledge
Taylor & Francis Group

LONDON AND NEW YORK

First published 2013
by Routledge
27 Church Road, Hove, East Sussex, BN3 2FA

Simultaneously published in the USA and Canada
by Routledge
711 Third Avenue, New York, NY 10017

Routledge is an imprint of the Taylor & Francis Group, an informa business

British Library Cataloguing in Publication Data
A catalogue record for this book is available from the British Library

Library of Congress Cataloging in Publication Data
A catalog record for this book has been requested

ISBN: 978-1-84872-083-1 (hbk)
ISBN: 978-0-20309-769-4 (ebk)

Typeset in Times
by Saxon Graphics Ltd, Derby

MIX
Paper from responsible sources
FSC
www.fsc.org   FSC® C004839

Printed and bound in Great Britain by the MPG Books Group

For Steve – always [JLW]

For Uncle David [TAG]

Contents

List of contributors

Dominic Abrams
School of Psychology
University of Kent
Canterbury
Kent

Emma Alleyne
CORE-FP
School of Psychology
Keynes College
University of Kent,
Canterbury
Kent, CT2 7NP

Emma Bradford
Institute of Psychology, Health and Society
Waterhouse Building, Block B, 2nd Floor
University of Liverpool
Brownlow Street
Liverpool L69 3GL
United Kingdom

David L. Burton
Smith College School for Social Work
302 Lilly Hall
Northampton, MA 01063

Vince Egan
Forensic Section
School of Psychology
University of Leicester
106 New Walk
Leicester
LE1 7EA

Scott Decker
School of Criminology & Criminal Justice
Arizona State University
411 North Central Avenue, Ste. 600, MC: 4420
Phoenix, AZ 85004-0685

Louise Dixon
School of Psychology
Frankland Building
University of Birmingham
Edgbaston
Birmingham
B15 2TT

Leigh Harkins
School of Psychology
Frankland Building
University of Birmingham
Edgbaston
Birmingham
B15 2TT

Karen Hennigan
Assistant Research Professor of Psychology
Department of Psychology
Seeley G. Mudd Building
1015 3620 South McClintock Ave.
University of Southern California
Los Angeles, CA 90089-1061

Lucy Lemanski
Institute of Psychology, Health and Society
Waterhouse Building, Block B, 2nd Floor
University of Liverpool
Brownlow Street
Liverpool L69 3GL
United Kingdom

Brian Lickel
Associate Professor
University of Massachusetts, Amherst
Department of Psychology
441 Tobin Hall
Amherst, MA 01003

Stephen Lock
Head of Group Business Protection
Old Mutual plc
Old Mutual Place
2 Lambeth Hill
London
EC4V 4GG, UK

Liam E. Marshall
Rockwood Psychological Services
303 Bagot Street, Suite 403
Kingston, ON, Canada, K7K 5W7

William L. Marshall
Rockwood Psychological Services
303 Bagot Street, Suite 403
Kingston, ON, Canada, K7K 5W7

David Pyrooz
School of Criminology & Criminal Justice
Arizona State University
411 North Central Avenue, Ste. 600, MC: 4420
Phoenix, AZ 85004-0685

Jo Thakker
School of Psychology
Faulty of Arts and Social Sciences
The University of Waikato
Gate 1, Knighton Road
Private Bag 3105
Hamilton 3240
New Zealand

Eduardo A. Vasquez, Ph.D.
School of Psychology
Keynes College
University of Kent
Canterbury, Kent
CT2 7NP, United Kingdom

G. Tendayi Viki
School of Psychology
University of Kent
Canterbury
Kent

Margaret Wilson
Institute of Psychology, Health and Society
Waterhouse Building, Block B, 2nd Floor
University of Liverpool
Brownlow Street
Liverpool L69 3GL
United Kingdom

Jane L. Wood
CORE-FP
School of Psychology
Keynes College
University of Kent,
Canterbury
Kent, CT2 7NP

Preface

Having conducted research examining individual criminal activity for a number of years, it has been striking how many offenders refer to the influence that their group affiliations had on their offending careers. Of course, this may simply be a way of justifying their crimes. But for some, it may be a valid argument: research has shown that being a member of a group can influence people to become more criminal than they would if they acted alone (e.g. Bendixen *et al.*, 2006; Klein *et al.*, 2006). So, it seems that there are people who at the individual level, may or may not be especially criminally inclined, yet as group members they create alarm for governments, neighborhoods, and entire social structures. Terrorist groups, street gangs, and organized crime groups are well-known and well-feared entities – justifiably so. And the existence of such groups suggests that there is something dynamic about group membership that amplifies or elicits individual criminal inclinations.

To date, few texts have focused specifically on why group membership is relevant to individual criminal behavior. The purpose of this book is to begin to bridge this gap by presenting the actual and potential influence that group membership has in criminal events and the treatment of offenders. Although an examination of group crime is established in some areas of research, the influence of group membership is yet to be fully synthesized in other forensic topics, and this is reflected in some of our chapters. Our aim is therefore to emphasize the importance that should be given to group membership when considering individual criminal behavior and its treatment.

The book is organized into three parts. In the first part we examine the psychology of groups and group crime. In the first chapter Tendayi Viki and Dominic Abrams set the scene by providing an in-depth examination of the powerful influence that group membership can have on individuals. The authors provide social psychological theoretical and empirical explanations of the compelling and enduring influence that group membership has on our individual thoughts, feelings, and behavior. Thus, this chapter provides an important empirically based backdrop for taking group influences into account when examining individual's criminal activity.

In Chapter 2 we begin to examine specific criminal groups. Jane Wood and Emma Alleyne consider the group processes that underpin street gang membership.

Gang structure, leadership, female membership, and the motivation for joining gangs are examined in turn. The authors provide a critical examination of the ability of existing theories to explain gang membership and speculate on the role that psychological theory and research could play in advancing our understanding of street gangs.

Chapter 3 expands on the concepts raised in Chapter 2 by examining specific psychological influences on the group aggression of street gangs. Eduardo Vasquez, Brian Lickel, and Karen Hennigan consider how group-based aggression as seen in a street gang context may be facilitated by psychological processes such as rumination. The authors speculate how rumination may promote not only inter-gang aggression but also the targeting of innocent individuals without provocation. The chapter evaluates models of displaced aggression and the authors hypothesize the value of considering the ruminative thinking of gang members when tackling gang membership and aggression.

The fourth chapter concludes Part 1 of the book by examining the psychology of group sexual offending. The authors, Leigh Harkins and Louise Dixon, consider the psychological factors that contribute to individuals' involvement in group sexual offenses against children and adults. The chapter evaluates how individual, sociocultural, and situational factors contribute to group sexual offending and examines these in context (e.g. rape committed during war, pedophile organizations, and rape in a fraternity setting). The authors also consider specific factors that promote group sexual offending such as male bonding and discuss the contribution that theories of group behavior can offer to group perpetrated sexual offending.

Part 2 focuses on criminal networks and crime. In Chapter 5 Margaret Wilson, Emma Bradford, and Lucy Lemanski take a critical view of terrorism by examining how terrorist networks emerge from the group influences exerted on individuals. The chapter considers the motivations and benefits that underpin membership of terrorist groups and whether people enter terrorist groups as innocents or as individuals with a cause to address. The authors note how terrorist organizations may be initiated and maintained through subtle psychological influences on individual members and challenge some of the prevailing assumptions regarding motivations to become terrorists.

Vincent Egan and Steven Lock continue the criminal network theme by providing an engaging discussion of organized crime in Chapter 6. The authors define organized crime and describe how it is embedded in criminal activity such as drug and people trafficking. The chapter describes the social context in which organized crime emerges and the social and cultural motivations for its continuance. The authors highlight the importance of organized crime networking, the consequences of organized crime activities, the fluidity and adaptability of organized crime group structure, and the methods that individuals employ to maintain their status in the criminal hierarchy of an organized crime network.

Chapter 7 concludes Part 2 of the book. Marie Griffin, David Pyrooz, and Scott Decker evaluate an international body of research that examines prison gangs. The authors evaluate findings that explain how prison gangs form, their activities, the interface between prison and street gangs and the impact that such groups have on prisons and prisoners. This chapter concludes by considering the myriad of problems associated with accurately identifying prison gang members and the consequences for prisoners who are identified as such.

In Part 3 we present the final two chapters of the book which focus on the relevance of groups in the treatment of offenders. In Chapter 8 William Marshall, David Burton, and Liam Marshall assess the positive value of group work in achieving treatment goals when treating mental disorders generally and sexual offenders specifically in a clinical setting. The authors point out that group work is considered by some to be more effective than individual therapy. They also highlight how a positive group environment that challenges and supports offenders works to maximize treatment benefits for individuals. The importance of group cohesiveness and group expressiveness are emphasized as essential pre-conditions to facilitate a positive change in offenders that will benefit society by a reduction in offending.

In the final chapter Jo Thakker concludes the book by examining the importance of existing group membership in terms of reducing criminal offending. The chapter contemplates the important role that an individual's group membership (e.g. religious, ethnic, or even group commitment) can have on the success of treatment and rehabilitation. This chapter also highlights that an individual's religious beliefs may be used in treatment as a foundation for rehabilitation as the individual searches for a meaning in his/her life. By discussing these and other potential group membership influences, this chapter provides a critical examination of whether group membership is/should be considered when devising or implementing interventions to prevent future offending and draws the book to a positive and yet thought provoking close.

References

Bendixen, M., Endresen, I. M., and Olweus, D. (2006). Joining and leaving gangs: selection and facilitation effects on self-reported antisocial behaviour in early adolescence. *European Journal of Criminology, 3,* 85–114.

Klein, M. W., Weerman, F. M., and Thornberry, T. P. (2006). Street gang violence in Europe. *European Journal of Criminology, 3*, 413–437.

Acknowledgements

The potential influences of groups on individuals in committing crime and in reducing crime are extensive. It is no mean feat to collate and evaluate the complex evidence associated with group influences on offenders. So, we owe a huge debt to all the authors in this book for the time, thought and considerable effort they devoted to producing such thought provoking chapters that are not only so high in quality, but also accessible to all levels of readership. We also owe many thanks to those who have offered support and advice when we needed it most. We would like to thank our own group – the forensic research team for providing such a positive environment in which to work. We would also like to thank our colleagues – from various institutions – who have shaped our thinking on aspects of forensic psychology over the years. Those who spring to mind in specific relation to the ideas that led to the formation of this book are Tony Beech, Scott Decker, Bill Marshall, Tony Ward and the many members of the Eurogang network. Special thanks go to Tara Stebnicky for initially supporting our efforts to get this book off the ground and also Raz, Sharla and Louise at Psychology Press for dealing with the various queries and amendments that we proposed. Finally, we would like to thank our families (Doreen, Lydia, Becca, Sam, and Bobs [JLW]; Jim [TAG]) for their love, friendship and support.

Part 1

The psychology of groups and group crime

1 The social influence of groups on individuals

G. Tendayi Viki and Dominic Abrams,
University of Kent, United Kingdom

Part of the human experience is having a certain level of self-awareness or a sense of self (Lewis, 1990). Indeed, self-concept is considered a psychological resource that can influence life situations and life outcomes (Byrne, 1996; Harris, 1995; Oyserman, 2004). Historically, a large proportion of research in psychology has examined the role of social influence on the self by focusing almost exclusively on the individual as a unit of analysis (Allport, 1924; Zajonc, 1980). This approach is consistent with the dominant western legal tradition that also focuses on individual accountability via the concepts of *actus rea* and *mens rea* (Hamdani, 2007). However, such an approach often ignores the fact that human beings are also social animals (Brooks, 2011; Aronson, 2003). William James (1890/1950) argued that people's self-concept can be strongly influenced by the various social relationships they have. People may experience shifts in identity depending on the social context and whom they are interacting with (Abrams & Hogg, 2004). Thus, in as much as the self can be thought of as unique, the self is also social in nature.

In fact, the importance of social life to human beings cannot be over-emphasised. Even apparently individualistic concepts such as self-esteem can be viewed through a social lens. Leary and colleagues argue that self-esteem often indicates people's perceptions of how other people view them, reflecting one's perception of their level of social inclusion versus exclusion (Leary & Downs, 1995; Leary *et al.*, 1995; see also Kirkpatrick & Ellis, 2004). Further to this, individuals can derive their self-esteem from their group memberships. For example, basking in reflected glory (or BIRGing) is a process through which individuals increase their association with successful groups (e.g. sports teams; Cialdini *et al.*, 1976). It is also important to note that it is not only physically present groups that can exert their influence. Individuals act on the basis of their group membership even when other group members are absent (Hogg & Abrams, 1988).

Group membership plays an important role in criminal behavior. Several examples of this can be cited including religion-based terrorism (Taylor & Louis, 2004 – see also Wilson *et al.*, Chapter 2), gang membership (Wood & Alleyne, 2010), football violence (Stott *et al.*, 2006) and deviant sub-cultures (Holt, 2010). Social norms also prescribe how serious certain crimes are perceived to be, and how people should respond to certain types of criminals. This is reflected, for example, in social attitudes towards acquaintance rape (Abrams *et al.*, 2003), compared to social attitudes toward paedophilia (Sample & Bray, 2006). In this chapter, we will explore the influence that groups have on individual behavior. We present theoretical arguments and empirical evidence concerning important psychological processes through which groups affect individual behavior (i.e. social categorization). Understanding such processes can provide a context for further examining how group membership can influence criminal activity. In this regard, our goal is to provide the theoretical and empirical backdrop to the rest of the chapters in this book.

Accounts of groups as overarching individuals

At one theoretical extreme, there are researchers who argue that the group supersedes the individual (e.g. Wundt, 1916). According to these researchers social phenomenon such as religion, language and customs cannot be understood through the analysis of the thoughts and beliefs of individuals. Durkheim (1898) argued that social forces or social facts have a life of their own that overrides individual members of society. Furthermore, such social phenomena are not the same as individual attitudes or beliefs and cannot be understood as an aggregate of individual attitudes.

Similar arguments have also been proposed in some criminological theorizing on the social factors that cause criminal behavior. The dominant theories here include cultural deviance theories (Shaw & McKay, 1942), strain theories (Merton, 1938) and theories of social disorganization (Thrasher, 1927). According to these theories criminal behavior emerges as a result of powerful social factors. For example, Thrasher (1927) argued that economic instability leads to *social disorganization*, which then leads to a breakdown in social institutions (e.g. church, family and schools). Such a breakdown then results in a weakening of the institutions that control social behavior and a subsequent increase in criminality. However, these criminological theories describe social forces that result in criminal behavior without directly considering the psychology of the individual actors in this context (see Wood & Alleyne, 2010 for a review). Although it may be the case that certain social factors increase the likelihood of criminal behavior, these factors do not *necessarily* result in criminality (Caroll *et al.*, 2001).

There is no denying the powerful effects of groups on individuals. The conformity experiments of Solomon Asch provide a powerful example of this (Asch, 1951). However, it is important to explore the psychological processes through which group membership influences individual behavior. Such an exploration is not similar to the denial or neglect of the social group that is found in some psychological research and theorizing (e.g. Allport, 1924). Rather, it is a synthesis that recognizes that people have both personal and social identities (Turner *et al.*, 1994). What is important is to examine when, why and how social identities come to influence individual action. The remainder of this chapter will focus on this question by examining theoretical approaches and empirical evidence.

The social group as a comparative context

One view of the group's influence on the individual posits that the group provides a comparative context through which individuals come to understand themselves and make decisions about their behavior (Baumeister, 1999; Higgins, 1987; Steele, 1988; Tesser, 1988). This approach includes topics such as self-regulation, self-evaluation, self-affirmation and reputation enhancement (Caroll *et al.*, 2001). For example, self-discrepancy theory argues that people make comparisons between their current state and an external reference point, such as significant others (Higgins, 1987). According to this theory, people are motivated to reduce any discrepancy between their current state and the state to which they aspire. In this regard, the group can influence behavior through the individual's motivation to reduce any discrepancy between their current state and that of a valued social group.

Similarly self-evaluation maintenance theory endorses the view that people seek to maintain or increase a positive self-evaluation (Tesser, 1988). This process may involve a psychological contrast between the self and others. In order to maintain a positive self-evaluation people make comparisons on dimensions that are relevant to their self-evaluation and feel good when they are different from or more successful than others (Tesser, 1988). For dimensions that are less relevant to their self-evaluation, people are happy to bask in the reflected glory of the success of others. In other words, people avoid similarity with others on dimensions that are relevant for self-evaluation and seek personal distinctiveness on relevant attributes (Abrams & Hogg, 2004; Ciadini *et al.*, 1976). In this context, the group influences behavior via individuals' motivation to seek a positive self-evaluation.

One way to obtain such a positive self-evaluation is through reputation enhancement (Emler & Reicher, 1995). Reputation enhancement theory posits that an individual chooses a particular self-image they want to enhance in front of a certain audience (Caroll *et al.*, 2001; Emler & Reicher, 1995). This audience then provides feedback that allows the individual to maintain a certain identity within their community. Delinquency and criminal behavior can thus be viewed as being motivated by social goals related to reputation enhancement (Emler & Reicher, 1995). This makes such reputations social phenomena that are produced via social processes (Caroll *et al.*, 2001). According to Hopkins and Emler (1990), people must be part of a connected and stable community in order to develop their reputations. Further, contact with like-minded peers provides a highly influential audience with regard to reputation enhancement and maintenance (Emler & Reicher, 1995).

An interesting aspect of the above theories is that there is no in-depth discussion of social identity, group process or even intergroup relations. However, Hogg (2004: 203) argues that groups only exist 'by virtue of there being outgroups'. To understand the impact of group membership on individual behavior, it is important to consider the meta-context in which groups exist. This combination of *intra*group and *inter*group processes gives rise to social identities and their subsequent influence on individual behavior (Hogg & Abrams, 1988). It is also important to note that some criminal activity emanates from intergroup conflict (e.g. terrorism or gang violence – as noted in this volume). As such, the role of intergroup processes in criminal behavior cannot be ignored.

Social categorization and group behavior

According to Hogg (2004), any examination of group behavior requires the consideration of social categorization processes, and an analysis of the relationships between these social categories. The social identity approach (SIA), which includes social identity theory (SIT) and self-categorization theory (SCT), has been the most influential contemporary approach for exploring group process and intergroup relations (Hogg & Abrams, 1988; Tajfel & Turner, 1979; Turner, 1999). The core tenet of SIA is that part of a person's self-concept is derived from the social groups that they belong to (Hogg & Reid, 2006; Tajfel, 1972). Based on the work of Henri Tajfel (e.g. Tajfel, 1969; Tajfel et al., 1971), this approach views most group processes emanating from the basic psychological process of *categorization*. As a cognitive process, categorization is highly essential in perceptually organizing a potentially chaotic world (Bruner, 1957). Categorization provides a highly adaptive way to manage the infinite variety of stimuli in the world. This renders the world predictable and allows people to plan for current and future actions.

Social categorization is, therefore, the application of the basic categorization processes to social stimuli. According to SIT, social categorization serves two main purposes. First, social categorization allows people to understand their social environment. Categorization gives meaning to social stimuli and provides a 'causal understanding of the social environment' (Tajfel, 1978: 61). Second, social categorization serves a *self-referencing* function (Oakes, 2004). People need to have a meaningful self-concept or a meaningful interpretation of their place in a social structure. Social categorization provides individuals with an understanding of their social place and this knowledge influences attitudes and behavior (Oakes, 2004). For example, categorizing oneself as a gang member provides a meaningful understanding of one's relationship with members of other gangs, non-gang members and the police. This understanding then forms the basis for action in social contexts.

According to SCT, social categorization is based on prototypes. These prototypes are not necessarily a scientific set of attributes. Prototypes can be viewed as a fuzzy set of attributes which define a particular category's prototype (Turner et al., 1987). Such prototyping can be based on perceived 'typical' group members, but this is not necessarily the case. Sometimes prototypes can be extreme and non-representative of any member of the group (Hogg, 2004). These prototypes form the basis of the *meta-contrast principle* through which social categorization maximises the perceived similarities within the group and the perceived differences between groups (Turner, et al., 1994; Tajfel & Wilkes, 1963). Research shows that there is an asymmetry in this process, such that outgroups are perceived as being more homogenous than the ingroup (Bartsch & Judd, 1993; Judd & Park, 1988). This is referred to as the *outgroup homogeneity effect* (Judd & Park, 1988; Mullen & Hu, 1989). However, research also shows that minority groups tend to perceive the *ingroup* as more homogenous than the *outgroup* (Simon, 1992).

It is important to note that, because they serve to maximize differences between groups, prototypes are context dependent (Turner *et al.*, 1994). As such, the nature of the prototype can depend on which groups are being compared (e.g. our gang vs. another gang; or our gang vs. the police). Another important aspect of social categorization is that it involves the self in a comparative context with others (Hogg, 2004). In an intergroup context, a person can come to view herself as being more similar or even interchangeable with other ingroup members, and different from outgroup members (Hogg & Abrams, 1988). In the same way that outgroup members are stereotyped based on the perceived outgroup prototype, people will also categorize themselves and *self-stereotype* on the basis of the ingroup prototype (Turner *et al.*, 1994). This process is referred to as *depersonalization* and results in individuals viewing themselves in terms of the ingroup prototype rather than as unique individuals. Thus, depersonalization is what makes group behavior psychologically possible (Hogg, 2004).

In line with Tajfel's theorizing, SCT also highlights the notion that personal identities and social identities are mutually exclusive, but equally valid conceptions of the self (Oakes, 1996). Individuals cannot simultaneously act as unique individuals and group members. Furthermore, SCT provides an account of when individuals will act as group members. Researchers have found that people act as group members when social categories are *salient*. Category salience is determined by an interaction between the social *category-stimulus fit* and the persons *readiness* to perceive the categories (Oakes, 1987). Readiness refers to the relative accessibility of the social category based on a person's previous experience, knowledge, and motivations (Turner *et al.*, 1994). These factors mean that a person may be ready to use particular categories that are relevant and useful within the social context.

Category-stimulus fit is based on two factors: comparative fit and normative fit. *Comparative fit* is based on the notion that a set of stimuli will be categorised as belonging to one group when 'average differences between those stimuli are less than the average difference between them and the remaining stimuli that make up the frame of reference' (Turner *et al.*, 1994: 455). *Normative fit* is based on the content of the social categories. The idea is that it is not enough for there to be perceived difference. The difference must also be in the expected direction (Oakes *et al.*, 1991). For example, when comparing gang members and the police, differences in attitudes and behavior must be in the expected direction. On the basis of readiness and fit, social categorization occurs either due to the accessibility of the relevant category for the individual or because the situation renders the categories accessible (Hogg, 2004). When social categories are not salient, group behavior does not occur. Instead, individuals will act on the basis of their unique individual identities. However, when an ingroup – outgroup distinction is salient, individuals' actions become group-based rather than interpersonal (Oakes, 2004). That is, people treat members within a group (including themselves), as if they are interchangeable representatives of the group rather than unique individuals. This forms the basis for the social influence of groups on individual behavior.

Motivation and social categorization

As noted above, there are important motivational concerns that drive social categorization processes. People are motivated to have a positive view of themselves (the self-esteem hypothesis; Hogg & Abrams, 1988). People are also motivated to reduce their uncertainty about the world (Hogg, 2000). These motives of *self-enhancement* and *uncertainty reduction* lead people to seek positive social identities. In fact, Tajfel (1978) defined social identification as not only one's knowledge of the groups they belong to (i.e. self-categorization), but also the emotional value that one attaches to those groups. As such, people are motivated to be members of groups that are *positively distinct* (Abrams & Hogg, 2004). Research shows that such motivation often means that, to the extent that people identify with their ingroup, they are likely to exhibit a bias toward that ingroup.

Tajfel *et al.* (1971) demonstrated the ingroup bias effect using *minimal groups*. Minimal groups are groups without prior history that are created within a laboratory by researchers on the basis of virtually meaningless procedures (e.g. groups created by random allocation). This act of mere categorization appears to inspire the motive of self-enhancement which gives meaning even to the minimal groups, resulting in ingroup bias (Tajfel, 1972; Wilder, 1986). Due to the fact that the self and the group are now viewed as interchangeable, the group's goals and norms become the individual's goals and norms (Hogg & Reid, 2006). This creates the psychological process through which the social group influences individual behavior and the strength of this influence becomes apparent when it occurs even with meaningless group situations.

The social identity approach provides a comprehensive theoretical account of how groups come to influence individual behavior. Research in several domains has provided strong empirical support for the theoretical tenets of social identity theory and self-categorization theory. This research spans various domains ranging from decision making to deviance. Below we provide a review of some of this research and show how it can relate to the question of how groups may influence criminal behavior. This review is not meant to be comprehensive but to provide a flavour of research that further demonstrates the powerful effect of group membership on individual behavior.

Social identity and normative behavior

According to Hogg and Reid (2006), prototypes form the basis of group norms. What makes prototypes powerful in group behavior is the fact that they are shared among the group members. As noted above, these prototypes describe and prescribe the defining features of acceptable behavior from group members (Turner *et al.*,

1994). Thus, from a social identity perspective 'group prototypes are group norms' (Hogg & Reid, 2006: 11). This conception has implications for the notion that people follow norms because they fear the social sanctions that may come from norm violation (e.g. Rimal & Real, 2003). The social identity approach argues that people behave according to ingroup norms, not only because they fear negative judgements, but also because these ingroup norms have become part of the individual's internalized self-definition. Due to the fact that depersonalization results in individuals viewing themselves in terms of their group membership, conformity to the group's norms becomes a way to uphold one's self concept. Thus, the effects of norms are likely to be stronger for individuals who strongly identify with the group (see below and Abrams *et al.*, 1990).

The process through which social identification influences self-regulation is described in the social self-regulation model (SSR; Abrams, 1996). This model combines the research on social categorization and behavioral self-regulation. The model proposes that identity salience (self-categorization) and attention focus are separate elements in the regulation of social behavior. Four conditions are considered by the SSR model; high versus low identity salience and high versus low self-attention (Abrams & Hogg, 2004). When both identity salience and self-attention are low, behavior is more likely to be task focused. In contrast, when both identity salience and self-attention are high, behavior is more likely to be based on social identity (Fenigstein & Abrams, 1993). For example, in contexts in which there is consistent normative information from the ingroup, heightened self-attention may result in people engaging in self-stereotyping and ingroup bias (Abrams, 1996; Abrams & Hogg; 2004).

Social identity and social influence

In social situations people may seek objective information about reality from others (Cooper *et al.*, 2004). People may also seek to be accepted and may conform to social norms in order to gain social approval (Cooper *et al.*, 2004). These two forms of social influence are referred to as *informational* and *normative* social influence, respectively (Deutsch & Gerrard, 1955). However, research shows that people do not accept social influence from just any social group. People are more willing to accept influence from ingroups, especially those who are highly identified with the ingroup (Cooper *et al.*, 2004). This may partly account for why criminal behavior is higher among individuals who are gang members than it is even among the most prolifically offending non-gang youth (Klein *et al.*, 2006; Wood & Alleyne, 2010). Since individuals are more willing to accept influence from ingroup members social pressures towards criminality might be higher for people involved in gangs compared to those individuals who are not involved in gangs.

Informational social influence

Research on informational social influence has shown that in ambiguous situations, people look to others to gain an objective understanding of the world. For example,

Sherif (1935) placed groups of participants in a dark room and asked them to estimate the distance that was moved by a small light. This study examined a visual phenomenon known as the *autokinetic effect* in which people see the light to be moving when it is not. Sherif (1935) found that at the beginning people's estimates were very different from each other. However, after several trials when participants had heard each other's predictions, their estimates became more similar. This research suggests that when making objective decisions in ambiguous situations people tend to rely on others' judgements.

Interestingly, Abrams and colleagues found that informational influence is affected by the nature of the group that people are interacting with (Abrams *et al.*, 1990; Cooper *et al.*, 2004). In an experiment on the autokinetic effect, Abrams *et al.* (1990) manipulated the extent to which people viewed themselves as group members. They found that participants' estimates were more likely to converge in the condition in which participants viewed themselves as members of one group. Convergence was less likely to occur in the condition in which individuals viewed themselves as distinct from others. Thus, even when seeking objective information people are more likely to rely on the ingroup versus the outgroup (Cooper *et al.*, 2004).

Normative social influence

Normative influence is best indicated by the classic experiment by Solomon Asch (1951). In this study, people were asked to estimate the lengths of lines. Participants indicated their estimation after hearing estimates from others. The 'others' were all confederates of the experimenter and sometimes gave answers that were clearly wrong. Asch (1951) found that over 70 per cent of participants conformed with the wrong answer at least once. Similar to informational influence, research has also shown that normative influence is affected by the nature of the group people are doing the task with (Cooper *et al.*, 2004). Abrams *et al.* (1990) had people make their length estimates with either ingroup members or outgroup members. They found people were more likely to conform publicly (i.e. views presented in front of the group) but not privately (i.e. views expressed just to the researcher) when with an ingroup. In contrast, people were more likely conform privately (vs. publicly) when with outgroup members. This research shows that people value social approval from ingroup members (and so will agree with them, even if they believe they are wrong) more than they do from outgroup members.

Social identity and attitude-behavior consistency

Early social psychologists were engaged in a debate about whether attitudes and behavior were connected. Wicker (1969) argued that there was very weak evidence for such a relationship. Since then, research has provided evidence for situations in which attitudes might be predictive of behavior. For example, there is now an accepted notion that specific attitudes predict specific behaviors (Ajzen, 1991). Research has also highlighted the importance of social norms in attitude-behavior consistency. The theory of planned behavior (TPB) proposes that *subjective norms* (the importance attached to significant others' opinions) are as important as personal *attitudes towards the behavior* and *perceived behavioral control* (perception of ease or difficulty to perform behavior) in determining the behavioral intentions based on a particular attitude (Ajzen & Fishbein, 2000). However, research findings on the role of subjective norms have been inconsistent. Some studies have shown a role for subjective norms while other researchers have found no effects (Cooper *et al.*, 2004). This led Ajzen (1991) to conclude that attitudes and behavioral control may be more important than subjective norms in determining behavioral intentions.

Research from the social identity perspective has provided insights into when subjective norms play an important role. These researchers have argued that subjective norms are more likely to influence behavior when the relevant group membership is salient and important to the individual (Terry & Hogg, 1996). In their research, Terry and Hogg (1996) have shown that subjective norms only impact behavior when the referent group is an ingroup versus an outgroup. For example, Terry and Hogg (Study 1) found that group norms only influenced intentions to take exercise for individuals who identified strongly with referent group (i.e. university students). Terry and Hogg also showed that, in contrast to high identifiers, low identifiers were more likely to be influenced by personal factors.

In relation to criminal behavior, several researchers have applied the theory of planned behavior (e.g. Broadhead-Fearn & White, 2006; Tolman *et al.*, 1996). In contrast to what research has shown about the role of social factors in criminal behavior, these researchers have failed to find a role for subjective norms. Across most of this research perceived behavioral control has been the most important factor. For example, Tolman *et al.* (1996) examined TPB in the context of men's cessation of domestic violence. They found that perceived control was the strongest predictor of batterers' behavioral intentions. Similar results were found by Broadhead-Fearn and White (2006) in their research on rule-following behavior among homeless youths. It seems that future researchers in this area might consider the role of social identity in their TPB research. We propose that the consideration of social identity will produce research findings that people are more likely to be influenced by subjective norms emanating from the ingroup when deciding whether or not to engage in criminal behavior (cf. Terry & Hogg, 1996).

Social identity and pluralistic ignorance

Pluralistic ignorance refers to people's misperceptions of social norms (Prentice & Miller, 1996). This occurs when people privately reject a social norm but behave in a manner consistent with this norm because they perceive that others in their group accept the norm (O'Gorman, 1986). Prentice and Miller (1993) studied alcohol abuse at Princeton University and found that most students reported that they were personally not comfortable with the drinking habits of other students.

Interestingly, students were also found to rate other students as being more comfortable than themselves with student drinking habits. Such pluralistic ignorance has been implicated in criminal behavior. For example, Matza (1964) found pluralistic ignorance among members of juvenile gangs, who in private interviews expressed extreme discomfort with their criminal behavior when with the gang. Flezzani and Benshoff (2003) found that pluralistic ignorance was related to levels of sexual aggression among college students such that the higher the level of pluralistic ignorance, the greater the levels of sexual aggression. Examples of pluralistic ignorance have also been found in prison communities, where it may result in the development of anti-social behavior among inmates (Grekul, 1999), and less sympathetic behavior towards prisoners among prison officers (Kauffman, 1981). Interestingly, Grekul (1999) found that prison staff and inmates were more similar in their private attitudes than one would expect.

What is the role of social identity in pluralistic ignorance? This question is important because social identity theory argues that, to the extent the identity is salient, attitudes and behavior will always be consistent. Furthermore, this effect is likely to be stronger for people who identify strongly with their group. Reid *et al.* (2005) replicated the alcohol consumption study by Prentice and Miller (1993) at the University of California, Santa Barbara. They also assessed the extent to which participants viewed themselves as prototypical members of the ingroup (i.e. students). What they found was that students who considered themselves prototypical showed no signs of pluralistic ignorance. Their personal attitudes to alcohol consumption were the same as their perceived attitudes of the ingroup. In contrast, non-prototypical students showed pluralistic ignorance. Prototypicality was also related to self-reported drinking behavior, which was mediated by personal attitudes to drinking. Thus, students who viewed themselves as prototypical were more likely to report positive personal attitudes to drinking and also report higher levels of alcohol consumption.

The above research provides no support for *general* pluralistic ignorance, but shows that social identity plays a significant role. Future researchers in forensic contexts may want to consider social identity in their research. It may not be that gang members show pluralistic ignorance across the board. Prototypical or highly identified gang members may actually correctly perceive and endorse the group norm; and base their behavior on this perceived norm. In contrast, non-prototypical gang members (peripheral members or wannabes, see Wood & Alleyne, Chapter 2) may also correctly perceive but not endorse the group norm. Exploring social identity as a moderator will improve our understanding of pluralistic ignorance in group-based criminal behavior and also help in the designing of interventions targeting this behavior.

Social identity and group polarization

Group polarization refers to the consistent findings in social psychological research that people tend to polarize their attitudes after a discussion with a group of like-minded people (Isenberg, 1986; Moscovici & Zavalloni, 1969). This phenomenon was initially explored in Stoner's (1968) research on risk choices. Further research then demonstrated that this phenomenon extended beyond just decisions about risk, and includes group discussions about general attitude issues (Moscovici & Zavalloni, 1969). Indeed, Pynchon and Borum (1999) propose that group polarization might play a role in the development of attitudes in extremist groups involved in violence targeting civilian members of the public (see also Wilson *et al.*, Chapter 5).

Early attempts to account for group polarization focused on two main explanations. The first explanation is referred to as the *persuasive arguments* position (Burnstein, 1982). According to this explanation, people search for arguments in support of or against a particular attitude before stating their position (Burnstein & Vinokur, 1975). This search occurs prior to the group discussion. When the group finally comes together for the discussion people are more likely to be exposed to information they had not thought of before. Exposure to such new information is what results in attitude polarization because these new arguments strengthen people's initial opinions. The second explanation is referred to as the *social comparison* position (Jellison & Arkin, 1977). According to this theory, people are motivated to view themselves and present themselves in a socially favourable way (Sanders & Baron, 1977). This motivation is argued to result in what are termed 'band wagon' effects in which people shift to more extreme attitudes in order 'to hold a more favourable position than the rest of the group' (Cooper *et al.*, 2004: 253).

There is research evidence to support both the persuasive argument and the social comparisons positions (e.g. Kaplan & Miller, 1977; Blascovich *et al.*, 1975). However, reviewers have noted that neither explanation provides a full or sufficient account of all the results obtained in this field (Cooper *et al.*, 2004). A major issue concerns the fact that the two accounts form a *two-process dependency model* of group polarization (Hogg *et al.*, 1990). However, it is possible to provide a theoretical perspective that integrates both accounts and explains how they interact. The social identity approach offers such a solution by proposing that group polarization results from people conforming to a polarized norm from their ingroup. Discussions with ingroup members or information about ingroup member attitudes can result in a polarized norm being established, because the ingroup prototype is displaced away from the norms of contrasting groups. Group polarization then results from people conforming to this ingroup norm (Cooper *et al.*, 2004).

Several research studies have provided evidence that is consistent with the above argument. For example, Mackie (1986; see also Mackie & Cooper, 1984) found that people tend to view opinions from the ingroup as more extreme than the same opinions from outsiders. Furthermore, she found that people are more likely to polarize their attitudes in the direction of ingroup (vs. outsiders). This phenomenon was especially strong for individuals who identified with their ingroup. In support of the argument that polarization is the result of people conforming to a polarized norm, Mackie (1986) found a strong correlation between the extent of participants' attitude change (pre-test to post-test) and their estimates of the group norm. Interestingly, this correlation was only significant in the ingroup condition (Mackie, 1986).

Further evidence from the social identity approach was obtained by Hogg *et al.* (1990) who examined the intergroup context and noted that outgroup norms provide an important frame of reference for group polarization. In order to maximize intergroup differences, ingroup norms may be developed in a way that polarizes them away from relevant outgroup norms. Hogg *et al.* (1990) found that when people were confronted with a risky outgroup they developed a cautious ingroup norm. In contrast, when confronted with a cautious outgroup they polarized toward a risky ingroup norm (see also Turner *et al.*, 1989). These effects were partly explained by the extent to which people identified with their ingroup. As such, the research evidence seems to suggest that group polarization may indeed be a case of people conforming to polarized ingroup norms.

The development of ingroup norms that are polarized away from outgroups may provide a social identity based explanation for the development of criminal subcultures. These groups may be developing their norms by polarizing away from wider society (cf. Hogg & Reid, 2006). The above processes may actually lead to counterintuitive conclusions. In a recent paper, Dur and van der Weele (2011) argue that zero-tolerance policies to criminal behavior may not actually reduce crime due to the reduction of social signals that are tolerant to crime. Instead, they propose a new argument that is based on the dynamics of people's community social status. They argue that as zero-tolerance policies make it more costly to commit minor crimes (e.g. graffiti writing), 'gutless' people become less likely to commit these crimes. This then serves a signalling value that makes minor crimes an attractive alternative for 'tougher' people who would otherwise commit severe crimes (Dur & van der Weele, 2011).

Although not explicit in their paper, Dur and Van der Weele's (2011) argument appears to be consistent with the social identity perspective. The same types of crimes (i.e. minor crimes) take on a different social meaning depending on who is committing them. When perceived outgroups (e.g. the wider community) are committing these petty crimes, their identity value is reduced for people who value their social identity as 'tougher' people (e.g. gang members). However, when perceived outgroups now appear to be too scared to commit petty crimes, the identity value of these crime increases for 'tougher' people. This supports the argument that outgroup norms can form the basis for the ingroup to develop polarized norms (Hogg & Reid, 2006). Further research is needed to directly explore this question in forensic contexts.

Social identity and crowd behavior

Reicher (2004) describes crowds as the elephant man within the social sciences. He notes that crowds are viewed with a mixture of fascination and a perception that they are pathological. Despite this, crowd behavior is of significant importance in understanding the impact of groups on criminal behavior. Crowds are sometimes involved in criminal acts such as rioting, violence and destroying property (Stott *et al.*, 2008, 2006; Hoggett & Stott; 2010a). Early theorising about crowds viewed them as largely irrational, primitive and out of control (see Reicher, 2004 for a full review). The most prominent of these theories is that of Le Bon (1896) who argued that once individuals are part of a crowd they lose the ability to regulate their own behavior. Instead, they become immersed in the primitive psychology of the crowd and adopt a group mind which is largely irrational. Le Bon argued that people in crowds are open to contagion and their behavior can be largely unpredictable, violent and destructive. This view of crowds as irrational permeates much of early theorising; even in theoretical approaches that claim to focus on individuals (e.g. Allport, 1924).

Even as Le Bon's approach has started to fall into disrepute due to lack of consideration of group dynamics, his ideas still have a strong influence on public policy concerning crowd control. Hoggett and Stott (2010a) found that Le Bon's ideas are institutionalized in police crowd control training in the UK. Such ideas influence the decisions the police make about how to control crowds. Hoggett and Stott (2010b) found that when police hold the view that crowds are irrational, they are much more likely to employ strategies of mass containment or dispersal. Such approaches to crowd control have even received support from the UK High Court in 2005, which passed the judgement that mass containment of large crowds was legal in situations where there is potential for damage to property or violence (Hoggett & Stott, 2010a). However, the notion that crowds are irrational has been heavily criticized in more recent theorising and research.

Contemporary researchers have developed an alternative model of crowd behavior, based on social identity theory (e.g. Stott *et al.*, 2008; Reicher, 2004). This approach proposes that within crowds, behavior is based on a shared social identity among members of the group. Norms about appropriate behavior are derived from a shared prototype which emerges from these social categorization processes. Reicher (1982) notes that within crowds, group norms may be inferred from the behavior and attitudes of people that are viewed as prototypical group members. The key argument here is that people in crowds are not just a random collection of interacting individuals with a shared grievance. Rather, people in crowds are behaving as members of a particular social category, and their actions are informed by this group membership (Reicher 2004).

There is some empirical evidence to support this social identity model of crowd behavior. In their analysis of the St Pauls riot of 1980 in Bristol, Reicher and Potter (1985; see also Reicher, 1984) found that crowd behavior was not random. Rather there were limits to what people did. For example, violence first targeted only the police, and then only financial institutions and shops that were owned by people who were not from St Pauls. In fact, violence never went beyond the geographical boundaries of the St Pauls area. Members of the crowd also described themselves on the basis of their social identities which were defined in terms of being Black and being oppressed by the police (even though the majority of the crowd was white; Reicher, 2004). Such systematic behavior provides evidence that crowds are not primitive or irrational. Their behavior is informed by their social identity.

Further work by Reicher and colleagues has led to the development of the elaborated social identity model of crowd behavior (ESIM; Reicher, 1996; Stott & Reicher, 1998; Drury & Reicher, 2000). This model considers the role of intergroup relations in shaping and developing the social identity of the crowd. According to Reicher (2004), the context in which the social identity of the crowd forms is dynamic and is shaped by the behavior of relevant outgroups within the same context. Findings from several studies including tax protest (Drury & Reicher, 1999), football events (Hoggett & Stott, 2010a; Stott et al., 2006; Stott & Reicher, 1998) and student demonstrations (Reicher, 1996) show a pattern of results consistent with ESIM.

Research findings from Reicher and colleagues show that changes is crowd behavior often occur after interactions with the police, who already hold the view that the crowd is irrational. This generalization often results in heavy handed policing of even 'moderate' members of the crowd, who in turn perceive police behavior as illegitimate. These 'moderate' members then come to see the police as an oppositional outgroup and a previously disparate crowd becomes more cohesive in its willingness to challenge the police. This escalation serves to confirm police beliefs about crowds and results in the use of more force against the crowds. This cycle may then spiral down until violence and rioting occurs (see Reicher, 2004 for a full review).

In a study on difference in police tactics, Stott et al. (2006) examined football hooliganism during the Euro (2004) football tournament in Portugal. They found that in cities where policing was not heavy handed, football fans tended to self-police and no major incident of violence or rioting was recorded. In contrast, in cities where policing was 'high profile' (e.g. Albufeira), there were incidents of violence, including two reported riots. This study and the evidence cited above shows that crowd behavior is based on social identity and that this process is dynamic and responsive to the context and actions of relevant outgroups. Indeed, Hoggett and Stott (2010b) propose that police should be trained in using the strategy of 'negotiated management' rather than 'paramilitarism' in managing crowds. Negotiated management is arguably far less likely to result in the escalation of crowd behavior to violence and rioting (Stott et al., 2006).

Social identity and deviance from group norms

An important element of how groups influence individual behavior is the way they deal with deviance within their ranks. Deviance occurs when an individual departs from valued group norms. Groups are typically known to be highly intolerant of traitors. This is particularly true within criminal gangs where individuals who violate ingroup norms might meet with violent reprisals. Such norms against group deviance can also be used by criminals to regulate members of the local community through 'stop snitching' campaigns (Woldoff & Weiss, 2010). However, it is important to note that groups are not static entities that resist all forms of deviance. Groups also need to be able to adapt and change because such a capacity enables them to survive changes within their social environment

(Kurzban & Leary, 2001). According to Abrams *et al.* (2005), the evaluation of deviants is not necessarily based on objective violations of norms, but rather on the intergroup context in which the deviance is occurring.

The social identity approach to deviance is based on the notion that individuals prefer to be part of groups that are unified, valid and positive (Abrams *et al.*, 2005). On the basis of the metacontrast principle, people are able to maximise differences between the ingroup and outgroup, while minimizing the differences within the group (Turner *et al.*, 1994). The difficulty occurs when individuals categorized as ingroup members differ markedly from the rest of the group. Possible solutions to this problem include overlooking or disregarding the deviant ingroup member, reclassifying the deviant as an outgroup member or reassessing the categorization of the groups and redefining their boundaries (Abrams *et al.*, 2005; Spears *et al.* 1997b; Turner & Oakes, 1997). However, there are situations where the categorization is highly meaningful and people are not able to disregard or recategorize the deviant. In such situations, the challenge becomes how to deal with the deviant while maintaining ingroup norms.

The subjective group dynamics model (SGD) proposes that the maintenance of a positive and subjectively valid view of the ingroup in the face of deviance is achieved via a complementary process of intergroup and intragroup differentiation (Abrams *et al.*, 2005). According to SGD, the evaluation of ingroup members is based on a combination of descriptive and prescriptive norms (Marques *et al.*, 1998b). Descriptive norms operate on the basis of the metacontrast principle and help define the characteristics that are indicative of group membership (e.g. skin colour, uniforms, physical appearance; Marques *et al.*, 1999a). In contrast, prescriptive norms describe the behavior or attitudes that group members must uphold in order to maintain a positive social identity for the ingroup (Abrams *et al.*, 2005). Once the intergroup context has been established, individuals who violate prescriptive norms represent a threat to the ingroup's social standing (Pinto *et al.*, 2010). Therefore, such deviants are highly likely to be negatively evaluated by other members of the group.

Initial evidence in support of SGD comes from research on the 'black sheep effect'. This research has shown that people react more positively towards socially attractive ingroup members (e.g. people who engage in positive behavior); and more negatively toward unattractive ingroup members, in comparison to similar outgroup members (Marques *et al.*, 1988). This phenomenon has been found to be particularly strong among individuals who identify strongly with the ingroup (e.g. Branscombe *et al.*, 1993). Within forensic contexts, recent research by Gollwitzer and Keller (2010) found that people were more punitive towards repeat offenders from the ingroup in comparison to repeat offenders from the outgroup. The 'black sheep effect' is a good example of a sophisticated form of ingroup bias that deals with the existence of an undesirable ingroup member, while simultaneously maintaining the positive image of the ingroup (Pinto *et al.*, 2010). It is important to note that deviant group members are not always ejected from the ingroup. Marques *et al.* (2001) found that participants report a higher willingness to persuade the deviant to change when an ingroup (vs. outgroup) norm was violated.

In another study, Marques *et al.* (1998b) exposed participants to normative and deviant ingroup and outgroup members. These targets either violated or conformed to the ingroup's prescriptive norm. They found that overall, participants judged the ingroup as a whole more favourably than the outgroup. Participants also upgraded individuals who conformed to the ingroup's prescriptive norm and derogated individuals who violated this norm, regardless of whether these deviants were ingroup or outgroup members. These findings show that people are highly concerned with validating the ingroup norm. Furthermore, people were more likely to derogate when they were accountable to the ingroup, but not the outgroup. Research by Hutchison and Abrams (2003) further demonstrates that the derogation of deviants serves an ingroup stereotype maintenance function (see also Hutchison *et al.*, 2008).

The SGD model also proposes that deviance need not only be in the direction that is opposite to the ingroup norm (i.e. anti-norm deviance; Abrams *et al.*, 2000; see also Abrams *et al.*, 2002). Deviation can also be in the normative direction of the group (i.e. pro-norm deviance; Abrams *et al.*, 2000). Religious extremism is a good example of pro-norm deviance. Abrams *et al.* (2000) propose that while anti-norm deviants may be derogated as in the 'black sheep effect', pro-norm deviants will be evaluated as positively as or more positively than normative ingroup members (see also Wilson *et al.*, Chapter 5). In an experiment, Abrams *et al.* (2000) asked teenagers to evaluate a candidate from their own gender group. The participants were asked to compare gender normative targets, to targets that were either highly masculine or highly feminine. They found that participants rated the normative target more positively than the deviant targets. However, among the deviants, those who deviated in a pro-normative direction (e.g. a highly masculine male) were rated more positively than the anti-norm deviants. Similar findings were obtained in a study among employees in a major UK offshore bank (see Abrams *et al.*, 2005 for a review).

The above research indicates that deviance within groups can be regulated in various ways. From a social identity perspective the goal for the group is to maintain its positive distinctiveness. As such, groups are much more likely to react negatively and punish anti-norm deviance. In contrast, pro-norm deviance is likely to be rewarded. This may be problematic within gangs and extremist groups. Those individuals who are most extreme in their criminal behavior may be more likely to be highly regarded and respected (Anderson, 1999; Curry *et al.*, 2002).

Devalued identities

Deviance is related to another issue that is of interest to social identity researchers. This issue concerns how people cope with having negative or devalued social identities. As already noted, SIT proposes that people are motivated to belong to groups that are subjectively positive (Hogg & Abrams, 1988). However, groups do not exist in a social vacuum. Within any cultural meta-context individuals are often aware of how different groups are related to each other with regards to social status (Crocker & Quinn, 2004). In most cultures there are social groups that are devalued or stigmatized (see Solomon, 1986 for a review). According to Crocker and Quinn (2004), the differences between those with valued and devalued identities are often based on shared cultural values. In addition to this, members of devalued groups are aware of negative social stereotypes about them, and also aware of the existence of prejudice and discrimination against their group (Crocker & Major, 1989).

Several scholars have proposed that being a member of a devalued social group results in lowered self-esteem (see Crocker & Quinn, 2004 for a full review). For example, Schmidt and Branscombe (2002) argue that viewing oneself as a target of prejudice and discrimination harms self-esteem because people are forced to recognise that an important aspect of the self (i.e. their social identity) is not valued by important others in society. Indeed, research has shown that perceiving one's group as a target of discrimination results in lowered self-esteem and emotional well-being (see Major *et al.*, 2002 for a review). Similar findings have been reported in forensic contexts. For example, Apena (2007) noted the role of negative societal representations of blacks and how this may play a role in the lives and decisions of young black offenders in London. Similarly, Alarid and Vega (2010) noted the presence of devalued social identities and their negative consequences in a sample of young female convicted felons.

Other researchers reject the notion that being a member of a devalued group automatically leads to chronic levels of low self-esteem and well-being (e.g. Crocker & Quinn, 2004). In fact, research comparing African-Americans to European-Americans has found either no difference in self-esteem or higher self-esteem among African-Americans (see Crocker & Major, 1989 for a review). Crocker and Quinn (2004) argue that negative effects of devalued identities depend on social context and aspects of the immediate situation. For example, Crocker *et al.* (1991) found that African-American students were negatively affected by negative feedback from a white person, only when they thought the person was unaware of their race (i.e. blinds were down on a one-way mirror). When they thought the person was aware of their race, negative feedback had no effect on their self-esteem. Crocker *et al.* (1991) argue that this is because African-Americans could attribute the negative feedback to prejudice. Similar findings have been reported in studies on women (Major *et al.*, 2003) and in the context of students taking biased tests (Major *et al.*, 1998). Overall, these studies show that to the extent that people can attribute negative outcomes to the prejudice of others, their self-esteem is protected.

Research on stereotype threat has also shown that context is important for test performance (Steele, 1997). Over the last decade, a large body of research has shown that negative stereotypes may affect the performance of those to whom they apply (i.e. stereotype threat; Steele & Aronson, 1995). However, these effects are not general, and only occur if the stereotype is salient and relevant within the context (Rosenthal & Crisp, 2006). Studies have shown that when negative stereotypes are activated women perform worse on maths tasks (Spencer *et al.*, 1999) and choose low level career paths (Davies *et al.*, 2002). Research has also shown that black people perform worse on tasks described as intelligence tests and white people perform worse on tasks described as assessing athletic ability (Schmader *et al.*, 2008). It is important to note that stereotype threat has strong effects in certain circumstances; i.e. when the person really wants to succeed within the testing domain (Aronson *et al.*, 1999) or when the test is highly difficult such that it tests the very limits of a person's ability (Crocker & Quinn, 2004; Spencer *et al.*, 1999).

Researchers have also examined the role of ingroup identification on the consequences of devalued identities (McCoy & Major, 2003). For individuals who identify strongly with their group, the negative impact of devalued identities might be unavoidable. Spears *et al.* (1997a) found that high identifiers reacted differently to low identifiers when their group's social status was threatened. High identifiers were more likely to increase their levels of self-stereotyping, in comparison to low identifiers, when their group's status was threatened. This shows that high identifiers are highly committed to their group and the related identity. However, such commitment may have negative consequences. Using samples of women and Latinos, McCoy and Major (2003) found that the buffering effects of attributing negative outcomes to prejudice only worked for lower identifiers. For individuals who are highly identified with their group, attributing negative feedback to discrimination led to depressed emotion and lower self-esteem.

The research on devalued identities is consistent with the social identity approach which argues that the effects of group membership on behavior are context dependent (Oakes *et al.*, 1994), and also depend on the value that the individual attaches to the group (Hogg & Abrams, 1988). However, it is important to note that certain social situations repeat themselves and chronic exposure to the negative feelings related to devalued identities can have serious social consequences. Steele (1997) proposes that stereotype threat can lead to ethnic minority students disidentifying with school, and subsequently dropping out. This can have negative social consequences because dropping out of school has been found to be related to later criminal behavior (e.g. Thornberry *et al.*, 1985).

Dehumanization and its consequences

Social psychological research has found that people tend to essentialize social groups (Haslam *et al.*, 2000; Rothbart & Taylor, 1992). In other words, people have a tendency to believe that social categories are natural and to view social features, such as race, as reflecting an underlying essence (Rothbart & Taylor, 1992). Leyens *et al.* (2000) proposed that if people show ingroup bias and also essentialize groups, then people should attribute the best essence to their own group (i.e. the human essence). Leyens and colleagues (2000) refer to the tendency for people to perceive their ingroup as being more human in comparison to outgroups as *infrahumanization*. In a recent paper, Haslam (2006) differentiated between two types of *dehumanization*. The first type of dehumanization is *animalistic dehumanization*, which is the denial of *uniquely human attributes* such as moral sensibility. Such dehumanization results in people being viewed as animal-like. The second type is *mechanistic dehumanization*, which is the denial of *human nature* (e.g. interpersonal warmth and cognitive openness). This type of dehumanization results in people being viewed as machine-like.

Intergroup relations researchers have reported findings that show that people are much more likely to attribute humanity to their ingroup versus an outgroup. For example, Leyens and colleagues examined people's attributions of human emotions to groups. They found that people attribute more uniquely human emotions to their ingroup in comparison to outgroups (e.g. Leyens *et al.*, 2001; Paladino *et al.*, 2002). In a recent series of studies, Viki *et al.* (2006) examined the attribution of human-related versus animal-related words to the ingroup and outgroup. They found that human-related words were more likely to be attributed to the ingroup in comparison to the outgroup. These research findings suggest that people tend to dehumanize outgroups.

What are the consequences of such dehumanization? Viewing particular groups as being less than human can arguably be the basis for justifying their discrimination, ill treatment or social exclusion (Bar-Tal, 1990; Opotow, 1990; Staub, 2005). Bandura (1990) proposes that dehumanization is one of the factors related to moral disengagement. Such moral disengagement can be used to justify negative behavior against particular targets. Within intergroup contexts, Cuddy and colleagues (2007) found that people were less willing to help victims of Hurricane Katrina, if they dehumanized the victims. Research has also shown that when people dehumanize the outgroup, they are less likely to feel guilty about wrongs perpetrated by their ingroup against that outgroup (Zebel *et al*, 2008). Viki *et al.* (in press) found that when people dehumanized sex-offenders they were much more likely to recommend punitive punishments (e.g. castration). In other research, Viki (2011) found that people who dehumanized Muslims self-reported a higher proclivity to torture Muslim prisoners. Overall, the above research seems to indicate that dehumanization may influence individuals' social behavior by inhibiting the experience of moral emotions and the manifestation of moral behavior towards outgroups (see also Castano & Giner-Sorolla, 2006; Tam *et al.*, 2007; Vaes *et al*, 2003).

Group socialization

One aspect that is lacking from the research discussed so far is an examination of the temporal dimensions of group membership. The group socialization model clarifies the changes that happen in the relationship between the individual and the group over time (Levine & Moreland, 1994; Levine *et al.*, 2001; Moreland & Levine, 1982). This model is based on the assumption that the relationship between the group and the individual changes over time. The first phase is *investigation* where the group and the individual make decisions about whether to form a relationship. If this phase is successful then *entry* into the group occurs. The group then proceeds to *socialize* the individual until *acceptance* into the group is achieved. Over time the group and the individual engage in *role negotiation* through which their relationship is *maintained*. However, if there are any changes in commitment from either the group or the individual this can result in *divergence* and the eventual *exit* of the individual from the group. It is important to note that exit is not inevitable since the group can also *resocialize* the individual when divergence occurs (Levine *et al.*, 2001).

This group socialization model provides a useful temporal description of how individuals can become group members. Research evidence has supported this model in various contexts including how groups assimilate newcomers (Levine & Moreland, 1991), and group processes involved in the recruitment of new members (Levine *et al.*, 1997). Indeed, the accepted social behavior from ingroup members is different at different stages in the socialization process. Pinto *et al.* (2010) combined the subjective group dynamics model and the group socialization model in their research on deviance. They found deviance was more acceptable among new members of the group who were arguably still being socialized, in comparison to full members who were expected to know and conform to ingroup's prescriptive norms. As such, the effects of the group on an individual's behavior can depend on the group socialization process, reflecting changes over time (Levine *et al.*, 2001).

Conclusion

This chapter examined the social influence of groups on individuals. The vast amount of literature available on the topic illustrates the fact that social groups are important and have a strong influence of individuals. This influence is particularly strong when it comes from groups of which we are members, especially those groups with which we strongly identify. In this chapter, we examined the psychological processes that make group based behavior possible for individual actors. The social identity approach provides a powerful theoretical approach to group behavior, which is supported by a vast amount of research evidence. As noted earlier, our goal was not to provide an extensive review of this research literature. However, the research presented shows how social identity and self-categorization processes influence individual behavior. Examples of this include crowd behavior, conformity for social norms, group polarization, pluralistic ignorance, deviance, devalued identities and dehumanization.

The role of group processes in criminal behavior cannot be denied. Obvious examples include gang membership and religion-based terrorism. However, even criminal behavior that is less obviously 'groupy' can be the result of various social identity based processes. Examples of this include Caroll *et al.*'s (2001) work on reputation enhancement. As such, applied researchers in forensic contexts need to consider social identity and self-categorization processes. Research based on some of these theoretical tenets may lead to important discoveries about the psychological processes that underlie the influence of social groups on the criminal behavior of individuals.

References

Abrams, D. (1996). Social identity, self as structure and self as process. In W. P. Robinson (ed.), *Social Groups and Identities: Developing the Legacy of Henri Tajfel*. Oxford: Butterworth/Heinemann.

Abrams, D. and Hogg, M.A. (2004). Collective identity: group membership and self-perception. In M. B. Brewer & M. Hewstone (eds) *Self and Social Identity* (pp. 147–181). Oxford: Blackwell.

Abrams, D., Marques, J.M., Bown, N.J. and Dougill, M. (2002). Anti-norm and pro-norm deviance in the bank and on the campus: two experiments on subjective group dynamics. *Group Processes and Intergroup Relations, 5,* 163–182. DOI: 10.1177/136843020200 5002922.

Abrams, D., Marques, J.M., Bown, N.J. and Henson, M. (2000). Pro-norm and anti-norm deviance within and between groups. *Journal of Personality and Social Psychology, 78,* 906–912. DOI: 10.1037/0022-3514.78.5.906.

Abrams, D., Randsley de Moura, G.R., Hutchison, P. and Viki, G.T. (2005). When bad becomes good (and vice versa): why social exclusion is not based on difference. In D. Abrams, J.M. Marques and M.A. Hogg (eds) *Social Exclusion and Inclusion*. Philadelphia: Psychology Press.

Abrams, D., Viki, G.T., Masser, B. and Bohner, G. (2003). Perceptions of stranger and acquaintance rape: the role of benevolent and hostile sexism in victim blame and rape proclivity. *Journal of Personality and Social Psychology, 84,* 111–125. DOI: 10.1037/0022-3514.84.1.111.

Abrams, D., Wetherell, M.S., Cochrane, S., Hogg, M.A. and Turner, J.C. (1990). Knowing what to think by knowing who you are: self-categorization and the nature of norm formation, conformity, and group polarization. *British Journal of Social Psychology, 29,* 97–119 DOI: 10.1111/j.2044-8309.1990.tb00892.x.

Ajzen, I. (1991). The theory of planned behavior. *Organizational Behavior and Human Decision Processes, 50,* 179–211. DOI: 10.1016/0749-5978(91)90020-T.

Ajzen, I. and Fishbein, M. (2000). Attitudes and the attitude-behavior relation: reasoned and automatic processes. In W. Stroebe and M. Hewstone (eds) *European Review of Social Psychology* (pp. 1–33). DOI: 10.1080/14792779943000116.

Alarid, L.F. and Vega, O.L. (2010). Identity construction, self perceptions, and criminal behavior of incarcerated women. *Deviant Behavior, 31,* 704–728. DOI: 10.1080/01639620903415943.

Allport, F. (1924). *Social Psychology.* Boston: Houghton Mifflin.

Anderson, E. (1999). *Code of the Street: Decency, Violence and the Moral Life of the Inner City.* New York, NY: Norton and Company.

Apena, F. (2007). Being black and in trouble: the role of self-perception in the offending behavior of black youth. *Youth Justice, 7,* 211–228. DOI: 10.1177/1473225407082511.

Aronson, E. (2003). *The Social Animal.* New York: W.H. Freeman.

Aronson, J., Lustina, M.J., Good, C., Keough, K., Steele, C.M. and Brown, J. (1999). When white men can't do math: necessary and sufficient factors in stereotype threat. *Journal of Experimental Social Psychology, 35,* 29–46. DOI: 10.1006/jesp.1998 .1371.

Asch, S. E. (1951). Effects of group pressure upon the modification and distortion of judgment. In H. Guetzkow (ed.) *Groups, Leadership and Men*. Pittsburgh, PA: Carnegie Press.

Bandura, A. (1990). Mechanisms of moral disengagement. In W. Reich (ed.) *Origins of Terrorism: Psychologies, Ideologies, Theologies, States of Mind* (pp. 161–191). Cambridge: Cambridge University Press.

Bar-Tal, D. (1990). Causes and consequences of delegitimization: models of conflict and ethnocentrism. *Journal of Social Issues, 46,* 65–81. DOI: 10.1111/j.1540-4560.1990. tb00272.x.

Bartsch, R.A. and Judd, C.M. (1993). Majority–minority status and perceived ingroup variability revisited. *European Journal of Social Psychology, 23,* 471–483. DOI: 10.1002/ejsp.2420230505.

Baumeister, R.F. (ed.) (1999). *The Self in Social Psychology.* Philadelphia, PA: Psychology Press (Taylor & Francis).

Blascovich, J., Ginsburg. G.P. and Veach. T.L. (1975). A pluralistic explanation of choice shifts on the risk dimension. *Journal of Personality and Social Psychology, 31,* 422–429. DOI: 10.1037/h0076479.

Branscombe, N.R., Wann, D.L., Noel, J.G. and Coleman, J. (1993). In-group or out-group extremity: importance of the threatened social identity. *Personality and Social Psychology Bulletin, 19,* 381–388. DOI: 10.1177/0146167293194003.

Broadhead-Fern, D. and White, K. (2006). The role of self-efficacy in predicting rule following behaviors in shelters for homeless youth: a test of the theory of planned behavior. *Journal of Social Psychology, 146,* 307–325. DOI: 10.3200/ SOCP.146.3.307-325.

Brooks, D (2011). *The Social Animal – A Story of How Success Happens.* London: Short Books Ltd.

Bruner, J.S. (1957). On perceptual readiness. *Psychological Review, 64,* 123–152. DOI: 10.1037/h0043805.

Burnstein, E. (1982). Persuasion as argument processing. In H. Brandsttter, J.H. Davis and G. Stocker-Kreichgauer (eds) *Group Decision Making* (pp. 103–124). San Diego, CA: Academic Press.

Burnstein, E. and Vinokur, A. (1975). What a person thinks upon learning he has chosen differently from others: nice evidence for the persuasive-arguments explanation of choice shifts. *Journal of Experimental Social Psychology, 11,* 412–426. DOI: 10.1016/0022-1031(75)90045-1.

Byrne, B. (1996). *Measuring Self-concept across the Life Span.* Washington, DC: APA Press.

Carroll, A., Houghton, S., Hattie, J. and Durkin, K. (2001). Reputation enhancing goals: integrating reputation enhancement and goal setting theory as an explanation of delinquent involvement. In F. Columbus (ed.) *Advances in Psychology Research,* vol. 4. (pp. 101–129). Huntington, NY: Nova Science.

Castano, E. and Giner-Sorolla, R. (2006). Not quite human: infrahumanization in response to collective responsibility for intergroup killing. *Journal of Personality and Social Psychology, 90,* 804–818. DOI: 10.1037/0022-3514.90.5.804.

Cialdini, R.B., Borden, R.J., Thorne, A., Walker, M.R., Freeman, S. and Sloan, L.R. (1976). Basking in reflected glory: three (football) field studies. *Journal of Personality and Social Psychology, 34,* 366–375. DOI: 10.1037/0022-3514.34.3.366.

Cooper, J., Kelly, K.A. and Weaver, K. (2004). Attitudes, norms, and social groups. In M.B. Brewer and M. Hewstone (eds) *Social Cognition.* Oxford, UK: Blackwell Publishers.

Crocker, J. and Major, B.M. (1989). Social stigma and self-esteem: the self-protective properties of stigma. *Psychological Review, 96,* 608–630. DOI: 10.1037/0033-295X.96.4.608.

Crocker, J. and Quinn, D.M. (2004). Psychological consequences of devalued identities. In M.B. Brewer and M. Hewstone (eds) *Self and Social Identity, Perspectives on Social Psychology* (pp. 203–231). Malden: Blackwell Publishing.

Crocker, J., Voelkl, K., Testa, M. and Major, B.M. (1991). Social stigma: affective consequences of attributional ambiguity. *Journal of Personality and Social Psychology, 60,* 218–228. DOI: 10.1037/0022-3514.60.2.218.

Cuddy, A.J.C., Rock, M.S. and Norton, M.I. (2007). Aid in the aftermath of Hurricane Katrina: inferences of secondary emotions and intergroup helping. *Group Processes and Intergroup Relations, 10,* 107–118. DOI: 10.1177/1368430207071344.

Curry, G.D., Decker, S.H. and Egley, A. (2002). Gang involvement and delinquency in a middle school population. *Justice Quarterly, 19,* 275–292. DOI: 10.1080/07418820200095241.

Davies, P.G., Spencer, S.J., Quinn, D.M. and Gerhardstein, R. (2002). Consuming images: how television commercials that elicit stereotype threat can restrain women academically and professionally. *Personality and Social Psychology Bulletin, 28,* 1615–1628. DOI: 10.1177/014616702237644.

Deutsch, M. and Gerard, H.B. (1955). A study of normative and informational social influences upon individual judgment. *Journal of Abnormal and Social Psychology, 51,* 629–636. DOI: 10.1037/h0046408.

Drury, J. and Reicher, S. (1999). The intergroup dynamics of collective empowerment: Substantiating the social identity model of crowd behavior. *Group Processes and Intergroup Relations 2,* 1–22. DOI: 10.1177/1368430299024005.

Drury J. and Reicher, S. (2000). Collective action and psychological change: the emergence of new social identities. *British Journal of Social Psychology 39,* 579–604. DOI: 10.1348/014466600164642.

Dur, R. and van der Weele, J. (2011). *Status-seeking in Criminal Subcultures and the Double Dividend of Zero-tolerance.* IZA Discussion Paper Series, No. 5484. Bonn, Germany. Available at SSRN: http://ssrn.com/abstract=1765649 (accessed 10 April 2012).

Durkheim, E. (1898). Individual and collective representations. In *Sociology and Philosophy,* (pg. 1–34). New York: Free Press.

Emler, N. and Reicher, S. (1995). *Adolescence and Delinquency: The Collective Management of Reputation.* Oxford: Blackwell.

Fenigstein, A. and Abrams, D. (1993). Self-attention and the egocentric assumption of shared perspectives. *Journal of Experimental Social Psychology, 29,* 287–303. DOI:10.1006/jesp.1993.1013.

Flezzani, J.D. and Benshoff, J.M. (2003). Understanding sexual aggression in male college students: the role of self-monitoring and pluralistic ignorance. *Journal of College Counseling, 6,* 69–79. Available at: http://libres.uncg.edu/ir/uncg/f/J_Benshoff_Understanding_2003.pdf (accessed 12 April 2012).

Gollwitzer, M. and Keller, L. (2010). What you did only matters if you are one of us: offenders' group membership moderates the effect of criminal history on punishment severity. *Social Psychology, 41,* 20–26. DOI: 10.1027/1864-9335/a000004.

Grekul, J. (1999). Pluralistic ignorance in a prison community. *Canadian Journal of Criminology, 41,* 65–83. Available at: http://www.highbeam.com/doc/1G1-56328378.html (accessed 10 April 2012).

Hamdani, A. (2007). Mens rea and the cost of ignorance. *Virgina Law Review, 93*, 415–457. Available at: http://www.virginialawreview.org/content/pdfs/93/415.pdf (accessed 10 April 2012).

Harris, J. (1995). Where is the child's environment? *Psychological Review, 102*, 458–489. DOI: 10.1037/0033-295X.102.3.458.

Haslam, N. (2006). Dehumanization: an integrative review. *Personality and Social Psychology Review, 10*, 252–264. DOI: 10.1207/s15327957pspr1003_4.

Haslam, M., Rothschild, L. and Ernst, D. (2000). Essentialist beliefs about social categories. *British Journal of Social Psychology, 39*, 113–127. DOI: 10.1348/014466600164363.

Higgins, E.T. (1987). Self-discrepancy: a theory relating self and affect. *Psychological Review, 94*, 319–340. DOI: 10.1037/0033-295X.94.3.319.

Hogg, M.A. (2000). Subjective uncertainty reduction through self-categorization: a motivational theory of social identity processes. *European Review of Social Psychology, 11*, 223–255. DOI: 10.1080/14792772043000040

Hogg, M.A. (2004). Social categorization, depersonalization, and group behavior. Self and social identity. In M.B. Brewer and M. Hewstone (eds) *Self and Social Identity, Perspectives on Social Psychology* (pp. 203–231). Malden: Blackwell Publishing.

Hogg, M.A. and Abrams, D. (1988). *Social Identifications: A Social Psychology of Intergroup Relations and Group Processes.* London: Routledge.

Hogg, M.A. and Reid, S.A. (2006). Social identity, self-categorization, and the communication of group norms. *Communication Theory, 16*, 7–30. DOI: 10.1111/j.1468-2885.2006.00003.x.

Hogg, M.A., Turner, J.C. and Davidson, B. (1990). Polarized norms and social frames of reference: a test of the self-categorization theory of group polarization. *Basic and Applied Social Psychology, 11*, 77–100. DOI: 10.1207/s15324834basp1101_6.

Hoggett, J. and Stott, C. (2010a). The role of crowd theory in determining the use of force in public order policing. *Policing & Society, 20*, 223–236. DOI: 10.1080/10439461003668468.

Hoggett, J. and Stott, C. (2010b). Crowd psychology, public order police training and the policing of football crowd. *Policing: An International Journal of Police Strategies & Management, 33*, 218–235. DOI: 10.1108/13639511011044858.

Holt, T.J. (2010). Examining the role of technology in the formation of deviant subcultures. *Social Science Computer Review, 28*, 466–481. DOI: 10.1177/08944393093 51344.

Hopkins, N. and Emler, N. (1990). Social network participation and problem behavior in adolescence. In K. Hurrelmann and F. Losel (eds) *Health Hazards in Adolescence* (pp. 385–407). The Hague: De Gryuter.

Hutchison, P. and Abrams, D. (2003). Ingroup identification moderates stereotype change in reaction to ingroup deviance. *European Journal of Social Psychology, 33*, 497–506. DOI: 10.1002/ejsp.157.

Hutchison, P., Abrams, D., Gutierrez, R. and Viki, G.T. (2008). Getting rid of the bad ones: the relationship between group identification, deviant derogation, and stereotype maintenance. *Journal of Experimental Social Psychology, 44*, 874–881. DOI:10.1016/j.jesp.2007.09.001.

Isenberg, D.J. (1986). Group polarization: a critical review and meta-analysis. *Journal of Personality and Social Psychology, 50*, 1141–1151. DOI: 10.1037/0022-3514.50.6.1141.

James, W. (1890/1950). *The Principles of Psychology.* New York: Dover.

Jellison, J.M. and Arkin, R.M. (1977). Social comparison of abilities: a self-presentational approach to decision making in groups. In J.M. Suls and R.L. Miller (eds) *Social Comparison Processes*. New York: Halsted Press.

Judd, C.M. and Park, B. (1988). Out-group homogeneity: judgments of variability at the individual and group levels. *Journal of Personality and Social Psychology, 54*, 778–788: DOI: 10.1037/0022-3514.54.5.778.

Kaplan. M.F. and Miller. C.E. (1977). Judgments and group discussion: effect of presentation and memory factors on polarization. *Sociometry, 40*, 337–343. Available at http://www.jstor.org/pss/3033482 (accessed 10 April 2012).

Kauffman, K. (1981). Prison officers' attitudes and perceptions of attitudes: a case of pluralistic ignorance, *Journal of Research in Crime and Delinquency, 18*, 272–294. DOI: 10.1177/002242788101800205.

Kirkpatrick, L.A. and Ellis, B.J. (2004). An evolutionary-psychological approach to self-esteem: multiple domains and multiple functions. In M.B. Brewer and M. Hewstone (eds), *Self and Social Identity* (pp. 52–77) Malden: Blackwell Publishing

Klein, M.W, Weerman, F.M. and Thornberry, T.P. (2006). Street gang violence in Europe. *European Journal of Criminology, 3*, 413–437. DOI: 10.1177/1477370806067911.

Kurzban, R. and Leary, M.R. (2001). Evolutionary origins of stigmatization: the functions of social exclusion. *Psychological Bulletin, 127*, 187–208. DOI: 0.1037/0033-2909.127.2.187.

Le Bon, G. (1896). *The Crowd: A Study of the Popular Mind*. London: T. Fisher Unwin.

Leary, M.R. and Downs, D.L. (1995). Interpersonal functions of the self-esteem motive: the self-esteem system as a sociometer. In M. Kernis (ed.) *Efficacy, Agency, and Self-esteem* (pp. 123–144). New York: Plenum.

Leary, M.R., Tambor, E.S., Terdal, S.K. and Downs, D.L. (1995). Self-esteem as an interpersonal monitor: the sociometer hypothesis. *Journal of Personality and Social Psychology, 68*, 518–530. DOI: 10.1037/0022-3514.68.3.518.

Levine, J. M. and Moreland, R.L. (1991). Culture and socialization in work groups. In L B. Resnick, J.M. Levine and S.D. Teasdale (eds) *Perspectives on Socially Shared Cognition* (pp. 257–279), Washington, D.C.: American Psychological Association.

Levine, J.M. and Moreland, R.L. (1994). Group socialization: theory and research. In W. Stroebe and M. Hewstone (eds) *European Review of Social Psychology* (pp. 305–336). Chichester: Wiley. DOI: 10.1080/14792779543000093.

Levine, J.M., Moreland, R.L. and Choi, H-S (2001). Group socialization and newcomer innovation. In M.A. Hogg and R.S. Tindale (eds) *Blackwell Handbook of Social Psychology: Group Processes* (pp. 86–106). Oxford, England: Blackwell Publishers.

Levine, J. M., Moreland, R. L. and Ryan, C. (1997). Group socialization and intergroup relations. In C. Sedikides, J. Schopler and C. Insko (eds) *Intergroup Cognition and Intergroup Behavior* (pp. 283–308). Mahwah, N.J.: Erlbaum.

Lewis, M. (1990). Self-knowledge and social development in early life. In L. Pervin (ed.) *Handbook of Personality: Theory and Research* (pp. 277–300). New York: Guilford Press.

Leyens, J.Ph., Paladino, P.M., Rodriguez, R.T., Vaes, J., Demoulin, S., Rodriguez, A.P. and Gaunt, R. (2000). The emotional side of prejudice: the attribution of secondary emotions to ingroups and outgroups. *Personality and Social Psychology Review, 4*(2), 186–197. DOI: 10.1207/S15327957PSPR0402_06.

Leyens, J.P., Rodriguez, A.P., Rodriguez, R.T., Gaunt, R., Paladino, M.P., Vaes, J. and Demoulin, S. (2001). Psychological essentialism and the differential attribution of uniquely human emotions to ingroups and outgroups. *European Journal of Social Psychology, 31*, 395–411. DOI: 10.1002/ejsp.50.

McCoy, S.K. and Major, B. (2003). Group identification moderates emotional responses to perceived prejudice. *Personality and Social Psychology Bulletin, 29*, 1005–1017. DOI: 10.1177/0146167203253466.

Mackie, D.M. (1986). Social identification effects in group polarization. *Journal of Personality and Social Psychology, 50*, 720, –728. DOI: 10.1037/0022-3514.50.4.720.

Mackie, D.M. and Cooper, J. (1984). Attitude polarization: the effects of group membership. *Journal of Personality and Social Psychology, 46*, 575–585. DOI: 10.1037/0022-3514.46.3.575.

Major, B., McCoy, S.K. and Quinton, W. (2002). Antecedents and consequences of attributions to discrimination: theoretical and empirical advances. In M.P. Zanna (ed.) *Advances in Experimental Social Psychology* (vol. 34, pp. 251–349). San Diego: Academic.

Major B., Quinton W.J. and Schmader T. (2003). Attributions to discrimination and self-esteem: impact of social identification and situational ambiguity. *Journal of Experimental Social Psychology, 39*, 220–231. DOI: 10.1016/S0022-1031(02) 00547-4.

Major, B., Spencer, S., Schmader, T., Wolfe, C. and Crocker, J. (1998). Coping with negative stereotypes about intellectual performance: the role of psychological disengagement. *Personality and Social Psychology Bulletin, 24*, 34–50. DOI: 10.1177/0146167298241003.

Marques, J.M., Abrams, D., Paez, D. and Hogg, M.A. (2001). Social categorization, social identification, and rejection of deviant group members. In M.A. Hogg and R.S. Tindale (eds) *Blackwell Handbook of Social Psychology (Vol. 3): Group Processes* (pp. 400–424). Oxford, England: Blackwell.

Marques, J.M., Abrams, D., Paez, D. and Martinez-Taboada, C. (1998a). The role of categorization and in-group norms in judgments of groups and their members. *Journal of Personality and Social Psychology, 75*, 976–988. DOI: 10.1037/0022-3514.75.4.976.

Marques, J.M., Paez, D. and Abrams, D. (1998b). Social identity and intragroup differentiation as subjective social control. In S. Worchel, J.F. Morales, D. Paez and J.-C. Deschamps (eds) *Social Identity: International Perspectives* (pp. 124–141). New York: Sage.

Marques, J.M., Yzerbyt, V.Y. and Leyens, J.-P. (1988). The black sheep effect: judgmental extremity towards ingroup members as a function of group identification. *European Journal of Social Psychology, 18*, 1–16. DOI: 10.1002/ejsp.2420180102.

Matza, D. (1964). *Delinquency and Drift*. New Jersey: Transaction Press.

Merton, R.K. (1938). Social structure and anomie. *American Sociological Review, 3*, 672–682. Available at: http://www.jstor.org/pss/2084686 (accessed 10 April 2012).

Moreland, R.L. and Levine, J.M. (1982). Socialization in small groups: temporal changes in individual-group relations. In L. Berkowitz (ed.) *Advances in Experimental Social Psychology* (vol. 15, pp. 137–192). New York: Academic Press.

Moscovici, S. and Zavalloni, M. (1969). The group as a polarizer of attitudes. *Journal of Personality and Social Psychology, 12*, 125–135. DOI: 10.1037/h0027568.

Mullen, B. and Hu, L. (1989). Perceptions of ingroup and outgroup variability: a meta-analytic integration. *Basic and Applied Social Psychology, 10*, 233–252. DOI: 10.1207/s15324834basp1003_3.

Oakes, P. (1987). The salience of social categories. In J.C. Turner, M.A. Hogg, P.J. Oakes, S.D. Reicher and M.S. Wetherall (eds) *Rediscovering the Social Group: A Self-categorization Theory* (pp. 117–141). Oxford: Blackwell.

Oakes, P. (1996). The categorization process: cognition and the group in the social psychology of stereotyping. In W.P. Robinson (ed.) *Social Groups and Identities: Developing the Legacy of Henri Tajfel* (pp. 95–120). Bodmin, Cornwall, UK: Butterworth-Heinemann

Oakes, P. (2004). The root of all evil in intergroup relations? Unearthing the categorization process. In M.B. Brewer and M. Hewstone (eds) *Social Cognition: Perspectives on Social Psychology* (pp. 102–119). Malden: Blackwell Publishing.

Oakes, P.J., Turner, J.C. and Haslam, S.A. (1991). Perceiving people as group members: the role of fit in the salience of social categorizations. *British Journal of Social Psychology*, *30*, 125–144. Available at: http://psycnet.apa.org/psycinfo/1991-33130-001 (accessed 10 April 2012).

O'Gorman, H. (1986). The discovery of pluralistic ignorance: an ironic lesson. *Journal of the Historic and Behavioral Sciences*, *22*, 333–347. DOI: 10.1002/1520-6696(198610)22:4<333::AID-JHBS2300220405>3.0.CO;2-X.

Opotow, S. (1990). Moral exclusion and injustice: an introduction. *Journal of Social Issues, 46*, 1–20. DOI: 10.1111/j.1540-4560.1990.tb00268.x.

Oyserman, D. (2004). Self-concept and identity. In M.B. Brewer and M. Hewstone (eds) *Self and Social Identity: Perspectives on Social Psychology* (pp. 5–24). Malden, MA: Blackwell.

Paladino, M.P., Leyens, J.Ph., Rodriguez, R.T. and Rodriguez, A.P. (2002). Differential association of uniquely and non-uniquely human emotions with the ingroup and the outgroup. *Group Process and Intergroup Relations, 5*, 105–117. DOI: 10.1177/1368430202005002539.

Pinto, I.R., Marques, J.M., Levine, J.M. and Abrams, D. (2010). Membership status and subjective group dynamics: who triggers the Black Sheep effect? *Journal of Personality and Social Psychology, 9*, 107–119. DOI: 10.1037/a0018187.

Prentice, D.A. and Miller, D.T. (1993). Pluralistic ignorance and alcohol use on campus: some consequences of misperceiving the social norm. *Journal of Personality and Social Psychology, 64*, 243–256. DOI: 10.1037/0022-3514.64.2.243.

Prentice, D.A. and Miller, D.T. (1996). Pluralistic ignorance and the perpetuation of social norms by unwitting actors. In M.P. Zanna (ed.) *Advances in Experimental Social Psychology* (vol. 28, pp. 161–209). New York: Academic Press. DOI: 10.1016/S0065-2601(08)60238-5.

Pynchon, M.R. and Borum, R. (1999). Assessing threats of targeted group violence: contributions from social psychology. *Behavioral Science and the Law 17*, 339–355. Available at: http://works.bepress.com/randy_borum/33 (accessed 10 April 2012).

Reicher, S. (1982). The determination of collective behavior. In H. Tajfel (ed.) *Social Identity and Intergroup Relations*. Cambridge: Cambridge University Press, and Paris: Maison des Sciences de l'Homme.

Reicher, S. (1984). The St Paul's 'riot': an explanation of the limits of crowd action in terms of a social identity model. *European Journal of Social Psychology, 14*, 1–21. DOI: 10.1002/ejsp.2420140102.

Reicher, S.D. (2004). The psychology of crowd dynamics. In M.B. Brewer and M. Hewstone (eds) *Social Cognition: Perspectives on Social Psychology* (pp. 232–258). Malden: Blackwell Publishing.

Reicher, S. (1996). The crowd century: reconciling theoretical failure with practical success. *British Journal of Social Psychology, 35*, 535–553. DOI: 10.1111/j.2044-8309.1996.tb01113.x.

Reicher, S. and Potter, J. (1985). Psychological theory as intergroup perspective: a comparative analysis of 'scientific' and 'lay' accounts of crowd events. *Human Relations, 38*, 167–189. DOI: 10.1177/001872678503800206.

Reid, S.A., Cropley, C. and Hogg, M.A. (2005). *A self-categorization explanation of pluralistic ignorance*. Top three paper presented at the International Communication Association, New York.

Rimal, R.N. and Real, K. (2003). Understanding the influence of perceived norms on behaviors. *Communication Theory, 13*, 184–203. DOI: 10.1111/j.1468-2885.2003.tb00288.x.

Rosenthal, H.E.S. and Crisp, R.J. (2006). Reducing stereotype threat by blurring intergroup boundaries. *Personality and Social Psychology Bulletin, 32*, 501–511. DOI: 10.1177/0146167205281009.

Rothbart, M and Taylor, M. (1992). Category labels and social reality: do we view social categories as natural kinds? In G.R. Semin and K. Fiedler (eds) *Language, Interaction and Social Cognition*. London: Sage.

Sanders, G. S. and Baron, R.S. (1977). Is social comparison irrelevant for producing choice shifts? *Journal of Experimental Social Psychology*, 13, 303–315. DOI: 10.1016/0022-1031(77)90001-4.

Sample, L.L. and Bray, T.M. (2006). Are sex offenders different? An examination of rearrest patterns. *Criminal Justice Policy Review, 17*(1), 83–102. DOI: 10.1177/0887403405282916.

Schmader, T., Johns, M. and Forbes, C. (2008) An integrated process model of stereotype threat effects on performance. *Psychological Review, 115*, 336–356. DOI: 10.1037/0033-295X.115.2.336.

Schmidt, M.T. and Branscombe, N.R. (2002). The internal and external causal loci of attributions to prejudice. *Personality and Social Psychology Bulletin, 28*, 620–628. DOI: 10.1177/0146167202288006.

Shaw, C.R. and McKay, H.D. (1942). *Juvenile Delinquency and Urban Areas*. Chicago: The University of Chicago Press.

Sherif, M. (1935). A study of some social factors in perception. *Archives of Psychology, 27*, 187. Available at: http://www.brocku.ca/MeadProject/Sherif/Sherif_1935b.html (accessed 10 April 2012).

Simon, B. (1992). The perception of ingroup and outgroup homogeneity: reintroducing the social context. In W. Stroebe and M. Hewstone (eds), *European Review of Social Psychology* (vol. 3, pp. 1–30). Chichester, UK: Wiley.

Solomon, H.M. (1986). Stigma and western culture: a historical approach. In S.C. Ainlay, G. Becker and L. Coleman (eds) *The Dilemma of Difference: A Multidisciplinary View of Stigma* (pp. 59–76). New York: Plenum.

Spears, R., Doosje, B. and Ellemers, N. (1997a). Self-stereotyping in the face of threats to group status and distinctiveness: the role of group identification. *Personality and Social Psychology Bulletin, 23*, 538, –553. DOI: 10.1177/0146167297235009.

Spears, R., Oakes, P.J., Ellemers, N. and Haslam, S.A. (eds) (1997b). *The Social Psychology of Stereotyping and Group Life*. Oxford: Basil Blackwell.

Spencer, S.J., Steele, C.M. and Quinn, D.M. (1999). Stereotype threat and women's math performance. *Journal of Experimental Social Psychology, 35*, 4–28. DOI: jesp.1998.1373.

Staub, E. (2005). *The Roots of Evil: The Origins of Genocide and Other Group Violence.* Cambridge: Cambridge University Press.

Steele, C.M. (1988). The psychology of self-affirmation: sustaining the integrity of the self. In L. Berkowitz (ed.) *Advances in Experimental Social Psychology* (vol. 21, pp. 261–302). New York: Academic Press.

Steele, C.M. (1997). A threat in the air: how stereotypes shape the intellectual identities and performance of women and African-Americans. *American Psychologist, 52*, 613–629. DOI: 10.1037/0003-066X.52.6.613.

Steele, C.M. and Aronson, J. (1995). Stereotype threat and the intellectual test performance of African-Americans. *Journal of Personality and Social Psychology, 69*, 797–881. DOI: 10.1037/0022-3514.69.5.797.

Stoner, J.A.F. (1968). Risky and cautions shifts in group decisions: the influence of widely held values. *Journal of Experimental Social Psychology, 4*, 442–459. DOI: 10.1016/0022-1031(68)90069-3.

Stott, C. and Reicher, S. (1998). Crowd action as intergroup process: introducing the police perspective. *European Journal of Social Psychology, 26*, 509–529. DOI: 10.1002/(SICI)1099-0992(199807/08)28:4<509::AID-EJSP877>3.0.CO;2-C.

Stott, C.J., Adang, O.M., Livingstone, A. and Schreiber, M. (2006). Variability in the collective behavior of England fans at Euro2004: public order policing, social identity, intergroup dynamics and social change. *European Journal of Social Psychology, 37*, 75–100. DOI: 10.1002/ejsp.338.

Stott, C.J., Adang, O.M., Livingstone, A. and Schreiber, M. (2008). Tackling football hooliganism: a quantitative study of public order, policing and crowd psychology. *Psychology Public Policy and Law, 52*, 2, 111–138. DOI: 10.1037/a0013419.

Tam, T., Hewstone, M., Cairns, E., Tausch, N., Maio, G.R. and Kenworthy, J. (2007). The impact of intergroup emotions on forgiveness in Northern Ireland. *Group Processes and Intergroup Relations, 10*, 119–136. DOI: 10.1177/1368430207071345.

Tajfel, H. (1969). Cognitive aspects of prejudice. *Journal of Social Issues, 25*, 79-97. DOI: 10.1111/j.1540-4560.1969.tb00620.x

Tajfel, H. (1972). Social categorization. In S. Moscovici (ed.) *Introduction à la psychologie sociale* (vol. 1, pp. 272–302). Paris: Larousse.

Tajfel, H. (ed.) (1978). *Differentiation between Social Groups: Studies in the Social Psychology of Intergroup Relations.* London: Academic Press.

Tajfel, H., Billig, M., Bundy R.P. and Flament, C. (1971). Social categorization and intergroup behavior. *European Journal of Social Psychology, 1*, 149–177. DOI: 10.1002/ejsp.2420010202.

Tajfel, H. and Turner, J.C. (1979). An integrative theory of intergroup conflict. In W.G. Austin and S. Worchel (eds) *The Social Psychology of Intergroup Relations* (pp. 33–47). Monterey, CA: Brooks/Cole.

Tajfel, H. and Wilkes, A.L. (1963). Classification and quantitative judgment. *British Journal of Psychology, 54*, 101–114. DOI: 10.1111/j.2044-8295.1963.tb00865.x.

Taylor, D.M. and Louis, W. (2004). Terrorism and the quest for identity. In F.M. Moghaddam and A.J. Marsella (eds) *Understanding Terrorism: Psychosocial Roots, Uncertainty and Identification Consequences, and Interventions* (pp. 169–185). Washington, DC: American Psychological Association.

Tesser, A. (1988). Toward a self-evaluation maintenance model of social behavior. In L. Berkowitz (ed.) *Advances in Experimental Social Psychology* (pp. 181–227). San Diego, CA: Academic Press.

Terry, D.J. and Hogg, M.A. (1996). Group norms and the attitude-behavior relationship. A role for group identification. *Personality and Social Psychology Bulletin, 22,* 776–793. DOI: 10.1177/0146167296228002.

Thornberry, T.P., Moore, M. and Christenson, R.L. (1985). The effect of dropping out of high school on subsequent criminal behavior. *Criminology, 23,* 3–18. DOI: 10.1111/j.1745-9125.1985.tb00323.x.

Thrasher, F. (1927). *The Gang: A Study of 1,313 Gangs in Chicago.* Chicago: University of Chicago Press.

Tolman, R.M., Edleson, J.L. and Fendrich, M. (1996). The applicability of the theory of planned behavior to abusive men's cessation of violent behavior. *Violence and Victims, 11,* 341–354. Available at: http://www.ingentaconnect.com/content/ springer/vav/1996/00000011/00000004/art00005 (accessed 10 April 2012).

Turner, J.C. (1999). Some current issues in research on social identity and self-categorization theories. In N. Ellemers, R. Spears and B. Doosje (eds) Social ID Entity Context, Commitment, Content (pp. 6–34). Oxford: Blackwell.

Turner, J.C. and Oakes, P.J. (1997). The socially structured mind. In C. McGarty and S.A. Haslam (eds.) *The Message of Social Psychology.* Oxford: Blackwell.

Turner, J.C., Hogg, M.A., Oakes, P.J., Reicher, S.D. and Wetherell, M.S. (1987). *Rediscovering the Social Group.* Oxford: Basil Blackwell.

Turner, J.C., Oakes, P.J., Haslam, S.A. and McGarty, C. (1994). Self and collective: cognition and social context. *Personality and Social Psychology Bulletin, 20,* 454–463. DOI: 10.1177/0146167294205002.

Turner, J.C., Wetherell, M.S. and Hogg, M.A. (1989). Referent informational influence and group polarization. *British Journal of Social Psychology, 28,* 135–147. DOI: 10.1111/j.2044-8309.1989.tb00855.x.

Vaes, J., Paladino, M.P., Castelli, L., Leyens, J-P. and Giovanazzi, A. (2003). On the behavioral consequences of infrahumanization: the implicit role of uniquely human emotions in intergroup relations. *Journal of Personality and Social Psychology, 85,* 1016–1034. DOI: 10.1037/0022-3514.85.6.1016.

Viki, G.T. (2011). Dehumanization and self-reported proclivity to torture: the mediating role of perceived threat. Unpublished manuscript: University of Kent.

Viki, G.T., Winchester, L., Titshall, L., Chisango, T., Pina, A. and Russell, R. (2006). Beyond secondary emotions: the infrahumanization of outgroups using human-related and animal-related words. *Social Cognition, 24,* 753–775. DOI: 10.1521/soco.2006.24.6.753.

Viki, G.T., Fullerton, I., Ragget, H., Tait, F. and Wiltshire, S. (in press). The role of dehumanization in attitudes toward the social exclusion and rehabilitation of sex offenders. *Journal of Applied Social Psychology.*

Wicker, A.W. (1969). Attitudes versus actions: the relationship of verbal and overt behavioral responses to attitude objects. *Journal of Social Issues, 25,* 41–78. DOI: 0.1111/j.1540-4560.1969.tb00619.x.

Wilder, D.A. (1986). Social categorization: implications for creation and reduction of intergroup bias. In L. Berkowitz (ed.) *Advances in Experimental Social Psychology: Vol. 19* (pp. 293–355). New York: Academic Press

Woldoff, R. and Weiss, K. (2010). Stop snitchin': exploring definitions of the snitch and implications for urban black communities. *Journal of Criminal Justice and Popular Culture, 17,* 184–223. Available at: http://www.albany.edu/scj/jcjpc/vol17is1/Woldoff 7_6.pdf (accessed 10 April 2012).

Wood, J. and Alleyne, E. (2010). Street gang theory and research: Where are we now and where do we go from here? Special Issue: Group Processes and Aggression. *Aggression and Violent Behavior*, 15(2), 100–111. DOI: 10.1016/j.avb.2009.08.005.

Wundt, W. (1916). *Elements of Folk Psychology: Outlines of a Psychological History of the Development of Mankind.* London: Allan & Unwin.

Zajonc, R.B. (1980). Cogntion and social cognition: a historical perspective. In L. Festinger (ed.) *Retrospections on Social Psychology* (pp. 180–204). New York: Oxford University Press.

Zebel, S., Zimmermann, A., Viki, G.T. and Doosje, B. (2008). Dehumanization and guilt as distinct but related predictors of support for reparation policies. *Political Psychology*, *29*, 193–219. DOI: 10.1111/j.1467-9221.2008.00623.x.

2 Street gangs

Group processes and theoretical explanations

Jane L. Wood and Emma Alleyne,
University of Kent, UK

Gang involvement, gang membership, and gang activity are attractive, media popular topics. Media attention has generated an asymmetry in news outlets (Spergel, 1995; Sullivan, 2006) creating glamorous media images of gang membership (Przemieniecki, 2005). So, it is not surprising when youth admire gang members, mimic them, and aspire to join gangs (Hughes & Short, 2005). If they do join a gang they are likely to become more violent than they were previously even if they already associated with prolifically offending peers (Klein *et al.*, 2006). Consequently, researchers have strived to explain street gangs in a plethora of research spanning pretty much the last century.

Existing literature provides much about the circumstances in which gangs form and flourish (see Wood & Alleyne, 2010, for review). For example, gangs probably form to fulfill adolescent needs such as: peer friendship, pride, identity development, enhancement of self-esteem, excitement, acquisition of resources, as well as goals that may not – due to low socio-economic environments – be available legitimately (Goldstein, 2002). Gangs offer a strong psychological sense of community, a physical and psychological neighborhood, a social network, and social support (Goldstein, 1991). In essence, gangs form for the same reasons that any groups form (Goldstein, 2002). In this chapter we consider research and theories regarding gang formation, structure, and behavior. In particular, we consider the group processes that underpin and explain these important facets of gang culture, and suggest theoretical pathways to fill these gaps.

Defining a gang

The recognition that 'No two gangs are just alike' (Thrasher, 1927: 36) instigated a heated and ongoing debate about gang definitions (see Esbensen *et al.*, 2001, for review). Definitions are vital since without them we cannot know what researchers refer to. Research founded on *assumed* understandings only create ambiguity and create distorted media and public officials' views of gangs (Horowitz, 1990). A gang is a group but a group is not necessarily a gang and the lack of consensus about this difference has dogged gang research for decades (see Spergel, 1995, for review).

A main impasse in agreeing a definition is whether criminal activity should be a defining feature of a gang (e.g. Bennett & Holloway, 2004). Certainly, if criminal activity is excluded then there will be 'good' and 'bad' gangs (i.e. those criminally active and those not). But this will only exacerbate the chaos that infects the definition debate. For example, Everard (2006) notes that in Glasgow, groups of teenagers labeled as 'gangs' claimed that they banded together to *stay out* of trouble. So, how can researchers consider such a group in the same vein as they do those involved in drive-by shootings? Equally, such definitions run the risk that non-offending youth will be stigmatized by the label 'gang' and gain a 'gangster' identity (Bullock & Tilley, 2002). A defining feature of any entity is surely *who* wants to examine it. Those interested in gangs include the police, criminologists, task force agents, and, more recently, forensic psychologists. And the main reason why they are interested in gangs is their criminal activity. Gangs may differ on many dimensions, (e.g. size, member age etc.) but one aspect they all share *is* their criminality. Thus, we argue that criminal activity represents the *core* definitional feature of a gang.

The Eurogang network has reached a consensus on definition (Weerman *et al.*, 2009) and makes an important distinction between gang 'descriptors' and gang 'definers.' Descriptors are descriptive (e.g. ethnicity, age, gender, special clothing and argot, location, group names, crime patterns, and so on; Klein, 2006) and should not influence definition. Definers, however, are central to characterizing a gang. The Eurogang definition offers four defining elements: *durability* (at least several months), *street orientation* (away from home, work, school), *youthfulness* (adolescence or early twenties), and *identity via illegal activity* (criminal activity). Thus, the definition states that: 'a street gang (or troublesome youth group corresponding to a street gang elsewhere) is any durable, street-oriented youth group whose identity includes involvement in illegal activity' (Weerman *et al.*, 2009: 20). This consensus is vital for the future of gang research since a definition is more than a description of what we mean. It is a research tool – an 'instrument' – that 'underlies all other instruments' (Weerman *et al.*, 2009: 6). Without the vital parameters set by a definition even the best researchers' efforts and best research designs will be seriously hindered by a common misunderstanding of meaning.

GROUP PROCESSES

Gang membership and structure

Research examining member characteristics has focused primarily on the age (e.g. Rizzo, 2003), gender (see below), and ethnic origins (e.g. Gatti *et al.*, 2005) of gang members. Gang members in the United States and the United Kingdom are overwhelmingly young on entry to the gang (12 – 18 years old; e.g. Rizzo, 2003). Some continue gang membership well into their 20s or even older (e.g. Bullock and Tilley, 2002). Research examining ethnic composition has found that some gangs are homogeneous (e.g. Bullock & Tilley, 2002), whilst others are heterogeneous (e.g. Gatti *et al.*, 2005). This inconsistency supports the notion that gangs simply reflect the ethnic make-up of their neighborhoods (Bullock & Tilley, 2002).

The media portray gangs as highly organized with a clear structure, leadership, and committed membership. In fact, 'Street gangs generally are alike, and yet there is much difference among them' (Klein & Maxson, 2006: 194). For instance, gangs may have a haphazard organizational structure or they may have a written constitution (Decker, 2001). Most have rules and group meetings and some even take a political interest by actively supporting specific candidates (Decker, 2001). Some gangs own legitimate businesses, which may also launder money from drug sales, whilst others have no legitimate business interests (Decker, 2001). Many gangs have subgroups; smaller factions based on friendship, school attendance, common residence, or similarities in age, gender, or ethnicity (Klein & Maxson, 2006). Membership is often transient leaving many gangs with an unstable structure (e.g. Thornberry *et al.*, 2003).

To lend coherence to our understanding of gang structures, Klein and Maxson (2006) derived a taxonomy of five gang types: Traditional gangs; Neotraditional gangs; Compressed gangs; Collective gangs and Speciality gangs. *Traditionals* have existed for more than 20 years and generally exceed 100 members with a wide age range (e.g. 9 – 30+ years). Probably due to size they usually have subgroups, formed by age groups or area. They are territorial, identify strongly with their area, and their criminal activity is generally versatile. *Neotraditionals* are similar to Traditionals but have existed for less than 10 years. They are medium or large in size (generally 50 – 100 members, but may have hundreds) and often have subgroups, again according to age or area. Members may be very young or much older. Like Traditionals, Neotraditionals are territorial and versatile in criminality. *Compressed* gangs are smaller with up to 50 members, no subgroups, and have existed for less than 10 years. Age ranges are narrow (generally only 10 years between youngest and oldest), they may or may not be territorial but again they are versatile in crime. *Collectives* are similar to Compressed gangs but are bigger with a wider age-range. They have existed for 10 – 15 years and membership usually exceeds 100, but can be less. They do not normally have subgroups, they may or may not be territorial, and, again, their criminality is versatile. Due to chaotic membership they have fewer distinguishing characteristics than other gangs. *Speciality* gangs differ from all other gangs because they concentrate on specific offenses which are the group's main focus. They are small (50 or less), seldom have subgroups, have existed for less than 10 years, and have a clearly defined territory. Their ages are generally similar (less than 10 years range) but can be wider.

Leadership, status, and female membership

The image of a gang having a charismatic leader is not supported by research. The group norms of gangs mean that they generally function as a group and are unlikely to have stable leadership (Klein & Maxson, 2006). Indeed, many gang members are hostile to the idea of a leader (Decker & Van Winkle, 1996). When it does occur, leadership is quite informal, and functions on the person's potential to satisfy the gang's needs (Decker & Van Winkle, 1996).

Thrasher (1927) noted differential levels of gang membership: an inner circle, rank and file, and fringe members. This remains; gangs have a fluid hierarchy of members and youth on the periphery (e.g. Alleyne & Wood, 2010; Curry *et al.*, 2002; Esbensen *et al.*, 2001). Unsurprisingly, intra-gang norms dictate that core members have higher status; generally earned by violent acts against rival gangs (Decker & Van Winkle, 1996). Core members often have lower levels of: school performance, judged intelligence, impulse control, desire for rehabilitation, and interests outside the gang (Klein, 1971). They are also more likely to be: psychopathic, dependent on their group, willing to fight, and get others into trouble or skip school. Core members show more commitment to their group through – for example – participation in spontaneous activities, clique involvement, and group contribution (Klein, 1971). Predictably then, given their commitment to the gang, core members are most resistant to rehabilitation (Klein & Maxson, 2006). And since cohesiveness is often commensurate with criminality (i.e. the one increases levels of the other; Klein & Maxson, 2006), it seems that the gang members who are least likely to change will also be those who are most criminally active.

Researchers concentrate mainly on male gang members, and neglect and/or trivialize female membership (Moore & Hagedorn, 2001; Moloney *et al.*, 2011). Levels of female membership differ between gangs and across time. For instance, in the U.S. in 1970 10 per cent of gang members were thought to be female (Miller, 1975), by 2001 it was 37 per cent (Peterson *et al.*, 2001), which is reflected in current findings of 36 per cent for both the U.S. (Gover *et al.*, 2009) and the U.K. (Alleyne & Wood, 2010). Collapsing across findings probably puts the overall female gang membership at about 25 per cent (Klein & Maxson, 2006). Unsurprisingly, recent increases in female members have generated public concern and media attention (Moloney *et al.*, 2011). So, quite why researchers have neglected roughly a quarter of gang members is unclear.

Some argue that female members are viewed as pale imitations of their male counterparts (e.g. Spergel, 1995) with little gang-role other than as sexual objects serving male members (e.g. Sanchez-Jankowski, 1991). However, others report two distinct categories of female membership: 'she' gangs – solely female groups who concentrate on violence and crime (Pitts, 2008); or females in mixed groups who are active and assertive; standing equal to the males (Young *et al.*, 2007). Females also earn respect and status just as males do – by achieving the gang's aims (Decker & Van Winkle, 1996) – and may be considerably violent (Curry *et al.*, 1994). Alternatively, females may take ancillary roles by hiding guns or drugs for male members (Pitts, 2008) or acting as 'bait' to attract rival gang members into vulnerable situations (Decker & Van Winkle, 1996). Although females generally commit fewer crimes than male members, they do so at a higher rate than non-gang males or females (e.g. Esbensen & Huizinga, 1993). They may commit property and status crimes (i.e. age-related, such as underage drinking), but are most likely to commit drug-related offenses (Moore & Hagedorn, 2001).

Although female gang membership is neglected by research, it is an important area of study – now more than ever. Changes in family structure, particularly in poorer communities in the last decades (Decker & Van Winkle, 1996) mean that women are often lone parents. And so the increase in female gang membership over the past decades may have far reaching effects on the intergenerational transmission of gang membership, and must not be ignored by future research.

Motivation for membership and gang activity

Underprivileged youth may be enticed into gangs because of the opportunity to gain respect and status (Anderson, 1999; Klein & Maxson, 2006; Alleyne & Wood, 2010). Knox (1994) maintains that gangs exert two types of tempting social influence: coercive power – the threat or use of force and violence; and the power to pay, buy, or impress. As mentioned, young boys admire gang members, mimic them, and aspire to membership (Hughes & Short, 2005). This admiration may be reinforced by films depicting rewards for gang-like behaviors (Przemieniecki, 2005). So, youth may be attracted to gangs because they see a chance to acquire resources and satisfy goals that cannot be obtained legitimately within low-income environments (Goldstein, 2002). On achieving power and resources via membership, youth may also acquire higher peer status. Research shows that gang members (Anderson, 1999; Klein & Maxson, 2006; Alleyne & Wood, 2010) and peripheral youth (not full members), value status highly (Alleyne & Wood, 2010). This suggests that on-the-cusp youth aspire to the status that fully fledged gang members possess. Attraction may also be mutual since gangs often select/recruit members who are already delinquent (Thornberry *et al.*, 2003; Gordon *et al.*, 2004; Alleyne & Wood, 2010). Thus, the gang's interest in delinquent youth may positively reinforce behavior condemned by others (e.g. parents, schools etc.), and this may raise the youth's self esteem (see Dukes *et al.*, 1997).

Once a member, a youth's criminal behavior is set to increase. One of the most robust findings in criminological research is that gangs are disproportionately delinquent and violent (Thornberry, 1998). Gang members commit more crime (especially violent crime) than even prolifically offending non-gang delinquents (Tita & Ridgeway, 2007) and are more involved in drug dealing and use (Klein & Maxson, 2006). In the U.S., gang members are more likely than non-gang youth to carry a gun to school, possess illegal weapons, and use a gun to commit crime (Miller & Decker, 2001; Decker & Curry, 2002). The link between gangs and violence is so profound that fluctuations in murder and violent crime levels in U.S. cities such as: Chicago (Curry, 2000), Cleveland and Denver (Huff, 1998), Los Angeles (Howell & Decker, 1999), Miami (Inciardi & Pottieger, 1991), Milwaukee (Hagedorn, 1994), and St Louis (Miller & Decker, 2001) have been attributed to variations in gang activity. In Europe, gang, compared to non-gang violence, occurs in public, involves more weapons, more assailants, and more victims (often accidentally) not known to their assailants (Klein, *et al.*, 2006; see also Vasquez *et al.*, Chapter 3). In the U.K. at least half of the 55 murders of youth aged 13-19 in 2007 – 08 in London were thought to be gang-related (Home Affairs Committee,

2009) leading the government to issue anti-gang guidance to schools (BBC, 2010).

Most gangs are territorial (e.g. Klein & Maxson, 2006), using graffiti and threats to stamp ownership on their territory (Spergel, 1995; Alleyne, 2010), and, as mentioned above, gang members value status (Alleyne & Wood, 2010). Together, these findings suggest that acquiring and maintaining territory and status (gang and individual members) may motivate criminality. Perceived threats from others to status and territory are typically counteracted by a group response (Abelson *et al.*, 1998). Threats may stem from rival gangs and authority figures such as the police. So, it is not surprising that gang members hold anti-authority attitudes (Kakar, 2005; Lurigio *et al.*, 2008; Alleyne & Wood, 2010). It is possible that conflict between gangs and authority figures stem from *vicarious personalism* (Cooper & Fazio, 1979) where authority actions are perceived as directed specifically at their gang. Members then react with violence, which then cements gang relations, and increases cohesion and commitment. Even interventions attempting to reduce group cohesion may be construed as oppositional threat and paradoxically reinforce the gang's status and cohesion (Klein & Maxson, 2006).

Theoretical explanations of gang membership

Research offers a plethora of reasons why youth join gangs. Existing theories stem mostly from criminological perspectives (see Wood & Alleyne, 2010 for a review). However, no one theory fully explains gang membership. For instance Thrasher (1927) argued that *social disorganization* leads to the breakdown of conventional social institutions such as the school, the church, and most importantly, the family. Thrasher neatly set the failure of conventional institutions in opposition to the thrill and excitement that gangs offer 'the thrill and zest of participation in common interests, more especially corporate action, in hunting, capture, conflict, flight and escape' (1927: 32 – 33).

Shaw and McKay (1931) developed Thrasher's (1927) concepts by proposing that socially disorganized neighborhoods *culturally transmit* criminal traditions. For Shaw and McKay (1931), families in poor inner-city areas have low levels of functional authority over children, who, once exposed to delinquent traditions, succumb to delinquency. In this cultural climate, gang membership provides satisfying alternatives to unsatisfactory legitimate conventions.

Sutherland (1937), recognizing the prevalence of criminal behavior across social classes, developed a theory of *differential association*. Sutherland asserts that youth develop attitudes and skills to become delinquent by learning from individual 'carriers' of criminal norms and argued that a principal part of this criminal learning comes from small social groups such as gangs. Burgess and Akers' (1966) *social learning theory* built on and expanded Sutherland's work by introducing the concept of reinforcement for delinquency and proposed that deviancy will directly stem from the amount, frequency, and probability of its reinforcement. Mixing with delinquent others will therefore provide the opportunity for delinquency to be reinforced and continue. In 1998 Akers expanded the theory to also take environmental factors into account when explaining deviant behavior. *Strain theory* (Merton, 1938) argues that society sets universal goals and then offers opportunities to achieve them to a limited number of people. The resulting inequality creates a strain on cultural goals. This, Merton proposes, leads to anomie (Durkheim, 1893); a breakdown in the cultural structure due to divisions between prescribed norms and people's ability to adhere to them (Merton, 1938). Cohen (1955) saw gang members as working class youth who experience strain and status frustration. Status frustration may be ameliorated as youth associate with similar others to 'strike out' against middle class ideals and form delinquent subcultures where instant gratification, fighting, and destructive behavior become the new values.

Although *differential opportunity* (Cloward & Ohlin, 1960) is often considered a general theory of delinquency, it began life as a theory of gangs (Knox, 1994). Cloward and Ohlin (1961), like Merton (1938), explain class differences in opportunity, but unlike Merton, they argue that opportunity *for* delinquency is also limited. They argue that Sutherland also failed to consider that access to 'criminal schools' varies across the social structure. Consequently, they unite two sociological traditions; *access to legitimate means* (Merton 1938; Cohen 1955) and *access to illegitimate means* (Sutherland 1937).

Control theory (Gottfredson & Hirschi 1990; Hirschi 1969) neatly diverts attention from why offenders offend, to why conformists *do not* offend. Whilst strain theory concentrates on the *presence* of negative cultural relationships in delinquency, control theory focuses on the *absence* of key relationships (Agnew, 1992; Klemp-North, 2007). The central contention is that people are inherently disposed to offend due to short-term gains (e.g. immediate money) and that crime satisfies desires in the quickest and simplest ways possible (Gottfredson & Hirschi, 1990). A breakdown in social bonds or inadequate psychological support during childhood leaves a child free to act on his/her natural inclinations without adverse emotional consequences. Adequate child rearing necessitates: monitoring the child's behavior and recognizing and punishing deviant behavior, creating 'a child more capable of delaying gratification, more sensitive to the interests and desires of others, more independent, more willing to accept restraints on his activity and more unlikely to use force or violence to attain his ends' (Gottfredson & Hirschi, 1990: 97).

Empirical evidence

A wealth of research supports the theories outlined above. For example, youth are thought to join gangs because membership compensates for environmental shortfalls (e.g. low employment opportunities) by providing illegitimate means to goals (Klemp-North, 2007). Research also shows that youth living in highly delinquent neighborhoods are more likely to become delinquent than youth in low delinquency areas (e.g. Hill *et al.*, 2001). Gang members are also more exposed to negative environmental influences, such as drug taking and delinquent peer groups (e.g. Klemp-North, 2007) and neighborhoods with existing gangs (Spergel, 1995).

In terms of familial influences, research shows that gang members' families are often disorganized and gang members have often lost contact with a parent(s) due to death, separation, or divorce (Klemp-North, 2007). If families are intact, gang members often experience poor parental management (Thornberry *et al.*, 2003; Sharp *et al.*, 2006) or levels of physical punishment that cause them to leave home or retaliate with similar aggression (Klein, 1995). Further, gang members' families are often criminally active (e.g. Eitle *et al.*, 2004) and youth are likely to become criminal if exposed to law-breaking attitudes early in life, over a prolonged period of time, and from people they like (e.g. Sutherland & Cressey, 1960). Furthermore, familial gang members (i.e. parents, siblings, etc.) increase the risk of joining a gang (Spergel, 1995) since familial criminality (Eitle *et al.*, 2004; Sharp *et al.*, 2006), and gang-involved families (Spergel, 1995) provide environments that reinforce gang-related and delinquent behavior (Thornberry *et al.*, 2003).

Research also shows that poor performance in and commitment to school facilitates gang membership (e.g. Thornberry *et al.*, 2003). Gang members often have a low IQ (Spergel, 1995) and/or learning disabilities (Hill *et al.*, 1999), which may adversely affect the youth's ability to flourish at school. In turn, this can generate low commitment to school life and a positive future (e.g. Brownfield, 2003) by endorsing perceptions that legitimate opportunities are unavailable.

If youth cannot integrate into legitimate societal institutions (e.g. school/work), they may be tempted into deviant peer groups (Hill *et al.*, 1999). Delinquent peers and the pressure they exert substantially increase chances that youth will become involved in delinquency (e.g. the confluence model – Dishion *et al.*, 1994; Monahan *et al.*, 2009) and gang membership (e.g. Esbensen & Weerman, 2005).

Individual differences: psychological perspectives of gang membership

Although an abundance of excellent research supports the above theories, critics point out their tendency to see people as vessels to be filled with society's impositions (Emler & Reicher, 1995). There is also evidence that refutes several theoretical propositions. For instance, children raised in the same household are 'variably prone' to gang involvement and gang members just as easily emerge from wealthier backgrounds (Spergel, 1995). Another problem is that we understand little about why most lower class youth eventually lead law-abiding lives despite their economic status remaining static (Goldstein, 1991). We also do not know why it is that 33 per cent of youth from deprived areas, who have experienced significant trauma (e.g. acrimonious divorce, domestic violence, family estrangement from siblings), have never offended (Webster *et al.*, 2006).

Moreover, far from rebelling against middle class norms, many gang members endorse middle class values (e.g. Sikes, 1997) and spend a lot of time engaged in conventional pursuits such as trying to find a job, sporting activities, and committing to a positive future by, for example, enlisting in the Navy (Hughes & Short, 2005). Research also shows that parental supervision has a very modest relationship with gang membership (LeBlanc & Lanctot, 1998). Moreover, evidence shows that it is legitimate social controls that urge gang members to stop offending. Gang members leave the gang in favor of fatherhood (Moloney *et al.*, 2009), motherhood (Moloney *et al.*, 2011), and employment (Sampson & Laub, 2001). In addition, the classic study conducted by Short and Strodtbeck (1965) found no support for many of the theories outlined above and challenged assumptions that gangs oppose white, middle class American culture since many ethnic minorities adhere to their own cultures and simply ignore the majority culture that they apparently contest.

Each of these findings highlights the importance of individual differences and the psychological processes that underpin differential behavior of gang members and youth generally. So far, research has paid little attention to individual differences and the psychology of gang membership (Thornberry *et al.*, 2003). Some work has examined personality traits and identified that youth with psychopathic tendencies (i.e. high hyperactivity, low anxiety, and anti-social tendencies) living in disorganized neighborhoods (i.e. with a high turnover of residents) are five times more likely to become gang members than youth without such personality traits (Dupéré *et al.*, 2007). They are also less sensitive to parental attempts at supervision (Dupéré *et al.*, 2007) and even more vulnerable to gang membership if they live in an adverse family environment (Lacourse *et al.*, 2006). As noted earlier, we already know that certain psychological factors are important in gang membership (e.g. attitudes, IQ levels, learning difficulties, mental health problems, and low self-esteem). Psychology, clearly, has much to offer gang research, but so far it has been rather quiet on the topic (see Wood & Alleyne, 2010 for a review). Below we outline some of the classic psychological theories that could illuminate our understanding of gangs.

Social learning theory

Psychological theories such as Bandura's (1977) social learning theory can offer insight into gang membership. Bandura maintained that behavior may be learned via direct and vicarious learning and that their emergence may also be influenced by physical factors such as genes and hormones. So, aggression could be learned via direct observations (e.g. familial abuse, neighborhood delinquency) or vicarious experiences (e.g. television). The behavior can be triggered by factors such as: aversion (thereby causing anger), modeling (e.g. another being rewarded for aggression), incentives (i.e. gaining financial rewards), and/or instructions (i.e. being told to aggress by superior others – e.g. gang leaders). A behavior is repeated if it is reinforced (e.g. rewards such as money, peer approval, and elevated status) and if moral issues can be resolved by justifying the action (e.g. rival gang members deserve to be attacked).

Research lends support to social learning theory concepts by showing that factors such as peer criminality and delinquency (Winfree *et al.*, 1994; Lahey *et al.*, 1999; Esbensen *et al.*, 2001; Thornberry *et al.*, 2003; Klein & Maxson, 2006), parental criminality (Winfree *et al.*, 1994; Eitle *et al.*, 2004; Klein & Maxson, 2006), peer attitudes, peer pressure and the individual's negative moral attitudes (Winfree *et al.*,

1994; Esbensen *et al.*, 2001; Sharp *et al.*, 2006), are more capable of distinguishing gang members from non-gang youth than demographic characteristics (i.e. gender, ethnicity, place of residence, etc.). However, social learning theory fails to specify *how much* individuals need to favor crime before they adopt criminal lifestyles (such as gang membership) since people generally hold beliefs that justify crime only in certain situations (Agnew, 1995; Akers, 1997).

Social identity theory

Another psychological theory that can shed light on gang membership is *social identity theory* (Tajfel, 1974 – see Viki and Abrams, Chapter 1, for a more in-depth discussion). Research suggests that an individual's self-concept is partly composed of their social and psychological group(s) membership (Tajfel, 1974; Turner, 1982). And so this theory outlines the functional significance of group membership to individual identity, which may then be expressed with respect to group membership, (Turner, 1982; Sherman *et al.*, 1999). Within the group, determinants of social identity include processes such as in-group-out-group distinctions (e.g. favoritism vs. discrimination) and shared attitudes, values, and beliefs of members (Goldstein, 2002). The group itself has a collective identity, which the group defends against perceived threats (Emler & Reicher, 1995). And social psychologists show how intergroup competitive and discriminatory behavior can be provoked by the mere awareness of an out-group (e.g. Tajfel & Turner, 1979). This idea was neatly demonstrated by the classic 'Robbers Cave experiment' (Sherif *et al.*, 1961), where even arbitrarily created groups – whose members did not know each other – resulted in in-group favoritism and out-group discrimination. Sherif suggested that the perceived threat of an out-group to goal attainment provoked group solidarity during intergroup competition (Dion, 1979).

Social identity theory has much to offer gang research – especially in terms of their group processes (Klein & Maxson, 2006). However, in the study of gangs we also need to understand psychological processes at the individual level. For instance, we need to understand where the inclination to join deviant and violent groups originates and why it might differ between say two youth from the same family (Spergel, 1995). Certainly group membership may foster and develop aspects of a youth's character, but to understand gangs fully we also need to understand more about the psychological processes that underlie an individual's *inclination* for deviance.

Interactional theory

Addressing the gang issue more specifically, *interactional theory* (Thornberry, 1987; Thornberry & Krohn, 2001; Thornberry *et al.*, 2003) builds on earlier criminological theories by proposing that gang membership involves a reciprocal relationship between the individual and: peer groups, social structures (i.e. poor neighborhood, school and family environments), weakened social bonds, and a learning environment that fosters and reinforces delinquency. This theory therefore links concepts from control theory and social learning theory. As discussed previously, control theory argues that people become deviant when their bonds to society weaken and social learning theory maintains that crime is learned and positively reinforced. Interactional theory therefore offers a *developmental* explanation of delinquency where control, learning, and delinquency factors are reciprocal and influence the individual across his/her lifespan (Thornberry *et al.*, 2003).

As noted earlier, Thornberry and colleagues (2003) maintain that gang membership can result from *selection* where gangs select and recruit existing delinquents (Lahey *et al.*, 1999; Craig *et al.*, 2002). It also argues that membership occurs through *facilitation* where gangs offer opportunities for delinquency to non-delinquent youth (Gatti *et al.*, 2005; Gordon *et al.*, 2004; Thornberry *et al.*, 1993), and *enhancement* where gang members are recruited from a population of youth who are more antisocial than non-gang youth before membership, but become even more so following membership (Gatti *et al.*, 2005; Thornberry *et al.*, 1993).

Interactional theory examines gang membership from a unique perspective. It considers that not all members are delinquent before joining a gang and how gang membership facilitates/escalates delinquency. However, this theory also has its limitations. So far it does not provide insight into the specific psychological processes that *motivate* gang membership and neither does it explain why youth leave a gang. Research shows that risk factors from social *and* environmental domains, (i.e. the individual, family, school, peer, and neighborhood factors), as discussed earlier, increase the likelihood of joining a gang. And the more risk factors a youth experiences, the more prone s/he will be to gang membership (Hill *et al.*, 2001; Howell & Egley, 2005). Since most gang research is conducted with adolescent samples, Howell and Egley argue that the pathway to gang membership is well underway in childhood and so early key factors that precede acknowledged risk factors are unknown. Howell and Egley (2005) therefore propose that interactional theory be expanded to include risk factors in younger age groups. Nonetheless, interactional theory offers a fruitful way forward for developing gang theory and gang research.

Current research and theoretical developments

No one theory fully explains gang development. A good theory should be able to explain and predict behavior (e.g. Newton-Smith, 2002). It should be coherent, consistent, and unify aspects of a diverse phenomenon to provide a clear and logical account of the world. Theory knitting refers to integrating the best *existing* ideas into a new framework (Ward & Hudson, 1998). It involves identifying both common and unique ideas from existing theories to preserve good ideas (Ward & Beech, 2004). An integrated theory of gang membership should therefore bring together the good ideas contained in current theories into a model with explanatory power and *testable* hypotheses. Such a model will facilitate the examination of specific aspects of gang membership and the further development of theory.

A unified theory of gang involvement

A *Unified Theory of Gang Involvement* (Wood & Alleyne, 2010;) is the latest comprehensive model that brings together both criminological and psychological factors to membership. It draws together concepts from criminological theory and integrates them with relevant *psychological* factors (see Figure 2.1) and includes

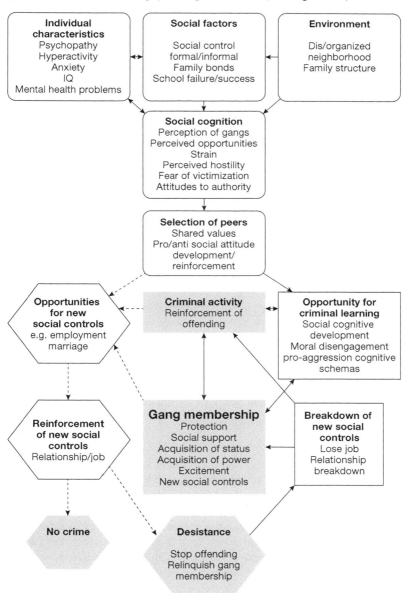

Figure 2.1 A unified theory of gang involvement.

concepts from similar models (e.g. Howell & Egley, 2005) to provide a comprehensive framework to guide empirical work. It illustrates the pathway into criminality and/or gang membership but it also illustrates non-criminal pathways, and pathways out of criminality and/or gang membership. Hence the model offers a rounded conceptualization of criminality, gang membership, and non-criminal involvement. And it is this inclusion of alternative pathways together with key psychological and criminological factors which distinguishes it from other similar models

Individual, social, and environmental influences

As the model shows, *social factors, individual characteristics*, and *environment* are important starting points for social development. Family structure and type of neighborhood inter-relate since families with poor or unstable structures (i.e. frequent house moves and/or changes in parental partners) potentially live in disorganized neighborhoods. However, the model also considers *organized* neighborhoods as starting points for gang membership, since individual factors (e.g. psychopathic personality traits, low IQ levels, learning difficulties, mental health problems, and low self-esteem) may facilitate gang membership even if the neighborhood and family are stable. Environmental factors influence social factors such as formal and informal control. Disorganized neighborhoods may be difficult to police (formal control) and informal social controls (e.g. parental supervision) may be difficult due to family structure. This may weaken family bonds. Since poorly supervised youth are less likely to succeed at school, a breakdown in informal controls means the youth's school performance is likely to suffer. Organized neighborhoods may have more formal social control and more stable families, but individual factors such as psychopathic traits etc. (outlined above) will present social problems for families, challenge informal social controls, and place a strain on family bonds. These individual factors may also adversely affect a youth's school performance and the school's ability to manage the youth. In turn, school failure, weakened family bonds, and social controls may impact on a youth's levels of anxiety, mental health problems, and self esteem.

Social cognitive factors

Personal and social factors will shape the youth's *social perception* of his/her world. Gang activity in the neighborhood will inform a youth's attitudes and beliefs about gang membership and crime. If gangs are not active in the neighborhood, youth may develop perceptions of gang membership and crime from media images (see above) or from vicarious experiences of school friends who live in gang-active neighborhoods. Accompanying perceptions of gangs will be perceptions of legitimate opportunities. Difficulties or failure at school may impact on self-esteem and create negative perceptions of legitimate opportunities – leading to strain. Neighborhoods peppered with gangs and crime may create fear of victimization, which coupled with perceptions of limited opportunities, may create perceptions of the world as a hostile place. Negative attitudes to authority may form if youth attribute school failure to officials rather than the self. And if crime is high in the neighborhood, and formal social control is low, youth may develop hostile or even contemptuous perceptions of the police as failing (or not bothering) to protect people in poor neighborhoods. Perceptions of social environment, shared values such as a mutual like/dislike of school, mutual attitudes to authority, and mutual fear of victimization will feed into the youth's selection of peers.

Peer selection

Selection of peers will be based on commonalities and these will strengthen existing attitudes and social cognitions. Youth who flourish at school and who have a solid relationship with parents are likely to associate with peers who share these attributes (regardless of neighborhood structure and crime rates). These associations will strengthen pro-social moral standards and capitalize on legitimate opportunities for social controls such as employment, solid romantic relationships, and parenthood. This legitimate pathway will strengthen existing informal social controls and provide opportunities to progress, for example, in the workplace. On the other hand, even if youth are doing well at school and have solid familial backgrounds they may associate with delinquent peers due to the lure of protection, excitement, status, and power. However, this association may be fleeting since it conflicts with the youth's fundamental pro-social attitudes, morality, and school success. These youth may also find that the rest of the group does not view them as 'fitting in.' In short, they may do little more than 'flirt' with a more deviant lifestyle.

Learning to be criminal: opportunities

Associating with delinquent peers offers an *opportunity for criminal learning* and involvement in crime will reinforce these learning curves. By mixing with delinquents, existing anti-social attitudes will also be reinforced. To become criminally active a youth will need to set aside any existing pro-social moral standards s/he may have, and cognitively reconstruct harmful behavior (e.g. gang violence) into acceptable behavior. This process is known as moral disengagement (Bandura *et al.*, 1996). By associating with delinquent others, any existing pro-aggression beliefs and attitudes will be reinforced by peer approval, and lead to positive appraisals of personal deviance. This process will promote the development of information processing biases and deficits in a pro-aggressive direction, and be stored in memory as cognitive schemas to guide future behavior. Such schemas develop primarily during childhood (Huesmann, 1998), but have a lifetime influence and are resistant to change (Anderson & Bushman, 2002; see Collie *et al.* (2007) for a review). Thus, the younger the child is when s/he becomes deviant the more *critical* and *enduring* will be the influence. As the youth becomes more involved in criminal activity he/she may also experience an increase in self esteem (from peer reinforcement), and strengthened bonds with delinquent peers. In turn, this reinforces his/her resolve for continued criminal activity.

Gang membership

The model shows how youth may become involved in criminal activity but avoid joining a gang. Criminal activity may occur *independently of*, or *simultaneously to,* gang membership. However, gang membership is likely to occur for reasons *over and above* those involved in becoming delinquent. Gang membership offers protection; possibly from threats from competing criminal entities (e.g. rival drug dealers); it provides social support, offers elevated status, the chance to acquire power, and potentially, excitement. Accompanying gang membership may be rules or social controls that members adhere to – thus providing a form of familial environment. Once a member, the youth has additional opportunities for criminal learning and criminal activity. Of course, hand in hand with these new opportunities for 'personal enhancement' come additional chances of victimization and these may lead gang member youth to desire a gang-free life.

Desistance of offending and leaving the gang

As the model shows (see Figure 2.1), desistance may occur at the criminal activity, or the gang member stage. The youth may give up criminal activity/gang membership in favor of employment and/or stable relationships. Of course these opportunities may be unfavorably influenced if the youth has been prosecuted for criminal acts. In this case the youth's criminal inclinations will either dispel (from fear of further legal sanctions) or strengthen (from the obstruction that prosecution places on legitimate opportunities). If, however, legitimate activities are reinforced (e.g. opportunities to advance in employment) the youth's resolve to desist from crime may strengthen and continue. If, however, they collapse (i.e. employment is lost or a relationship breaks up) then the youth may return to criminal involvement and/or gang membership.

This model has the potential to expand research findings at a psychological and criminological level. Because it includes pathways of non-involvement in crime and gangs and concepts of desistance, it allows us to make *meaningful comparisons.* And, as Klein (2006) observes, comparisons are too rare in the gang literature. Comparisons can be made between gang members, between abstaining and remaining gang members, and between gang and non gang members. It is also possible to compare neighborhoods by examining the individual characteristics, social factors, and social cognitions of youth living in organized and disorganized areas. Most importantly, it presents the integration of gang related concepts into a coherent structure that integrates criminological and psychological ideas and provides *testable hypotheses* for future work.

Conclusion

In this chapter we have considered the group processes of gang membership. We have examined the norms, roles, relations, social influences, and behavioral effects of gang membership. We have shown that research is dogged by definitional difficulties and that current theoretical approaches have both value and limitations. As a result, we come to the conclusion that empirical research guided by each of the theoretical approaches above reflects the strength and weaknesses of the theory that steers it. Nonetheless, street gang research has so far provided a wealth of empirical findings that offer much to consider. However, one of the problems with such a wealth of work is that confusion flourishes as gang researchers strive to select the best theoretical path forward. This can result in what seems to be more of a competition between theories than a concerted effort to develop and merge the best theoretical propositions. The arguments we present show the gaps in the literature and we suggest that the only real way to plug them is to take a multidisciplinary approach to the problem. By working together to identify reasons why youth join gangs, diverse disciplines will expand our knowledge and develop deeper and more meaningful explanations. Gang membership is complex and diverse and it will only be through the concerted efforts of interdisciplinary approaches to research that we will begin to unravel the vital criminological and psychological strands that construct it.

References

Abelson, R. P., Dasgupta, N., Park, J., & Banaji, M. R. (1998). Perceptions of the collective other. *Personality and Social Psychology Review, 2,* 243–250. DOI: 10.1207/s15327957pspr0204_2.

Agnew, R. (1992). Foundation for a general strain theory of crime and delinquency. *Criminology, 30,* 47–87. DOI: 10.1111/j.1745-9125.1992.tb01113.x.

Akers, R. L., (1997). *Criminological Theories: Introduction and Evaluation* (2nd edn). Los Angeles: Roxbury.

Akers, Ronald L. (1998). *Social Learning and Social Structure: A General Theory of Crime and Deviance.* Boston: Northeastern University Press.

Alleyne, E. (2010). *Gang Membership: Behavioural, Social and Psychological Characteristics* (Doctoral dissertation). University of Kent, Canterbury, UK.

Alleyne, E. and Wood, J. (2010). Gang involvement: psychological and behavioral characteristics of gang members, peripheral youth, and non-gang youth. *Aggressive Behavior*, 36, 423–436. DOI: 10.1002/ab.20360.

Anderson, E. (1999). *Code of the Street: Decency, Violence and the Moral Life of the Inner City.* New York, NY: Norton and Company.

Anderson, C. A. and Bushman, B. J. (2002). Human aggression. *Annual Review of Psychology, 53,* 27–51.

Bandura, A. (1977). *Social learning theory.* Englewood Cliffs, NJ: Prentice-Hall, Inc.

Bandura, A., Barbaranelli, C., Caprara, G. V., and Pastorelli, C. (1996). Mechanisms of moral disengagement in the exercise of moral agency. *Journal of Personality and Social Psychology, 71,* 364–374. DOI: 10.1037/0022-3514.71.2.364.

BBC news online (2010, March 11) Anti-gang guidance from government offered to schools. Retrieved from http://news.bbc.co.uk/1/hi/education/8560806.stm (accessed 30 March 2012).

Bennett, T. and Holloway, K. (2004). Gang membership, drugs and crime in the UK. *British Journal of Criminology, 44,* 305–323. DOI: 10.1093/bjc/azh025.

Brownfield, D. (2003). Differential association and gang membership. *Journal of Gang Research,* 11, 1–12. http://www.ngcrc.com/ngcrc/page2.htm.

Bullock, K. and Tilley, N. (2002). Shootings, gangs and violent incidents in Manchester: developing a crime reduction strategy. *Crime Reduction Research Series Paper, Vol. 13.* London, UK: Home Office.

Burgess, R. and Akers, R. L. (1966). A differential association-reinforcement theory of criminal behavior. *Social Problems, 14*: 363–383.

Cloward, R. and Ohlin, L. (1960). *Delinquency and Opportunity.* NY: Free Press.

Cohen, A. K. (1955). *Delinquent Boys: The Culture of the Gang.* Glencoe, IL: The Free Press.

Collie, R. M., Vess, J., and Murdoch, S. (2007). Violence-related cognition: current research. In C. Hollin and M. McMurran (series ed.) and T. A. Gannon, T. Ward, A. R. Beech and D. Fisher (vol. ed.), *Wiley Series in Forensic Clinical Psychology: Aggressive Offenders' Cognition Theory Research and Practice* (pp. 179–197). Chichester, U.K.: Wiley.

Cooper, J. and Fazio, R. H. (1979). The formation and persistence of attitudes that support intergroup conflict. In W. G. Austin and S. Worchel (eds), *The Social Psychology of Intergroup relations* (pp. 149–159). Belmont, CA: Wadsworth, Inc.

Craig, W. M., Vitaro, F., Gagnon, C., and Tremblay, R. E. (2002). The road to gang membership: characteristics of male gang and non-gang members from ages 10 to 14. *Social Development, 11,* 53–68. DOI: 10.1111/1467-9507.00186.

Curry G. D., (2000). Self-reported gang involvement and officially recorded delinquency. *Criminology, 38,* 1253–1274. DOI: 10.1111/j.1745-9125.2000.tb01422.x.

Curry, D., Ball, R.A. and Fox, R.J. (1994). *Gang Crime and Law Enforcement Recordkeeping.* Research in Brief. Washington, DC: U.S. Department of Justice, Office of Justice Programs, National Institute of Justice.

Curry, G. D., Decker, S. H. and Egley, A. (2002). Gang involvement and delinquency in a middle school population. *Justice Quarterly, 19,* 275,–292. DOI: 10.1080/07418820200095241.

Decker, A. H. (2001). The impact of organizational features on gang activities and relationships. In M. W. Klein, H. -J. Kerner, C. L. Maxson and E. G. M. Weitekamp (eds), *The Eurogang Paradox: Street Gangs and Youth Groups in the U.S. and Europe* (pp. 21–39). Dordrecht: Kluwer Academic Press.

Decker, S. H. and Curry, G. D. (2002). Gangs, gang members and gang homicides: organized crimes or disorganized criminals. *Journal of Criminal Justice, 30,* 343–352. DOI: 10.1016/S0047-2352(02)00134-4.

Decker, S. H. and Van Winkle, B. (1996). *Life in the Gang: Family, Friends, and Violence.* New York: Cambridge University Press.

Dion, K. L. (1979). Intergroup conflict and intragroup cohesiveness. In W. G. Austin and S. Worchel (eds), *The Social Psychology of Intergroup Relations* (pp. 211–224). Belmont, CA: Wadsworth, Inc.

Dishion, T. J., Patterson, G. R. and Griesler, P. C. (1994). Peer adaptations in the development of antisocial behavior: a confluence model. In L. R. Huesmann (ed.), *Aggressive Behavior: Current Perspectives* (pp. 61–95). New York, US: Plenum Press.

Dukes, R. L., Martinez, R. O. and Stein, J. A. (1997). Precursors and consequences of membership in youth gangs. *Youth and Society, 29,* 139–165. DOI: 10.1177/0044118X97029002001.

Dupéré, V., Lacourse, É., Willms, J. D., Vitaro, F. and Tremblay, R. E. (2007). Affiliation to youth gangs during adolescence: the interaction between childhood psychopathic tendencies and neighborhood disadvantage. *Journal of Abnormal Child Psychology, 35,* 1035–1045. DOI: 10.1007/s10802-007-9153-0.

Durkheim, E. (1893). *The Division of Labor in Society.* New York, NY: The Free Press.

Eitle, D., Gunkel, S. and Van Gundy, K. (2004). Cumulative exposure to stressful life events and male gang membership. *Journal of Criminal Justice, 32,* 95–the111. DOI: 10.1016/j.jcrimjus.2003.12.001

Emler, N. and Reicher, S. (1995). *Adolescence and Delinquency.* Oxford, UK: Blackwell Publishers Ltd.

Esbensen, F-A. and Huizinga, D. (1993). Gangs, drugs, and delinquency in a survey of urban youth. *Criminology, 31,* 565–589. DOI: 10.1111/j.1745-9125.1993.tb01142.x.

Esbensen, F-A. and Weerman, F. M. (2005). Youth gangs and troublesome youth groups in the United States and the Netherlands: a cross-national comparison. *European Journal of Criminology, 2,* 5–37. DOI: 101177/1477370805048626

Esbensen, F-A., Winfree, L. T., Jr., He, N., and Taylor, T. J. (2001). Youth gangs and definitional issues: when is a gang a gang, and why does it matter? *Crime and Delinquency, 47,* 105–130. DOI: 10.1177/0011128701047001005.

Everard, S. (2006). Streetwise teens gang together to avoid trouble and stay safe. Retrieved March 30, 2006, from the Joseph Rowntree Foundation press room website: http://www.jrf.org.uk/pressroom/releases/200206.asp

Gatti, E., Tremblay, R. E., Vitaro, F., and McDuff, P. (2005). Youth gangs, delinquency and drug use: a test of the selection, facilitation, and enhancement hypotheses. *Journal of Child Psychology and Psychiatry, 46,* 1178–1190. DOI: 10.1111/j.1469-7610.2005.00423.x

Goldstein, A. P. (1991). *Delinquent Gangs: A Psychological Perspective.* Champaign, IL: Research Press.

Goldstein, A. P. (2002). *The Psychology of Group Aggression.* West Sussex, UK: John Wiley & Sons Ltd.

Gordon, R. A., Lahey, B. B., Kawai, E., Loeber, R., Stouthamer-Loeber, M., and Farrington, D. P. (2004). Antisocial behavior and youth gang membership: selection and socialization. *Criminology, 42,* 55–87. DOI: 10.1111/j.1745-9125.2004.tb00513.x.

Gottfredson, M. R. and Hirschi, T. (1990). *A General Theory of Crime.* Stanford, CA: Stanford University Press.

Gover, A. R., Jennings, W. G., and Tewksbury, R. (2009). Adolescent male and female gang members' experiences with violent victimization, dating violence, and sexual assault. *American Journal of Criminal Justice, 34,* 103–115. DOI: 10.1080/07418820802593345.

Hagedorn, J. M. (1994). Neighborhoods, markets, and gang drug organization. *Journal of Research in Crime and Delinquency, 31,* 264–294. DOI: 10.1177/0022427894031003002.

Hill, G. H., Lui, C., and Hawkins, J. D. (2001). *Early Precursors of Gang Membership: A Study of Seattle Youth.* Juvenile Justice Bulletin, Washington, DC: US Department of Justice, Office of Justice Program, OJJDP.

Hill, K. G., Howell, J. C., Hawkins, J. D., and Battin-Pearson, S. R. (1999). Childhood risk factors for adolescent gang membership: results from the Seattle Social Development

Project. *Journal of Research in Crime and Delinquency, 36,* 300–322. DOI: 10.1177/0022427899036003003.

Hirschi, T. (1969). *Causes of Delinquency.* Berkeley and Los Angeles, CA: University of California Press.

Home Affairs Committee (2009) *Knife Crime.* Seventh Report of Session 2008–09 HC112–I. London: HM Stationery Office.

Horowitz, R. (1990). Sociological perspectives on gangs: xonflicting definitions and concepts. In C. Ronald Huff (ed.), *Gangs in America.* Newbury Park, CA: Sage.

Howell, J. C. and Decker, S. H. (1999). *The Youth Gangs, Drugs, and Violence Connection.* Bulletin. Washington, DC: U.S. Department of Justice, Office of Justice Programs, Office of Juvenile Justice and Delinquency Prevention.

Howell, J. C. and Egley, A. Jr. (2005). Moving risk factors into developmental theories of gang membership. *Youth Violence and Juvenile Justice, 3,* 334–354. DOI: 10.1177/1541204005278679.

Huesmann, L. R. (1998). The role of social information processing and cognitive schema in the acquisition and maintenance of habitual aggressive behavior. In R. G. Geen and E. Donnerrstein (eds), *Human Aggression: Theories, Research and Implications for Social Policy* (pp. 73–109). San Diego, CA: Academic Press.

Huff, C. R. (1998). *Comparing the Criminal Behaviour of Youth Gangs and At-risk Youths.* Washington, DC: U.S. Department of Justice.

Hughes, L. A. and Short, J. F., Jr. (2005). Disputes involving youth street gang members: micro-social contexts. *Criminology, 43,* 43–76. DOI: 10.1111/j.0011-1348.2005.00002.

Inciardi, J. and Potteiger, A. (1991). Kids, crack and crime. *Journal of Drug Issues, 21(1),* 257–270. Retrived from http://www2.criminology.fsu.edu/~jdi/ (accessed 15 October 2011).

Kakar, S. (2005). Gang membership, delinquent friends and criminal family members: determining the connections. *Journal of Gang Research, 13,* 41–52.

Klein, M. W. (1971). *Street Gangs and Street Workers.* Englewood Cliffs, NJ: Prentice-Hall.

Klein, M. W. (1995). *The American Street Gang.* New York, NY: Oxford University Press.

Klein, M. W. (2006). The value of comparisons in street gang research. In J. F. Short and L. A. Hughes (eds), *Studying Youth Gangs* (pp. 129–143). Oxford, UK: Altamira Press.

Klein, M. W. and Maxson, C. L. (2006). *Street Gang Patterns and Policies.* New York, NY: Oxford University Press, Inc.

Klein, M. W., Weerman, F. M., and Thornberry, T. P. (2006). Street gang violence in Europe. *European Journal of Criminology, 3,* 413–437. DOI: 10.1177/147737080 6067911.

Klemp-North, M. (2007). Theoretical foundations of gang membership. *Journal of Gang Research,* 14, 11–26.

Knox, G. W. (1994). *An Introduction to Gangs.* Bristol, US: Wyndham Hall Press.

Lacourse, E., Nagin, D. S., Vitaro, F., Côté, S., Arseneault, L., and Tremblay, R. E. (2006). Prediction of early-onset deviant peer group affiliation: a 12-year longitudinal study. *Archives of General Psychiatry, 63,* 562–568. DOI: 10.1001/archpsyc.63.5.562.

Lahey, B. B., Gordon, R. A., Loeber, R., Stouthamer-Loeber, M., and Farrington, D. P. (1999). Boys who join gangs: a prospective study of predictors of first gang entry. *Journal of Abnormal Child Psychology, 27,* 261–276. DOI: 10.1023/B:JACP.0000039 775.83318.57.

LeBlanc, M. and Lanctot, N. (1998). Social and psychological characteristics of gang members according to the gang structure and its subcultural and ethnic makeup. *Journal of Gang Research, 5*, 15–28.

Lurigio, A. J., Flexon, J. L., and Greenleaf, R. G. (2008). Antecedents to gang membership: attachments, beliefs, and street encountes with the police. *Journal of Gang Research, 4*, 15–33.

Merton, R. K. (1938). Social structure and anomie. *American Sociological Review*, 3, 672–682. Retrieved from http://www.jstor.org/stable/208468 (accessed 10 April 2012).

Miller, W. (1975). *Violence by Youth Gangs and Youth Groups as a Problem in Major American Cities*. Washington, DC: U.S. Department of Justice, Law Enforcement Assistance Administration, National Institute for Juvenile Justice and Delinquency Prevention.

Miller, J. and Decker, S. H. (2001) Young women and gang violence: gender, street offending, and violent victimization in gangs. *Justice Quarterly* 18, 115–140. DOI: 10.1080/07418820100094841.

Moloney, M., Hunt, G., Joe-Laidler, K, and MacKenzie,K. (2011). Young mother (in the) hood: gang girls' negotiation of new identities. *Journal of Youth Studies*, 14, 1–19. DOI: 10.1080/13676261.2010.506531.

Monahan, K., Steinberg, L., and Cauffman, E. (2009) Affiliation with antisocial peers, susceptibility to peer influence, and desistance from antisocial behavior during the transition to adulthood. *Developmental Psychology, 45*, 1520–1530. DOI: 10.1037/a0017417.

Moore, J. and Hagedorn, J. (2001). *Female Gangs: A Focus on Research*. Juvenile Justice Bulletin, Washington, DC: US Department of Justice, Office of Justice Program, OJJDP.

Newton-Smith, W. (2002). *A Companion to the Philosophy of Science*. Oxford: Blackwell.

Papachristos, A. V. (2009). Murder by structure: dominance relations and the social structure of gang homicide. *American Journal of Sociology, 115*, 74–128. DOI: 10.1086/597791.

Peterson, D., Miller, J., and Esbensen, F., (2001). The impact of sex compositions in gangs and gang members' delinquency. *Criminology 39*, 2, 411–439. DOI: 10.1111/j.1745-9125.2001.tb00928.x.

Pitts, J. (2008). *Reluctant Gangsters: The Changing Shape of Youth Crime*. Devon, UK: Willan Publishing.

Przemieniecki, C. J. (2005). Gang behavior and movies: do Hollywood gang films influence violent gang behavior? *Journal of Gang Research, 12*, 41–71.

Rizzo, M. (2003). Why do children join gangs? *Journal of Gang Research, 11*, 65–74.

Sampson, R. J. and Laub, J. H. (2001). Understanding variability in lives through time: contributions of life course criminology. In A. Piquera and P. Mazerolle (eds), *Lifecourse Criminology: Contemporary and Classic Reading* (pp. 242–258). Belmont, CA: Wadsworth/Thomson Learning.

Sanchez-Jankowski, M. (1991). *Islands in the Street*. Berkeley, CA: University of California Press.

Sharp, C., Aldridge, J., and Medina, J. (2006). *Delinquent Youth Groups and Offending Behaviour: Findings from the 2004 Offending, Crime and Justice Survey*. Home Office Online Report 14/06, London, UK: Home Office.

Shaw, C. R. and McKay, H. D. (1931). *Social Factors in Juvenile Delinquency, 2*, 13. Washington DC: Government Printing Office.

Sherif, M., Harvey, O. J., White, B. J., Hood, W. R., and Sherif, C. W. (1961). *Intergroup Cooperation And Competition: The Robbers Cave Experiment.* Norman, OK: University Book Exchange.

Sherman, D. L., Hamilton, D. L., and Lewis, A. C. (1999). Perceived entitativity and the social identity value of group memberships. In D. Abrams and M. A. Hogg (eds), *Social Identity and Social Cognition* (pp. 80–110). Oxford: Blackwell.

Short, J. F., Jr. and Strodtbeck, F. L. (1965). *Group Process and Gang Delinquency.* Chicago, IL: University of Chicago.

Sikes, G. (1997) *8 Ball Chicks. A Year in The Violent World of Girl Gangs.* New York: Doubleday.

Spergel, I. A. (1995). *The Youth Gang Problem.* New York: Oxford University Press.

Sullivan, M. L. (2006). Are 'gang' studies dangerous? Youth violence, local context, and the problem of reification. In J. F. Short and L. A. Hughes (eds), *Studying Youth Gangs* (pp. 15–35). Oxford, UK: Altamira Press.

Sutherland, E. H. (1937). *The Professional Thief.* US: University of Chicago Press.

Sutherland, E. H. and Cressey, D. R. (1960). A theory of differential association. In *Principles of Criminology* (6th edn). Chicago: Lippincott.

Tajfel, H. (1974). Social identity and intergroup behaviour. *Social Science Information, 13,* 65–93. DOI: 10.1177/05390184740130020.

Tajfel, H. and Turner, J. C. (1979). An integrative theory of social conflict. In W. Austin and S. Worchel (eds), *The Social Psychology of Intergroup Relations* (pp. 33–48). Monterey, CA: Brooks/Cole.

Thornberry, T. P. (1987). Toward an interactional theory of delinquency. *Criminology, 25,* 863–891. DOI: 10.1111/j.1745-9125.1987.tb00823.x.

Thornberry, T. P. (1998). Membership in youth gangs and involvement in serious and violent offending. In R. Loeber and D. P. Farrington (eds), *Serious and Violent Offenders: Risk Factors and Successful Interventions* (pp. 147–166). Thousand Oaks, CA: Sage Publications.

Thornberry, T. P. and Krohn, D. (2001). The development of delinquency: an interactional perspective. In S. O. White (ed.), *Handbook of Youth and Justice* (pp. 289–305). New York, NY: Plenum.

Thornberry, T. P., Krohn, M. D., Lizotte, A. J., and Chard-Wierschem, D. (1993). The role of juvenile gangs in facilitating delinquent behavior. *Journal of Research in Crime and Delinquency, 30,* 55–87. DOI: 10.1177/0022427893030001005.

Thornberry, T. P., Krohn, M. D., Lizotte, A. J., Smith, C., and Tobin, K. (2003). *Gangs and Delinquency in Developmental Perspective.* Cambridge: Cambridge University Press.

Thrasher, F. (1927; 1963). *The Gang: A Study of 1,313 Gangs in Chicago.* Chicago: University of Chicago Press.

Tita, G. and Ridgeway, G. (2007). The impact of gang formation on local patterns of crime. *Journal of Research in Crime and Delinquency, 44,* 208–237. DOI: 10.1177/0022427806298356

Turner, J. C. (1982). Towards a cognitive redefinition of the social group. In H. Tajfel (ed.), *Social Identity and Intergroup Relations* (pp. 15–40). Cambridge: Cambridge University Press.

Ward, T. and Beech, A. R. (2004). The etiology of risk: a preliminary model. *Sexual Abuse: A Journal of Research and Treatment, 16,* 271–284. DOI: 10.1177/107906320401600402.

Ward, T. and Hudson, S. M. (1998). The construction and development of theory in the sexual offending area: a meta-theoretical framework. *Sexual Abuse: A Journal of Research and Treatment, 10,* 47–63. DOI:10.1177/107906329801000106.

Webster, C., MacDonald, R. and Simpson, M. (2006). Predicting criminality? Risk factors, neighbourhood influence and desistance. *Youth Justice, 6,* 7–22. DOI: 10.1177/1473225406063449.

Weerman, F. M., Maxson, C. L., Esbensen, F., Aldridge, J., Medina, J., and van Gemert, F. (2009), *Eurogang Program Manual Background, Development, and Use of the Eurogang Instruments In Multi-site, Multi-method Comparative Research.* Retrieved from the Eurogang Network website: https://www.escholar.manchester.ac.uk/uk-ac-man-scw:58536 (accessed 28 September 2011).

Winfree, L. T., Backstrom, T. V., and Mays, G. L. (1994). Social learning theory, self-reported delinquency, and youth gangs: a new twist on a general theory of crime and delinquency. *Youth and Society, 26,* 147–177. DOI: 10.1177/0044118X94026002001.

Wood, J. and Alleyne, E. (2010). Street gang theory and research: where are we now and where do we go from here? *Aggression and Violent Behavior, 15,* 100–111. DOI:10.1016/j.avb.2009.08.005.

Young, T., Fitzgerald, M., Hallsworth, S., and Joseph, I. (2007) *Guns, Gangs and Weapons.* London: Youth Justice Board.

3 Applying socio-psychological models to understanding displaced and group-based aggression in street gangs

Eduardo A. Vasquez, University of Kent,
Brian Lickel, University of Massachusetts, and
Karen Hennigan, University of Southern California

The following are two fictitious scenarios involving gang members:

> Three juvenile members of an urban gang are riding in a car and are about shoot at a group of rival gang-members as a reprisal for an earlier attack against one of their own. None of the three companions in the car was a target in the attack, and probably none of their current targets was involved in the violence against their gang. The three in the car, however, perceive all members of the rival group to be appropriate targets for revenge.

> Hector and three of his friends, all members of a street gang, confront a group of three teenage boys whom they suspect belong to a rival gang. Such confrontations typically involve fist fights. Hector, however, works in a fast-food restaurant and was reprimanded by his boss earlier that day. This angered Hector, who has not stopped thinking and ruminating about it all day long; he wants to vent his anger at someone. He carries a knife and is ready to stab a rival gang member.

These scenarios illustrate different manifestations of *displaced aggression* (Dollard *et al.*, 1939), defined as aggression towards innocent others or as aggression levels that are greater than what is justified by a prior provocation (see Marcus-Newhall *et al.*, 2000). We theorize that gang members and individuals who have strong links to gangs (i.e. gang-affiliated) are more likely to engage in various forms of displaced aggression, which might include drive-by shootings against rival gangs and beatings of siblings, peers, or romantic partners. Herein, we aim to 1) discuss how social-psychological processes involved in displaced aggression may be relevant for understanding some aspects of aggressive behavior by members of street gangs, and 2) propose general techniques that may reduce that behavior. These are important goals because most research on gangs has focused on aggression targeted directly at the instigators and has largely ignored the role that displaced aggression might play in gang violence. A better understanding of this phenomenon would facilitate the development of techniques aimed at decreasing such violence. Thus, an additional goal is to propose direct links between basic social-psychological and applied research in a serious, real-world problem, and thereby stimulate further inquiry into this topic.

In this chapter we first discuss the concept of displaced aggression. We subsequently discuss different types of this behavior, namely, *triggered displaced aggression* (TDA; Pedersen *et al.*, 2000), and *group-based or vicarious retribution* (Lickel *et al.*, 2006), and how they might contribute to gang-related aggression. Finally, we discuss and propose ways in which displaced aggression can be reduced.

Gang activity has been of interest to researchers for decades (e.g. Hagedorn, 1988; Short & Strodtbeck, 1965; Thrasher, 1927; see also Wood & Alleyne, Chapter 2). Many urban areas of the US experienced an alarming growth of gang activity and violence during the late 1980s and early 1990s and again from 2001 through 2007. The National Youth Gang Survey results, for instance, indicate that an estimated 788,000 gang members and 27,000 gangs were active in the United States in 2007 (Egley & O'Donnell, 2009). During the last five years in Los Angeles, California alone, there were over 23,000 violent gang crimes in the city, including 784 homicides, nearly 12,000 felony assaults, approximately 10,000 robberies and almost 500 rapes (Los Angeles Police Department, 2009). In the UK, in London alone, 55 teenagers died violently in gang-related incidents in 2007–2008 (House of Commons Home Affairs Committee, 2009). Importantly, there are indications that gang activities are on the rise in the UK (see Wood & Alleyne, Chapter 2).

Many imagine drive-by shootings as the typical form of gang-related aggression. Many also believe that such attacks will create an endless cycle of retributive inter-gang violence. Gang members, however, engage in a variety of different types of violent acts towards rivals and other targets. Such acts may have different motivations, such as competition in the drug trade (Cohen *et al.*, 1998; Decker & Van Winkle, 1996), upholding one's status within the gang (Short & Strodtbeck, 1965), or revenge (Decker, 1996). The focus of this chapter involves retaliatory behavior targeted towards individuals who have either not themselves committed an offense against the aggressor(s), but belong to a group who has, or individuals who receive a punishment that is more severe than is justified. We categorize such acts as displaced aggression because the targets, at least from an observer's point of view, are innocent or do not deserve the *level* of punishment that they receive. In the following sections, we discuss the concepts of displaced aggression and group-based retribution, which are relevant to understanding important aspects of gang violence.

Displaced aggression

In their book on frustration and aggressive behavior, Dollard *et al.* (1939) discuss the concept of displaced aggression, whereby an individual who encounters a provoking incident, but does not retaliate, subsequently aggresses against a target that is not the source of the provocation (i.e., is innocent). At least three factors can preclude aggression against the original source of a provocation and set a context for displacement (Dollard *et al.*, 1939): the unavailability of the provoking individual; intangible instigators (e.g. economic recessions); fear of retaliation from the provocateur. When any of these factors comes into play, aggression is displaced towards individuals who are safer and available for punishment.

A meta-analysis of the displaced aggression literature suggests that displaced aggression is a reliable phenomenon (Marcus-Newhall *et al.*, 2000), and that the more negative the setting in which previously provoked persons interact with their target, the greater the levels of aggression they displace (Marcus-Newhall *et al.*, 2000). This suggests that when individuals are provoked, subsequent aversive events play a role in triggering the displacement of aggression towards other persons.

Triggered displaced aggression

Empirical work on the impact of triggering events on displaced aggression has shown that provoked individuals can displace aggression towards targets who provide a second provocation, a phenomenon termed Triggered Displaced Aggression (TDA; Pedersen, *et al.*, 2000). TDA differs from the classic notion of displaced aggression in that in the former, the target of aggression provides a second provocation termed a *trigger* (Pedersen *et al.*, 2000). Thus, the aggressor encounters two provocations – a Time 1 or initial provocation and a subsequent (Time 2) trigger. In the TDA paradigm, even a mild trigger can produce high levels of aggression towards its source when it is preceded by a more intense initial provocation (Pedersen *et al.*, 2000; Vasquez *et al.*, 2005). Note TDA is conceptualized as displacement because the level of aggression is contingent upon a prior provocation, and the target is punished to a degree that violates norms of reciprocity and escalation of aggression. The tit-for-tat rule (Axelrod, 1984), for instance, guides retaliatory behavior such that aggression is typically reciprocated in *small* increments.

TDA can be explained using Berkowitz's Neo-associationistic model (Berkowitz, 1993). Researchers hypothesize that triggered displaced aggression occurs because provocations activate in long-term memory a network of aggression-related motives, cognitions, and emotions that prime or prepare individuals for aggressive responding. In consequence, the negative characteristics of any additional events become more salient and impactful, thus producing a stronger behavioral reaction.

Rumination and displaced aggression

Affective arousal from a provocation is likely to dissipate after a period of 15–20 minutes (Tyson, 1998). As a result, as the time lapse between provocation and trigger increases, the chances of displacing aggression decrease because individuals become less primed to interpret events negatively (see Bushman *et al.*, 2005). One would thus be hard pressed to explain instances when a juvenile, angered by a fierce argument with his/her parents, viciously attacks another teenager two hours later because of a minor misunderstanding. *Rumination*, however, can explain such situations because it can maintain negative affect and cognitive representations of instigating events. Rumination has been defined in at least two ways. One definition involves self-focused attention toward one's thoughts and feelings and their causes following aversive events (Lyubomirsky & Nolen-Hoeksema, 1995). Another definition involves continuous thinking about a provoking incident (Bushman *et al.*, 2005; Rusting & Nolen-Hoeksema, 1998). Rumination can increase as well as maintain angry feelings and aggression-related cognitions (Martin & Tesser, 1989; Rusting & Nolen-Hoeksema, 1998). As a result, ruminating persons remain aggressively primed for long periods of time and are more likely to displace aggression long after a provocation (Bushman *et al.*, 2005).

Several factors can produce ruminative thinking. Intense provocations, for example, can motivate rumination. In addition, anger is a high-activation emotion (Larsen & Diener, 1992), which may involve self-justification for experiencing it when provoked (Baumeister *et al.*, 1990). Thus, it may be especially difficult for angry persons to stop ruminative thought (Tice & Baumeister, 1993). More stable personality traits may also influence rumination. Individuals who *tend* to ruminate following aversive events are more likely to remain primed for aggression for long periods of time following a provocation, and thus, engage in displaced aggression (Denson *et al.,* 2006).

Gang members and displaced aggression

No research has examined if the processes that produce displaced aggression contribute to the aggressive behavior of gang members. We propose that various socio-psychological factors place gang members at a higher risk for displacing aggression. Displaced aggression involves aggressive priming via provoking situations that preclude retaliation against the original provocateur. Gang members may be more vulnerable than non-members to experiencing such situations because much of their behavior is not normative in conventional society, thereby creating conflict with other individuals, especially authority figures. Research also shows that gang members are more likely than non-gang youth to be victimized (Katz *et al.*, 2011), which suggests that they are also more likely to suffer provocations. Juveniles likely inhibit retaliation against authority figures, such as parents or the police (who may victimize them specifically – see Wood & Alleyne, Chapter 2), for various reasons (e.g. respect, fear of punishment). Younger gang members may be especially inhibited because they lack the physical size or self-efficacy to retaliate. Further, social environments that produce maladaptive behaviors and lifestyles (e.g. abuse) may also produce more negative affect (see Vigil, 1998). Long-term stressors may be a chronic source of aggressive priming, increasing the chances of displacing aggression. These processes are likely exacerbated by the aggressive nature of gangs, whose members develop habits for reacting to aversive events with aggression, and may have a greater tendency to seek an outlet when unable to retaliate.

The processes we have discussed may additionally impact inter-gang contact. Inter-gang contact does not always produce violence, and rivals at times simply exchange defiant looks and verbal attacks in order to defend their honor (Moore, 2002; Vigil, 1998, 2002). Previously provoked individuals, however, may escalate an encounter into violence because they are primed for aggressive responding.

Rumination may also play a greater role in displaced (as well as direct) aggression in gang members. This is because individuals who perceive anger as useful are more likely to ruminate (Averill, 1982; Tice & Baumeister, 1993). Gang members fit this category because they tend to learn that aggression is an appropriate response to provocations (Decker & Van Winkle, 1996; Moore, 2002), and that anger (and revenge fantasizing) is also a suitable emotion when provoked. In addition, gangs adopt codes or norms of honor that guide the appropriateness of behaviors (Klein, 1995; Moore, 2002; Vigil, 1998, 2002). They are cultures of honor wherein violations of various norms of conduct is disrespectful, highly provoking, and inviting and justifying retaliation (Cohen *et al.*, 1996). Thus, because provocation intensity is positively correlated with rumination (Horowitz, 1986), and because gangs are predisposed to react strongly to provocations, gang members are expected to ruminate more than non-members. Rumination may exacerbate aggressive responses by distorting cognitive representation of negative events, attributions of blame, and the resulting justifications for retaliation, and thus, serve as a mediator between of provocations and aggression.

Group-based retribution and violence

The available (though limited) evidence on group-based retribution suggests it is not the most common type of aggression expressed by gang members. The violence committed by gang members appears to occur primarily during interpersonal provocations (with fellow members as well as with non-gang members) and in the commission of crimes, rather than inter-gang retribution (e.g. Decker & Curry, 2002). Retributive inter-gang violence, however, has accounted for a significant percentage of gang-related violence in cities, such as Los Angeles (Klein & Maxson, 1989). Such aggression between gangs is an important public safety issue, especially when bystanders are hurt. Although it is tempting to attribute all such violence to gang-member pathology, such behavior is less surprising when viewed in the broader scope of human social life. Indeed, group-based retaliation is a widespread phenomenon ranging from organized war between nations to smaller scale 'vendettas' and 'blood feuds' (Daly & Wilson, 1988). Research shows that group-based retaliation is more likely when a centralized and coercive power that can exert external control of the parties involved in the altercation is lacking (Otterbein & Otterbein, 1965). As a result, aggrieved parties resort to 'self-help' to get justice. This self-help justice often takes the form of 'blood revenge' (e.g. Boehm, 1987) in which members of the group retaliate against not only the perpetrator, but also (or instead) other members of the perpetrator's group. Blood revenge is enhanced in cultural contexts in which there is competition over resources, and groups are motivated to appear strong to protect these resources (Daly & Wilson, 1988). As a result, the 'honor' of the group and its reputation for toughness and willingness to aggress against those who transgress against it are important (Boehm, 1987; Daly & Wilson, 1988).

These cultural contextual variables parallel some aspects of gang life (see Decker & Van Winkle, 2002; Klein, 1995). Gangs live at least partially outside the law, and thus, cannot easily appeal to authorities to help them resolve disputes with other groups. Furthermore, many gangs do have territory with both symbolic and practical value (e.g. an area in which drug sales are controlled). These conditions of low external control, the need for 'self-help' justice, and competition over turf would predict group-based aggression against rival gangs, as an aspect of group processes, rather than pathology.

The central issue for researchers on group-based aggression is to understand how people who are not directly involved in an initial provocation can nonetheless become involved in the conflict. There are two parts to this issue. First, why are people sometimes motivated to retaliate on behalf of others when they themselves have not been directly harmed? Second, why are out-group members beyond the direct perpetrator of a provocation sometimes considered appropriate targets for retaliation? When both of these conditions are met (i.e. retaliation by individuals not directly harmed and aggression against people not directly responsible for the initial provocation), the ground is potentially set for a cycle of retributive tit-for-tat inter-group violence. Note that this phenomenon can be categorized as displaced aggression because retaliatory behaviors are targeted at individuals who are not the original perpetrators. Nevertheless, retributive violence also shares similarities with direct forms of aggression because an attack against the in-group is perceived as an attack on the self, and people are believed to be thinking consciously about the ways in which the targets of retribution share blame for the provocation. Below we sketch the cognitive and affective processes and variables that are believed to come into play preceding acts of group-based retribution.

Is it an inter-group provocation? The first question is whether an event is coded as relevant to the group. Not all negative events produce group-based retribution. For instance, the intensity of a provocation moderates whether people attend to the event and consider its implications. The likelihood of retaliating on behalf of a fellow gang member is also likely to increase when the person harming the in-group member is categorized as a member of a relevant out-group. Because of past rivalry, any negative act from a member of a rival gang is likely to be viewed as an inter-group provocation, even when the act is primarily in an interpersonal dispute.

The importance of in-group identification in the motivation to retaliate. Once an event is perceived as inter-group in nature, there is the potential for people not directly harmed by the initial provocation to be motivated to retaliate on behalf of the group. Revenge may be targeted against the provocateur or his entire group. For the moment, we consider people's motivation for either form of retribution on behalf of their group. This motivation likely depends on several factors. One of these is the degree identification with the group. Group identification is a multifaceted concept, but can be defined in terms of a person's degree of attachment to members of an in-group, and the extent to which the group is an important valued aspect of personal identity (Brewer & Silver, 2000; Ellemers *et al.*, 1997).

Group identification may predict gang members' motivation for retaliation on behalf of the group for several reasons. First, by sharing strong attachments to in-group members who have been harmed, they may feel empathically driven anger (Davis, 1994). Gang members may feel motivated to help their harmed in-group members by retaliating against those who harmed them. Identification also matters because of the importance of the shared identity of the gang. Attacks from a rival gang or other group may threaten the valued identity of the gang. Given that individuals are motivated to maintain a positive group identity (Tajfel & Turner, 1979), these threats are likely to induce anger and the motivation to even the score to restore a valued identity. Indeed, research has shown that, outside the context of gangs, in-group identification predicts people's anger towards threatening out-groups (Stenstrom *et al.*, 2008) and shifting self-categorization away from the harmed in-group to another identity can reduce anger (Ray *et al.*, 2008). This group-based anger predicts the motivation for retaliation against the direct provocateur and against the entire group when the provocation has been framed in intergroup terms (e.g. Maitner *et al.*, 2006; Stenstrom *et al.*, 2008). Interestingly, retaliating on behalf of the group satisfies the need for retribution and reduces anger amongst other in-group members (Maitner *et al.*, 2006).

Another potentially important route to inter-gang retribution involves norms to aggress on behalf of the gang. It has been hypothesized (Lickel *et al.*, 2006) that there is a generalized norm of group-based retribution for all groups, which may be especially strong for gangs. Insofar as there is a strong norm of retribution on behalf of the gang, several things follow from this. First, we hypothesize that these normative influences are greatest for individuals who identify highly with the gang. Research on attitude-behavior consistency, for example, shows that individuals who are highly group-identified are more likely to exhibit behavior that is influenced by in-group norms (Terry & Hogg, 1996). Second, we expect that those who fail to retaliate on behalf of the gang will lose status and may be punished by the group. Third, we expect that retaliating on behalf of the gang increases respect and status within it. These norms may be particularly true for individuals who have a special role in upholding and embodying the norms of the group, and for peripheral gang members who are trying to prove themselves (Alleyne & Wood, 2010).

Finally, it is important to consider the potential role of pluralistic ignorance in the perception of norms of retributive violence in gangs. Pluralistic ignorance occurs when one misperceives the extent to which others share one's views by falsely assuming that one's own view is in the minority (Miller & McFarland, 1991; Prentice & Miller, 1993; see Viki & Abrams, Chapter 1). In a gang context, members may privately want to avoid acts that would escalate a confrontation with another gang, but believe that their view is in the minority. Because everyone is worried about the consequences of even broaching the idea of not retaliating, everyone keeps quiet, even if most prefer to avoid confrontation. We know of no studies on pluralistic ignorance in gang violence contexts, which points towards one avenue for future research and potential interventions.

Who is an appropriate target? – Perceptions of out-group entitativity. Anger and normative influences provide the motivation for group-based retribution. However, who should be the target for retribution? The perpetrator of the initial provocation is certainly an attractive target for retribution. Yet, other members of the perpetrator's group are often also considered appropriate targets. This spreading of retribution from the direct provocateur to other people is the hallmark of group-based retribution. Part of the answer concerns the initial framing of the provocation, when individuals discern whether this is an interpersonal incident between individuals whose group identities are (or are not) relevant to the self. This initial construal process highlights groups to which the provocateur belongs and which might be considered as targets for revenge.

We also hypothesize that people consider the nature of these groups and the ties amongst the group members when targeting their retaliation. In particular, we believe that people may attend to the perceived entitativity of the group, which refers to the perception of a group as a cohesive unit, tied together by common traits, values, and goals (Campbell, 1958; Hamilton & Sherman, 1996; Lickel *et al.*, 2000). In many ways, it is the perceptual side of group cohesiveness – it is in essence the lay person's analysis of the degree of cohesiveness and interdependence amongst members of a group. However, perceptions of entitativity can also be biased – when people are highly identified with their group and are feeling very angry about an intergroup provocation, they may be motivated to see the rival group as tight-knit even if its members are only loosely associated (Stenstrom *et al.*, 2008).

Group-based retribution in gangs: issues for future research

We propose several issues about inter-gang violence that should be addressed by future research. First, to what degree is group-based retribution a source of gang-related violence, and how can we identify individuals and gangs that are most likely to engage in this behavior? A second issue involves group identification. Although members of groups differ in their degree of identification, is there evidence that the more highly identified gang members actually commit much of this group-based violence? Apart from identification, are there other factors that influence retribution? Do gang leaders or new initiates face greater pressure to aggress on behalf of their group? Gangs differ in the ways that normative pressures are brought to bear on members. How do these 'loosely knit' groups induce compliance to engage in group-based retribution? Past research (Lickel *et al.*, 2000) shows that lay people perceive street gangs to be highly cohesive, on the par with families and sports teams. Research on actual gang cohesiveness, however, indicates that gangs are generally not close and cohesive groups (Klein & Maxson, 2006), though outside threat may be used to rally the group to action (Short & Strodtbeck, 1965).

Another set of questions involve perceptions of the rival out-groups. For instance, how do gangs discriminate whom they target? Do gang members perceive rival groups to be cohesive? Do these perceptions influence the way conflict with a rival group is expressed? Is it only rival gangs who they engage in group-based retaliation?

Research in the gang area has a long history of interest in concepts such as *core to fringe* gang members (that vary in their level of commitment to the group and involvement in activities – see also Wood & Alleyne, Chapter 2) and *gang cohesiveness* (heightened and maintained in part through inter-group conflict; see Klein & Maxson, 2006). The act of attacking any member of a rival gang in the context of a 'gang war' mentality (Unamoto, 2006) that can be observed on a large or on a small scale is routinely observed in the street gang context. However, there is little research at present that measures these constructs and tests these relationships empirically in the gang context. Future research in these areas may extend our knowledge in ways that can lead to a reduction in gang violence.

Reducing displaced aggression

Interventions that reduce rumination are expected to diminish aggression for at least three reasons. First, decreasing rumination is expected to reduce the amount of time that an individual is motivated and primed to aggress (Bushman *et al.*, 2005). Second, the opportunity for triggering events to interact with prior provocations to produce TDA is also expected to decrease (Bushman *et al.*, 2005). Third, avoiding rumination should also decrease revenge planning and the attributional processes that further motivate and justify violence.

Research investigating potentially effective means for reducing anger rumination is currently lacking. Reducing rumination, however, requires more than just the attempt of suppressing negative thoughts. For instance, under cognitive load, instructing individuals to avoid thinking about a provocation has the paradoxical effect of augmenting rumination (Wegner & Erber, 1992), apparently because conscious suppression tends to increase the availability of negative cognitions. Nevertheless, research on rumination suggests one can employ distracting behaviors and cognitions to reduce ruminative thinking (Bushman *et al.*, 2005; Fennell & Teasdale, 1984; Morrow and Nolen-Hoeksema, 1990). In previous research, strategies for distracting individuals to keep them from rumination have included exercise and listening to music (Thayer *et al.*, 1994). Other potentially useful behaviors include meditation, relaxation techniques, and hobbies. Such distractions reduce negative affect by reducing the accessibility of negative cognitions and/or drawing attention away from negative moods (Fennell & Teasdale, 1984; Rusting & Nolen-Hoeksema, 1998).

Little is known about the relative effectiveness of various distractions in reducing rumination in gang members. Indeed, certain distractions that might be helpful for non-gang members (e.g. reading, meditation) may be ineffective among gang members because they are less involved in sports or other conventional activities (Decker & Van Winkle, 1996). Nevertheless, distraction is potentially a cost-effective way to decrease aggression by decreasing rumination. Specific distracting activities would need to be tailored to specific preferences and idiosyncrasies of individuals (such as those with an interest and talent in art). Thus, we propose that research be conducted to assess the impact of rumination on aggression among gang members and to examine specific strategies for reducing ruminative thinking.

Reducing group-based aggression between gangs

The prior section discussed ways in which the skills and coping abilities of individual gang members can be addressed in ways that may reduce their propensity for aggression. With regards to inter-gang violence, however, gang prevention programs in the United States that have been evaluated have shown little success (Klein & Maxson, 2006), in part because of a general prevention focus that does not take into account group process factors that draw youth toward street gangs (Hennigan & Maxson, 2012). It is important to note that large scale longitudinal studies in the United States concur that gang joining is most prevalent in early adolescence (Thornberry *et al.*, 2003; Hill *et al.*, 1999) with the highest rates of joining during middle school years. Not coincidentally, these are ages when motivation to be a part of social groupings is heightened. In the next section, we consider three strategies for addressing group-based retribution in the gang context. First, we consider the effect of interventions to reduce gang cohesiveness and identification on the motivation for group-based retribution. Second, we discuss possible benefits of interventions to address norms of retribution in response to provocations. This is important because street gangs are social groups that gain strength and cohesion through intergroup conflict (Short & Strodtbeck, 1965; Klein, 1995), and gang members' aggression is related to group norms. Finally, we detail the likely benefits of positive interpersonal contact between members of gangs as a means of improving inter-gang attitudes and attitudes about intergroup violence.

Reducing gang cohesiveness and gang member identification

We believe that gang interventions should be carefully assessed with regard to their effects on gang-members' identification with the gang and the gang's cohesiveness. Insofar as these factors can be reduced, it should reduce the motivation for group-based retaliation. However, some interventions may have the paradoxical effect of increasing gang cohesiveness and identification. For example, as has been discussed elsewhere (Maxson *et al.*, 2003, 2005), aggressive policing may sometimes cause members of a gang to band together in the face of a common threat. Likewise, past community-based gang interventions which focused on activities of the gang as a unit (as described by Klein, 1995) may have also ironically led to increased gang cohesion and identification. Thus, in the long run, such programs might actually set the stage for more gang against gang violence. Conversely, there is optimism that other kinds of interventions, particularly jobs programs, may reduce gang cohesion and gang-member identification (Spergel, 2007). These programs provide gang members with another valued identity apart from the gang (in addition to providing money for themselves and family). As gang members become less identified with the gang, they are likely to both feel less anger when their gang is provoked and less normative pressure to retaliate on its behalf.

Intervening to affect norms of retribution in gangs

Another approach to gang interventions is to understand and reduce the normative pressure for retribution. Beyond the anger-driven motivation to retaliate, people in gangs may also retaliate because of normative expectations, even if they do not feel much desire to take revenge. This norm-based route to retribution may be different from an anger-based route. In particular, it seems likely that there will be value to investigating if gang members display *pluralistic ignorance* about their fellow-gang members' attitudes vis à vis retribution.

Sometimes, people in a group behave in accordance with a norm that is not as widely supported as they perceive. Pluralistic ignorance – this collective misperception of members of a group about the normative beliefs of the members of the group – can be an important target for behavior change, when it is discovered. For example, research on student alcohol use (Prentice & Miller, 1993) finds that in some schools, students perceive heavy drinking to be normative, when in fact a large majority of students would rather not drink heavily. Evidence (Schroeder & Prentice, 1998) indicates that when people learn about the true base-rates of people's attitudes and no longer suffer from pluralistic ignorance, drinking is reduced. In the context of norms in gangs regarding retribution to inter-gang provocations, a first step is to understand the extent to which there is pluralistic ignorance. It may be that members of gangs have an accurate understanding of the beliefs and attitudes of their fellow gang members. However, insofar as people in gangs tend to overestimate support for retribution and are guided by these misperceived norms, an intervention could be developed to raise people's awareness that they are not alone in their hesitance about retaliation. Interventions that utilize vivid first-person narratives, in addition to base-rate information, may be most successful. It is also important that those people that convey the information have credibility as a source, given that gang members are likely to distrust the truth of persuasive messages they perceive as coming from the police or other authorities with an antagonistic relationship to the gang.

Positive inter-group contact and the reduction of aggression

Another approach to reducing group-based retribution relies on the *contact hypothesis* (Allport, 1954), which proposes that direct contact between members of rival groups is crucial for reducing inter-group conflict. History and research have shown that such contact is generally, but not always, beneficial (Hewstone & Greenland, 2000; Pettigrew, 1998; Pettigrew & Tropp, 2000). For instance, it is not difficult to imagine how members of two rival gangs that are trying to end a feud can revert to violence if they perceive any threat from members of the out-group during an instance of inter-group contact. Researchers, however, have examined various processes involved in social categorization that are likely to produce positive outcomes of contact and a reduction in inter-group conflict (Brewer & Miller, 1984; Pettigrew, 1998).

The basic approach for employing contact to reduce inter-group conflict is to have members of the groups interact in a positive manner in order to generate positive affect and cognitions (towards and about the out-group members) that are generalizable to the out-group as a whole and can disrupt processes that motivate group members to retaliate against out-group members. An important process for positive contact is de-categorization, which reduces reliance on category-based information when forming impressions of and interacting with out-group members. Category-based interaction is likely to preclude the induction of positive affect and cognitions. Thus, the aim is to lead individuals who are members of rival groups to avoid perceiving each other as part of a hated out-group, and instead, interact on an interpersonal level. Although we can identify several top-down modes of information processing that may de-categorize, each with its own advantages and disadvantages, we focus on *personalization*, a bottom-up mode of information processing, as particularly useful for positive inter-group contact (Brewer & Miller, 1984).

During personalization the information about an out-group member that is encoded and employed during an interaction is not dominated by the relevant social category (e.g. a hostile rival gang), but rather, by unique attributes of that individual. Personalized interaction can reduce bias against the out-group member involved in the interaction (Berg & Wright-Buckley, 1988; Fiske & Neuberg, 1990). Its positive effects can extend (i.e. generalize) to the out-group when the out-group member with whom such interaction has occurred is perceived as being typical or representative of that particular category (Ensari & Miller, 2002; Hewstone & Brown, 1986). For instance, rather than keeping in mind character-istics of the rival gang, the two interacting gang members can focus on individual characteristics of the other person (e.g. favorite TV shows, level of enthusiasm) when forming an impression, thereby increasing the likelihood of positive out-comes.

Personalization is a complex construct consisting of a number of distinct bottom-up processes. We discuss herein only two modes of personalized interactions, self-other comparison and self-disclosure, because they have shown promise in reducing displaced aggression towards out-group members (Vasquez *et al.*, 2007). We additionally touch upon perspective taking as yet another process with the potential to reduce inter-gang violence.

Self-other comparison involves the comparison of one's personal attributes with those of another individual (Brewer & Miller, 1984). During such comparison, the out-group person involved in self-other comparison becomes individuated and de-categorized (i.e. perceived as an individual and less as a part of a category or group). Further, self-other comparison involves noticing similarities and differences between the self and the other person, which further reduces reliance on stereotypes, and increases out-group variability. In consequence, the evaluation of an out-group member is more likely to be based on unique characteristics and not on perceptions of the out-group, thereby reducing negative bias and prejudice (Miller, 2002).

Research shows that self-other comparison can reduce TDA towards out-group members (Vasquez *et al.*, 2007). Vasquez *et al.* (2007), for example, showed that relative to those who did not engage in self-other comparison, provoked participants who compared themselves with an out-group member on a list of personality traits displaced less aggression towards the out-group member.

Self-disclosure is another component of personalized interactions that refers to the sharing of intimate, personal information (Collins & Miller, 1994; Miller, 2002). As with self-other comparison, self-disclosure individuates and de-categorizes. It may also induce self-other comparison by eliciting comparisons between attributes of the other person and those of the self. Importantly, self-disclosure may have other beneficial effects, such as decreasing anxiety and increasing familiarity with the other individual. Inter-group anxiety is an important factor for inter-group relations. Anxiety, for instance, decreases the willingness to have contact with out-group members (Voci & Hewstone, 2003). It also interferes with the processes that produce beneficial outcomes (Plant & Devine, 2003). Decreasing anxiety can then lead to improved processing of individuating information (Rothbart & John, 1985; Sears, 1983). Anxiety and fear are likely to be important factors for inter-gang contact given the high levels of perceived (and real) threat that gangs encounter.

Importantly, self-disclosure additionally carries the implicit message that the discloser trusts the recipient (Steel, 1991; Worthy *et al.*, 1969) and increases liking for the discloser (Collins & Miller, 1994). It also may increase feelings of friendship (Cook, 1978; Pettigrew, 1998), and thus, reduce bias (Ensari & Miller, 2001, 2005; Miller, 2002). Importantly, self-disclosure has been shown to decrease triggered displaced aggression towards out-group members (Vasquez *et al.*, 2007).

It is also likely that gang prevention efforts can try to reduce violence toward out-group members by promoting perspective taking or empathy across social groups. To the extent that an ability to shift perspectives can be nurtured and reinforced in early adolescence, the ease by which one can engage in displaced aggression against innocent victims might be hampered. Previous research suggests that empathy-based interventions have the potential for reducing inter-gang aggression. In inter-group contexts, for instance, perspective taking has reduced inter-group bias and the reliance on out-group stereotypes (Galinsky & Moskowitz, 2000), as well as interpersonal aggression (Richardson *et al.*, 1994). Thus, we recommend that future research investigate the potential benefits of this process for reducing gang violence.

Research on the positive effects of personalization and de-categorization on aggression is still very limited, and several issues need to be addressed. Assessing such effects in aggressive contexts is important because we propose that de-categorization should increase perceptions of out-group variability, and thus, reduce entitativity. Lower levels of entitativity should diminish collective blame, thereby lowering levels of group-based retribution. Further, ensuring that the positive effects of personalization generalize to an out-group is also expected to reduce collective blame and the desire to retaliate against the out-group in general. If the processes that induce positive contact between members of rival gangs do not generalize to the out-group, it is likely that all members of a rival gang will continue to be perceived as deserving punishment. Moreover, it is important to understand how provocation intensity interacts with categorization processes. Gang violence is an extreme form of aggression, and members of gang with a history of violent conflict may be resistant to positive inter-group contact, especially those who identify very strongly with their gang.

Conclusions

Understanding gang-related processes and reducing gang violence are formidable challenges, thus motivating the task of examining the various factors that contribute to these phenomena. Herein, we have focused our discussion on displaced aggression and group-based retribution, both of which can target aggression against individuals who are not the original sources of provocations. We have proposed that members of street gangs have a greater risk of engaging in these categories of retaliatory behavior. In support of our proposals, we have discussed models of displaced aggression and group-based aggression and why we hypothesize that they may be useful for understanding some aspects of gang aggression, both at inter-personal and inter-group levels. We have also recommended general ways to reduce displaced aggression. One recommendation involves distracting activities that diminish ruminative thinking as a way to reduce aggressive priming and revenge planning. Other recommendations are more focused on reducing inter-gang violence and are based on processes that de-categorize members of rival gangs and promote positive inter-group contact that can generalize to the out-group. We additionally make the point that empirical studies that examine the proportion of violence that is accounted for by models of displaced aggression and group-based retribution are currently limited. Thus, we propose that future research address the issues we have mentioned in order to augment our understanding of gang-related aggression.

References

Alleyne, E. and Wood, J. L. (2010). Gang involvement: psychological and behavioural characteristics of gang members, peripheral youth, and non-gang youth. *Aggressive Behavior, 36*, 423–436. DOI: 10.1002/ab.20360.

Allport, G. W. (1954). *The Nature of Prejudice.* Oxford, England: Addison-Wesley.

Averill, J. R. (1982). *Anger and Aggression: An Essay on Emotion.* New York: Springer-Verlag.

Axelrod, R. (1984). *The Evolution of Cooperation.* New York: Basic Books.

Baumeister, R. F., Stillwell, A., and Wotman, S. R. (1990). Victim and perpetrator accounts of interpersonal conflict: autobiographical narratives about anger. *Journal of Personality and Social Psychology, 59,* 994–1005. DOI: 10.1037/0022-3514.59.5.994.

Berg, J. and Wright-Buckley, C. (1988). Effects of racial similarity and interviewer intimacy in a peer counseling analogue. *Journal of Counseling Psychology, 35,* 377–384. DOI: 10.1037/0022-0167.35.4.377.

Berkowitz, L. (1993). *Aggression: Its Causes, Consequences, and Control.* New York: McGraw-Hill.

Boehm, C. (1987). *Blood revenge: The Enactment and Management of Conflict in Montenegro and Other Tribal Societies.* Philadelphia: University of Pennsylvania Press.

Brewer, M. B. and Miller, N. (1984). Beyond the contact hypothesis: theoretical perspectives on desegregation. In N. Miller and M. B. Brewer (eds), *Groups in Contact: The psychology of Desegregation* (pp. 281–302). New York: Academic Press.

Brewer, M. B. and Silver, M. D. (2000). Group distinctiveness, social identification, and collective mobilization. In S. Stryker and T. Owens (eds), *Self, Identity, and Social Movements.* (pp. 153–171). Minneapolis, MN: University of Minnesota Press.

Bushman, B. J., Bonacci, A. M., Pedersen, W. C., Vasquez, E. A., and Miller, N. (2005). Chewing on it can chew you up: effects of rumination on triggered displaced aggression. *Journal of Personality and Social Psychology, 88,* 969–983. DOI: 10.1037/0022-3514.88.6.969.

Campbell, D. T. (1958). Common fate, similarity, and other indices of status of aggregates of persons as social entities. *Behavioral Science, 3,* 14–25. DOI: 10.1002/bs.3830030103.

Cohen, D., Nisbett, R. E., Bowdle, B. F., and Schwarz, N. (1996). Insult, aggression, and the southern culture of honor: An 'experimental ethnography'. *Journal of Personality and Social Psychology, 70,* 945–960. DOI: 10.1037/0022-3514.70.5.945.

Cohen, J., Cork, D., Engberg, J., and Tita, G. E. (1998). The role of drug markets and gangs in local homicide rates. *Journal of Homicide Studies, 2,* 241–262. DOI: 10.1177/1088767998002003007.

Collins, N. L. and Miller, L. C. (1994). Self-disclosure and liking: A meta-analytic review. *Psychological Bulletin, 116,* 457–475. DOI: 10.1037/0033-2909.116.3.457.

Cook, S. W. (1978). Interpersonal and attitudinal outcome in cooperating interracial groups. *Journal of Research and Development in Education, 12,* 97–113.

Daly, M., & Wilson, M. (1988). *Homicide: Foundations of Human Behavior.* New York: Hawthorne.

Davis, M. H. (1994). *Empathy: A Social Psychological Approach.* Boulder, CO: Westview Press.

Decker, S. H (1996). Collective and normative features of gang violence. *Justice Quarterly, 13,* 243–264.

Decker, S. H. and Curry, G. D. (2002). Gangs, gang homicides, and gang loyalty: organized crimes or disorganized criminals. *Journal of Criminal Justice, 30,* 343–352. DOI: 10.1016/S0047-2352(02)00134-4.

Decker, S. H. and Van Winkle, B. (1996). *Life in the Gang: Family Friends, and Violence.* New York, Cambridge.

Denson, T. F., Pedersen, W. C., and Miller, N. (2006). The displaced aggression questionnaire. *Journal of Personality and Social Psychology, 90,* 1032–1051. DOI: 10.1037/0022-3514.90.6.1032.

Dollard, J., Doob, L. W., Miller, N. E., Mowrer, O. H., and Sears, R. R. (1939). *Frustration and Aggression.* New Haven, CT: Yale University Press. DOI: 10.1037/10022-000.

Egley, A. Jr. and O'Donnell, C E. (2009). *Highlights of National Youth Gang Survey.* OJJDP Factsheet. U. S. Department of Justice, Office of Justice Programs, Office of Juvenile Justice and Delinquency Prevention NCJ 225185.

Ellemers, N., Spears, R., and Doosje, B. (1997). Sticking together or falling apart: in-group identification as a psychological determinant of group commitment versus individual mobility. *Journal of Personality and Social Psychology, 72,* 617–626. DOI: 10.1037/0022-3514.72.3.617.

Ensari, N., & Miller, N. (2001). Decategorization and the reduction of bias in the cross-categorization paradigm. *European Journal of Social Psychology, 31,* 193–216. DOI: 10.1002/ejsp.42.

Ensari, N., & Miller, N. (2002). The out-group must not be so bad after all: the effects of disclosure, typicality, and salience on intergroup bias. *Journal of Personality and Social Psychology. 83,* 313–329. DOI: 10.1037/0022-3514.83.2.313.

Ensari, N. and Miller, N. (2005.) Prejudice and inter-group attributions: the role of personalization and performance feedback. *Group Processes and Inter-group Relations, 8,* 391–410. DOI: 10.1177/1368430205056467.

Fennell, M. J. V. and Teasdale, J. D. (1984). Effects of distraction on thinking and affect in depressed patients. *British Journal of Clinical Psychology, 23,* 65–66.

Fiske, S. T. and Neuberg, S. L. (1990). A continuum of impression formation, from category-based to individuation processes: influences of information and motivation on attention and interpretation. In M. Zanna (ed.), *Advances in Experimental Social Psychology* (pp. 1–74). New York: Academic Press. DOI: 10.1016/S0065-2601 (08)60317-2.

Galinsky, A. D. and Moskowitz, G. B. (2000). Perspective-taking: Decreasing stereotype expression, stereotype accessibility, and in-group favoritism. *Journal of Personality and Social Psychology, 78,* 708–724. DOI: 10.1037/0022-3514.78.4.708.

Hagedorn, J. M. (1988). *People and Folks: Gangs, Crime, and the Underclass in a Rustbelt City.* Chicago: Lake View.

Hamilton, D. L. and Sherman, S. J. (1996). Perceiving persons and groups. *Psychological Review, 103,* 336–355. DOI: 10.1037/0033-295X.103.2.336.

Hennigan, K. M. and Maxson, C. (2012). New directions in street gang prevention for youth: the Los Angeles experience. In J. Sides (ed.), *Post-Ghetto: Reimagining South Los Angeles.* Forthcoming.

Hewstone, M. and Brown, R. J. (1986). Contact is not enough: An inter-group perspective on the 'contact hypothesis'. In M. Hewstone and R. J. Brown (eds), *Contact and Conflict in Inter-group Encounters* (pp. 1–44). Oxford, England: Blackwell.

Hewstone, M. and Greenland, K. (2000). Intergroup conflict. *International Journal of Psychology. Special Issue: Diplomacy and Psychology, 35,* 136–144. DOI: 10.1080/ 002075900399439.

House of Commons Home Affairs Committee (2009). *Knife Crime.* Seventh Report of Session 2008–09. HC112–I. London: HM Stationery Office.

Hill, K. G., Howell, J. C., Hawkins, J. D., and Battin-Pearson, S. R. (1999). Childhood risk factors for adolescent gang membership: results from the Seattle Social Development Project. *Journal of Research in Crime and Delinquency, 36,* 300–322. DOI: 10.1177/0022427899036003003.

Horowitz, M. J. (1986). *Stress Response Syndromes* (2nd edn). New York: Aronson.

Katz, C. M., Webb, V. J., Fox, K., and Shaffer, J. N. (2011). Understanding the relationship between violent victimization and gang membership. *Journal of Criminal Justice, 39,* 48–59. DOI: 10.1016/j.jcrimjus.2010.10.004.

Klein, M. W. (1995). *The American Street Gang.* New York: Englewood Cliffs, NJ: Prentice Hall.

Klein, M. W. and Maxson, C. L. (1989). Street gang violence. In M. E. Wolfgang and N. Weiner (eds) *Violent Crime, Violent Criminals* (pp. 198–234). Beverly Hills, CA: Sage.

Klein, M. W. and Maxson, C. L. (2006). *Street Gang Patterns and Policies.* New York: Oxford University Press.

Larsen, R. J. and Diener, E. (1992). Promises and problems with the circumplex model of emotion. *Review of Personality and Social Psychology, 13,* 25–59.

Lickel, B., Hamilton, D. L., Wieczorkowska, G., Lewis, A., Sherman, S. J., and Uhles, A. N. (2000). Varieties of groups and the perception of group entitativity. *Journal of Personality and Social Psychology, 78,* 223–246. DOI: 10.1037/0022-3514.78.2.223.

Lickel, B., Miller, N., Stenstrom, D. M., Denson, T. F., and Schmader, T. (2006). Vicarious retribution: the role of collective blame in intergroup aggression. *Personality and Social Psychology Review, 10,* 372–390. DOI: 10.1207/s15327957pspr1004_6.

Los Angeles Police Department (2009). Official web site: http://www.lapdonline.org/search_results/content_basic_view/1396 (accessed 2 May 2009).

Lyubomirsky, S. and Nolen-Hoeksema, S. (1995). Effects of self-focused rumination on negative thinking and interpersonal problem solving. *Journal of Personality and Social Psychology, 69,* 176–190. DOI: 10.1037/0022-3514.69.1.176.

Maitner, A., Mackie, D., and Smith, E. R. (2006). Evidence for the regulatory function of intergroup emotion: emotional consequences of implemented or impeded intergroup action tendencies. *Journal of Experimental Social Psychology, 42,* 720–728. DOI: 10.1016/j.jesp.2005.08.001.

Marcus-Newhall, A., Pedersen, W. C., Carlson, M., and Miller, N. (2000). Displaced aggression is alive and well: a meta-analytic review. *Journal of Personality and Social Psychology, 78,* 670–689. DOI: 10.1037/0022-3514.78.4.670.

Martin, L. L. and Tesser, A. (1989). Toward a motivational and structural theory of ruminative thought. In J. S. Uleman and J. A. Bargh (eds), *Unintended Thought* (pp. 306–326). New York: Guilford Press.

Maxson, C., Hennigan, K., and Sloane, D. (2003). For the sake of the neighborhood? Civil gang injunctions as a gang intervention tool in southern California, In S. Decker (ed.), *Policing Gangs and Youth Violence* (pp. 239–266). Belmont, CA: Wadsworth/Thomson Learning.

Maxson, C., Hennigan, K., and Sloane, D. (2005). It's getting crazy out there: can a civil gang injunction change a community? *Criminology and Public Policy, 4,* 577–606. DOI: 10.1111/j.1745-9133.2005.00305.x.

Miller, N. (2002). Personalization and the promise of contact theory. *Journal of Social Issues, 58,* 387–410. DOI: 10.1111/1540-4560.00267.

Miller, D. T. and McFarland, C. (1991). When social comparison goes awry: the case of pluralistic ignorance. In J. Suls and T. Wills (eds), *Social Comparison: Contemporary Theory and Research* (pp. 287–313). Hillsdale, NJ: Lawrence Erlbaum Associates, Inc.

Moore, J. W. (2002). *Going Down to the Barrio: Homeboys and Homegirls in Change.* Philadelphia: Temple University Press.

Morrow, J. and Nolen-Hoeksema, S. (1990). Effects of responses to depression on the remediation of depressive affect. *Journal of Personality and Social Psychology, 58,* 519–527. DOI: 10.1037/0022-3514.58.3.519.

Otterbein, K. F. and Otterbein, C.S. (1965). An eye for an eye, a tooth for a tooth: a cross-cultural study of feuding. *American Anthropologist, 67,* 1470–1482. DOI: 10.1525/aa.1965.67.6.02a00070.

Pedersen, W. C., Gonzales, C. and Miller, N. (2000). The moderating effect of trivial triggering provocation on displaced aggression. *Journal of Personality and Social Psychology, 78,* 913–927. DOI: 10.1037/0022-3514.78.5.913.

Pettigrew, T. F. (1998). Inter-group contact theory. *Annual Review of Psychology, 49,* 65–85. DOI: 10.1146/annurev.psych.49.1.65.

Pettigrew, T. F. and Tropp, L. R. (2000). Does inter-group contact reduce prejudice? Recent meta-analytic findings. In S. Oskamp (ed.), *Reducing Prejudice and Discrimination* (pp. 93–114). Mahwah, NJ: Lawrence Erlbaum Associates, Inc.

Plant, E. A. and Devine, P. G. (2003). The antecedents and implications of interracial anxiety. *Personality and Social Psychology Bulletin, 29,* 790–801. DOI: 10.1177/0146167203029006011.

Prentice, D. A. and Miller, D. T. (1993). Pluralistic ignorance and alcohol use on campus: some consequences of misperceiving the social norm. *Journal of Personality and Social Psychology,* 64, 243–256. DOI: 10.1037/0022-3514.64.2.243.

Ray, D., Mackie, D., Rydell, R., and Smith, E. (2008). Changing categorization of self can change emotions about out-groups. *Journal of Experimental Social Psychology, 44,* 1210–1213. DOI:10.1016/j.jesp.2008.03.014.

Rothbart, M. and John, O. P. (1985). Social categorization and behavioral episodes: a cognitive analysis of the effects of inter-group contact. *Journal of Social Issues, 41,* 81–104. DOI: 10.1111/j.1540-4560.1985.tb01130.x.

Richardson, D. R., Hammock, G. S., Smith, S. M., Gardner, W., and Signo, M. (1994). Empathy as a cognitive inhibitor of interpersonal aggression. *Aggressive Behavior, 20,* 275–289. DOI: 10.1002/1098-2337(1994).

Rusting, C. L. and Nolen-Hoeksema, S. (1998). Regulating responses to anger: effects of rumination and distraction on angry mood. *Journal of Personality and Social Psychology, 74,* 790–803. DOI: 10.1037/0022-3514.74.3.790.

Schroeder, C. M. & Prentice, D. A. (1998). Exposing pluralistic ignorance to reduce alcohol use among college students. *Journal of Applied Social Psychology, 28,* 2150–2180. DOI: 10.1111/j.1559-1816.1998.tb01365.x.

Sears, D. O. (1983). The person-positivity bias. *Journal of Personality and Social Psychology, 44,* 233–250. DOI: 10.1037/0022-3514.44.2.233.

Short, J. and Strodtbeck, F. (1965). *Group Processes and Gang Delinquency.* Chicago: University of Chicago Press.

Spergel, I. A. (2007). Reducing gang violence. *The Little Village Gang Project in Chicago.* New York: AltaMira Press.

Steel, J. L. (1991). Interpersonal correlates of trust and self-disclosure. *Psychological Reports, 68,* 1319–1320. DOI: 10.2466/PR0.68.4.1319-1320.

Stenstrom, D. M., Lickel, B., Denson, T. F., and Miller, N. (2008). The roles of in-group identification and out-group entitativity in inter-group retribution. *Personality and Social Psychology Bulletin. 34,* 1570–1582. DOI: 10.1177/0146167208322999.

Tajfel, H. and Turner, J. C. (1979). An integrative theory of intergroup conflict. In W. G. Austin and S. Worchel (eds), *The Social Psychology of Intergroup Relations.* Monterey, CA: Brooks-Cole.

74   *Eduardo A. Vasquez, Brian Lickel and Karen Hennigan*

Terry, D. J. and Hogg, M. A. (1996). Group norms and the attitude-behavior relationship: a role for group identification. *Personality and Social Psychology Bulletin, 22,* 776–793. DOI: 10.1177/0146167296228002.

Thayer, R. E., Newman, J. R., and McClain, T. M. (1994). Self-regulation of mood: strategies for changing a bad mood, raising energy, and reducing tension. *Journal of Personality and Social Psychology, 67,* 910–925. DOI: 10.1037/0022-3514.67.5.910.

Thornberry, T. P., Krohn, M. D., Lizotte, A. J., Smith, C. A., and Tobin, K. (2003). *Gangs and Delinquency in Developmental Perspective*. Cambridge: Cambridge University Press.

Thrasher, F. (1927). *The Gang*. Chicago: University of Chicago Press.

Tice, D. M. and Baumeister, R. E (1993). Controlling anger: self-induced emotion change. In D. M. Wegner and J. W. Pennebaker (eds), *Handbook of Mental Control* (pp. 393–409). Englewood Cliffs, NJ: Prentice Hall.

Tyson, P. D. (1998). Physiological arousal, reactive aggression, and the induction of an incompatible relaxation response. *Aggression and Violent Behavior, 3,* 143–158. DOI: 10.1016/S1359-1789(97)00002-5.

Unamoto, K. (2006). *The Truce: Lessons from an L.A. Gang War*. Ithaca, NY: Cornell University.

Vasquez, E. A., Denson, T. F., Pedersen, W. C., Stenstrom, D. M, and Miller, N. (2005). The moderating effect of trigger intensity on triggered displaced aggression. *Journal of Experimental Social Psychology, 41,* 61–67. DOI: 10.1016/j.jesp.2004.05.007.

Vasquez, E. A., Ensari, N. Pedersen, W. C., Yunzi Tan, R., and Miller, N. (2007). Personalization and differentiation as moderators of triggered displaced aggression towards out-group targets. *European Journal of Social Psychology, 33,* 297–319. DOI: 10.1002/ejsp.359.

Vigil, J. D. (1998). *Barrio Gangs: Street Life and Identity in Southern California*. Austin: University of Texas Press.

Vigil, J. D. (2002). *A Rainbow of Gangs*. Austin: University of Texas Press.

Voci, A. and Hewstone, M. (2003). Inter-group contact and prejudice toward immigrants in Italy: the mediational role of anxiety and the moderational role of group salience. *Group Processes & Intergroup Relations, 6,* 37–54. DOI: 10.1177/1368430203006001011.

Wegner, D. M. and Erber, R. (1992). The hyperaccessibility of suppressed thoughts. *Journal of Personality and Social Psychology, 63,* 903–912. DOI: 10.1037/0022-3514.63.6.903.

Worthy, M., Gary, A. L., and Kahn, G. M. (1969). Self-disclosure as an exchange process. *Journal of Personality and Social Psychology, 13,* 59–63. DOI: 10.1037/h0027990.

4   A multi-factorial approach to understanding multiple perpetrator sexual offending

Leigh Harkins and Louise Dixon,
University of Birmingham, United Kingdom

The effect of the group on individual behavior has long been recognized. As Zimbardo observes, 'You are not the same person working alone as you are in a group' (2007: 8). Indeed, the influence that specific situations, including being part of an identifiable group, can exert upon a person's behavior have been widely discussed in literature that has tried to understand why 'ordinary men' have engaged in heinous war crimes such as the holocaust (Browning, 2001), or aggressive and violent behavior between groups in prison (see Zimbardo, 2007). This chapter aims to describe a novel multi-factorial framework for understanding multiple perpetrator sexual offending. Within this model, factors hypothesized to affect and heighten the chances of an individual participating in multiple perpetrator sexual offending are highlighted with particular attention paid to the effects of group processes.

This chapter is concerned with the examination of 'multiple perpetrator' sexual offending, a term that has been previously used to coin all sexual assaults involving two or more offenders (Horvath & Kelly, 2009). This term is a preferable umbrella term for describing sexual assaults carried out by two or more assailants since specific subtypes may then be further identified (e.g. 'gang rape' to refer to groups that consistently operate together with select membership and shared group norms and identity).

Investigations of sexual offences have typically varied according to the age of the victim and degree of force or intrusiveness. Little empirical study has considered variation in terms of the number of perpetrators involved in such an offence. However, the paucity of research does not have a linear relationship with the occurrence of this crime, as the perpetration of multiple perpetrator sexual offences is considerably widespread. Although there are many methodological issues that effect the accuracy of rape prevalence in general (Koss, 1993), estimates of the rates at which multiple perpetrator sexual offences occur do exist. For example, Horvath and Kelly (2009) report multiple perpetrator rape accounting for a third to half of all rapes in South Africa and between 2 and 26 per cent of rapes in the US, depending on the type of sample accessed (see also Wright & West, 1981). Examining juvenile perpetrators, in a study of 495 allegations of sexual assault on strangers made to a metropolitan police station in the UK, 42 per cent were committed by more than one perpetrator (Woodhams, 2004).

The dynamics of multiple perpetrator sexual offences have been shown to be very different from cases involving lone perpetrators, as certain additional aspects are introduced including social processes, how others are inducted into the abuse, how roles within the abuse are allocated, and how secrecy is maintained (Finkelhor *et al.*, 1988). Although research into multiple perpetrator sexual offending is not extensive to date, a small number of studies have begun to develop understanding in this area. These will be described using a multi-factorial model of multiple perpetrator sexual offending which has been described elsewhere (Harkins & Dixon, 2010) and will be extended here.

Multi-factorial theory of multiple perpetrator sexual offending

Theoretical frameworks allow professionals to understand the nature of a problem as well as the course of action that should be taken to eliminate it (Loseke *et al.*, 2005). This chapter presents a conceptual framework of multiple perpetrator sexual offending, which is developed from knitting two theories of human violent behavior. The first originates from the work of Bronfenbrenner (1979), who documented the importance of etiological models to consider factors at each level of an ecological model (e.g. ontogenic; micro-; exo-; and macro-levels) to achieve a comprehensive explanation. This multifactor approach has been informative in understanding various types of individual offending behavior, such as child maltreatment and intimate partner violence (e.g. Cicchetti & Lynch, 1993; Dutton, 2006), and is highly likely to further facilitate the conceptualization of multiple perpetrator sexual crime.

The second perspective is the Proximal Confluence Model (White & Kowalski, 1998) which considers violence to result from the interaction of two people and the contextual environment. This perspective emphasizes the importance that the situation can have on perpetrators' behavior (see Zimbardo, 2007) illustrating that certain intrapersonal variables predict violence only in specific situations.

We therefore propose that any conceptualization of multiple perpetrator sexual offences should consider the role of multiple factors, including the interaction of the individual, and the sociocultural and situational context where the offence took place. Resultantly, we have constructed a multi-factorial model of multiple perpetrator sexual offending which is an adaptation of White and Kowalski's (1998) Proximal Confluence Model (see Harkins & Dixon, 2010). This multi-factorial model highlights the role of individual, socio-cultural, and situational factors (and the interaction between them) in explaining various forms of multiple perpetrator sexual offending (e.g. street gangs, war, pedophile organizations). Figure 4.1 depicts the overlapping layers of this model. It allows the integration of a number of explanatory theories to be aggregated and can be used to explain all different forms of aggression. Unlike the original White and Kowalski model, our adaptation does not place specific emphasis on victim characteristics as they are not hypothesized to play a specific role in explaining multiple perpetrator sexual offences. An adaptation of the Proximal Confluence Model has been previously proposed by Henry, Ward, and Hirshberg (2004) in their multi-factorial model of war time rape. Thus, Henry *et al.*'s (2004) theorizing

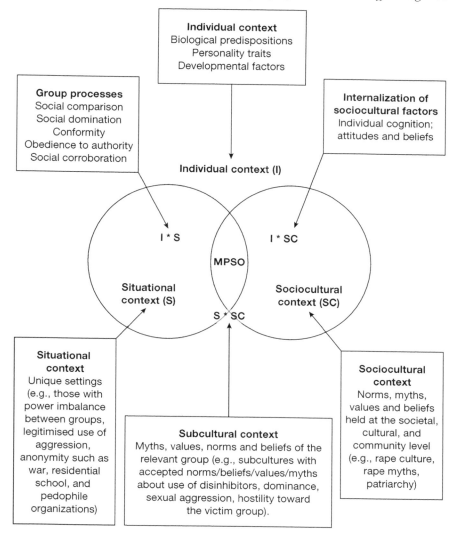

Figure 4.1 Multi-factorial model of multiple perpetrator sexual offending.

has heavily influenced our conceptualization of a generic model of multiple sexual offending.

Individual, sociocultural, and situational factors

As discussed above, for a phenomenon as complex and varied as multiple perpetrator sexual offending, a number of factors are likely to interact and play a contributory role in each type of offence. The literature examining the link between theoretical factors and multiple perpetrator sexual offending is limited. Therefore, the following explanation of each section of the model is based on the current available literature. We will now describe the model in its entirety (see Figure 4.1).

Individual context (I)

Several individual characteristics, such as personality traits, developmental factors, and sexual preferences, will inevitably play a role in whether someone engages in sexual violence. Irrespective of any other factors, each individual has to make the ultimate decision about whether they will engage in a multiple perpetrator sexual offence. In spite of cultures and situational contexts that are highly conducive to sexual violence against women, some individuals will refuse to engage in this behavior, even if there is extreme pressure to do so or if it could result in negative repercussions for them if they do not take part (Henry *et al.*, 2004; Price, 2001). Two factors that are likely to play a role in increasing the chances of taking part in such activities are discussed below.

Deviant sexual interest

Deviant sexual interest is likely to play a strong role in the initiation of some multiple perpetrator sexual offences. Although a number of etiological models exist to explain sexual offending (e.g. Marshall and Barbaree's [1990] Integrated Theory), these will not be covered here; for a comprehensive examination of theories of sexual offending see Ward *et al.* (2006). Deviant sexual interest (e.g. pedophilia or a sexual preference for rape) is the strongest predictor of sexual offences in meta-analyses of dynamic predictors of sexual recidivism (Hanson & Bussière, 1998; Hanson & Morton-Bourgon, 2005). Other researchers have found sexual deviance to be a predictor of violent (including sexual) recidivism as well (e.g. Quinsey *et al.*, 1995). Consequently it is likely this is an important driving force in at least some multiple perpetrator sexual offences.

In particular, it is likely that deviant sexual interest drives multiple perpetrator offences against children. Multiple perpetrator offending against children can occur in several different contexts, although little empirical evidence exists surrounding any of these. For example, child sex rings typically involve groups of men with shared knowledge of each other's deviant sexual interest in children, who then work together to find potential victims, share potential victims, and in some cases, engage in group abuse sessions with the victims (La Fontaine, 1993). In a study examining 55 sex rings, more than a third (35%, *n* = 19) of the individuals involved were found to have previous convictions for sexual offences (Burgess, 1984). The perpetrators involved in sex rings generally gain access to victims through their occupation, living situation, or through other children (Conradie, 2001). It is noted that the children are typically drawn into these activities as 'the adult engages the child in illicit activity through the abuse of adult power as well as misrepresentation of moral standards' (Burgess & Grant, 1988: 8). Therefore, as with other forms of sexual offences, it is likely that deviant sexual interests interact with other risk factors to increase the likelihood that multiple perpetrator rape will occur in some situations.

Leadership traits

It has been suggested that it is unusual for groups to come to a mutual decision to commit a sexual offence (Groth & Birnbaum, 1990). In many cases, leaders can play an important role in initiating the offences (Amir, 1971; Biljeveld *et al.*, 2007; Franklin, 2004; Porter & Alison, 2006), and they are thought to have varying degrees of influence over followers in multiple perpetrator sexual offences (Porter & Alison, 2001). It is likely that leaders emerge through their behavior rather than being appointed by other group members (Porter & Alison, 2006). Indeed in a study of gangs, Thrasher (1927) identified that leaders emerge as those willing to try new gang-related activities. Blanchard (1959) notes that leaders are usually the ones responsible for directing the others' attention towards sexual matters, and in the two groups he examined, it appeared that the leader was in fact sexually stimulated by the presence of the other group members. There may therefore be an interaction between the individual factors of leadership and sexual deviance. In examining leadership in prison, Schrag (1954) found that leaders were more generally violent and criminally mature offenders. Evidence suggests that leaders can be identified in a variety of multiple perpetrator sexual offences (Biljeveld *et al.*, 2007; Porter & Alison, 2001;'t Hart-Kerkhoffs *et al.*, 2010; Woodhams *et al.*, 2012). However it is unclear whether the same individuals who are leaders in terms of sexual activity are also those who lead general gang activity.

It has even been proposed that some multiple perpetrator rapes would not occur without the presence of the leader (Blanchard, 1959). Therefore, even in some situations which are conducive to rape, and in sociocultural contexts that support sexual violence, without the presence of an individual in the group with leadership qualities to direct the offending behavior, some multiple perpetrator sexual offences may not be initiated.

Sociocultural context (SC)

The influence of culture, social, and community factors are widely perceived as playing an important role in sexual and nonsexual behavior (Henry *et al.*, 2004; Wood, 2005). Such factors will play a greater or lesser role depending on the individual. Influences can include sexual inequality, and gender roles, as well as cultural norms, values, and beliefs about women, sex, and violence (White & Kowalski, 1998). All of these factors could influence the behavior of individuals in a group, including their sexual behavior. Examples of some pertinent factors that may operate at this level are given below.

Rape culture and rape myths

Sanday (2007) describes rape cultures as those that lack the social constraints to discourage sexual aggression or contain social arrangements that encourage sexual aggression. Wood (2005) describes a number of accepted cultural practices in South Africa that legitimize sexual violence against women (see also Brownmiller, 1975). 'Bride capture' is an example in which it is acceptable for a man to abduct and engage in forced sex with a woman that he wants to make his wife (Wood, 2005).

Rape myths are 'attitudes and beliefs that are generally false but widely and persistently held, and that serve to deny and justify male sexual aggression against women' (Lonsway & Fitzgerald, 1994: 134). Rape myths are used to justify the cultural practice of sexual victimization of women (Lonsway & Fitzgerald, 1994). A cluster of attitudinal variables have been identified as strong predictors of rape myth acceptance, such as gender role stereotyping, adversarial sexual attitudes, and acceptance of interpersonal violence (Burt, 1980). The multi-factorial model suggests that in combination with factors at other levels of the model, such socio-cultural factors can play an important role in increasing the likelihood of multiple perpetrator sexual offending occurring.

Patriarchy

Feminist theory asserts that males and females are conditioned differently as a result of rigid gender roles which influence one's expectations for sexual behavior (Henry *et al.*, 2004). From this perspective, masculinity is seen as dominant and powerful, whereas femininity is conceptualized as passive and submissive. Therefore the expectation is that the male will be the sexual seducer and the female will be seduced (Levine & Koenig, 1983). Hypermasculinity (exaggerated male stereotypical behaviors), considered to be an underlying cause of sexual aggression, is thought to arise as a result of such patriarchal societies (Malamuth *et al.*, 1991). Consequently, sex role patterns such as hypersexuality, aggressive masculinity, coercive sexuality as normal, and ideology of male dominance are disseminated by the media, culture, society, and community (Henry *et al.*, 2004; Russell & Finkelhor, 1984).

An ideology of male dominance is one aspect of a society that influences rape, according to Marshall and Barbaree (1990)'s integrated theory of sexual offending. Abel, Blanchard and Becker (1978) found that hyperidentification with a masculine role was common amongst rapists. Furthermore, sexually aggressive males are more likely to belong to a 'male subculture' which emphasizes masculine pursuits (Kanin, 1967) and hold double standards with respect to perceived appropriate male and female behavior (Kanin, 1969). Studies by Hunter and colleagues (2000) and Bourgois (1996) highlight the patriarchal attitudes and hostility that male offenders participating in multiple perpetrator rape hold toward their female victims. Indeed, hostility to women has proved an important factor in explaining rape in general (White & Koss, 1993). For example, Bourgois states how an interviewee legitimized his sexual violence with claims that he was teaching the females a lesson. Therefore, it is probable that such ideology will increase the likelihood of multiple perpetrator rape if internalized (i.e. consolidated as individual factors) by members of a group.

Situational context (S)

A variety of situational factors are likely to play a role in increasing sexual violence committed in groups. These include 'triggering' factors or those that would be expected to act as proximal disinhibitors in a given situation, irrespective of the presence of other vulnerabilities (Henry *et al.*, 2004). Thus, even if one's childhood circumstances provide resistance to being corrupted by sociocultural factors, strong situational factors may overpower these normally inhibiting factors to increase the chance of sexual aggression occurring (Marshall & Barbaree, 1990; Zimardo, 2007).

Green (2001) highlights the need to analyze and contextualize the setting itself. To illustrate, Zimbardo (2007: 211) claims that:

> Good people can be induced, seduced, and initiated into behaving in evil ways. They can also act in irrational, stupid, self-destructive, antisocial, and mindless ways when immersed in 'total situations' that impact human nature in ways that challenge our sense of the stability and consistency of individual personality, of character, and of morality.

Thus, research and theory that explain how a number of unique settings can influence the occurrence of multiple perpetrator sexual offending will now be discussed.

Unique settings

A number of specific settings are more conducive to multiple perpetrator sexual offending. For instance some settings represent particularly exaggerated sexuality (e.g. fraternities) or hostile masculinity (e.g. war).

War

The situational aspects of war are much different from non-war situations (Zimbardo, 2007). Wartime is an environment defined by aggression and violence that could potentially disinhibit one's self-regulatory mechanisms against sexual violence (Henry *et al.*, 2004). For example, Marshall and Barbaree (1990) note that wartime is a situation which has the potential to act as a disinhibitor. As such, it could permit even prosocial men to overcome normal restraints on their behavior in that it is characterized by violence and aggression, and the availability of weapons could instill a sense of power in individuals (Henry *et al.*, 2004). This is also compounded by the in-group/out-group mentality of war. In this setting, violence is acceptable and necessary in battle, and access to out-group (i.e. enemy), but not in-group women is common (Henry *et al.*, 2004). Baron *et al.* (1988) propose the Cultural Spillover Theory which can account for the widespread use of rape in wartime. They found that higher levels of legitimate violence – as in war – were directly related to rape. Evidence suggests that rape is common during war by a high proportion of men when there are few appropriate sexual outlets, high social support for rape, antagonistic attitudes towards the victim's group, and the perceived likelihood of punishment is low (Smuts, 1996).

Residential schools

Green (2001) suggests that problems with abuse in residential schools are embedded in issues of power and powerlessness, how children are perceived, sexuality and abuse, and social structures that influence morality and ideas about what is 'normal'. The Castle Hill School (a residential school for behaviorally disturbed boys) is one example of a documented case which initially involved a single perpetrator who managed to recruit more perpetrators until a unique setting was created in which 'virtually the whole organization became an instrument for the victimization of children' (La Fontaine, 1993: 227).

Goffman (1961) characterizes 'total institutions' as emphasizing uniformity, control, surveillance over care, development and individuality, and the emergence of separate and divisive staff and resident cultures. These characteristics were found in a majority of residential homes (Green & Parkin, 1999). In known cases where this has occurred, many of the institutions were located in fairly isolated communities with limited access to local communities (Green, 2001). The needs of the children were placed second to control and surveillance issues. It is not surprising then that children therefore were less likely to trust staff with sensitive information because of the perceived divide between staff and the children who resided there.

Pedophile organizations

Although pedophile support organizations do not routinely offend together, there are examples provided in the literature in which members of these organizations have direct and real-time input into the abuse of children (see Beech *et al.*, 2008). These groups tend to advocate (1) age of consent laws be abolished or lowered, (2) social harassment and prosecution of pedophiles be ended, and (3) the demythologizing of adult sexual behavior with children (De Young, 1988). Examination of the writings of these organizations highlight comments justifying offences against children (De Young, 1988; Durkin & Bryant, 1999) but also contain posts that are more social in nature in that they do not specifically discuss pedophilia (Malesky & Ennis, 2004).

The anonymity of computer-mediated communication used by such groups can heighten the expression of unpopular or extreme ideas, such as pedophilia (Baron & Kerr, 2003). Individuals with stigmatized attitudes can find corroboration for their ideas through the anonymity the Internet affords (McKenna & Bargh, 1998). Those who participate in newsgroups endorsing 'marginal' beliefs, have also been found to be more likely to feel greater social identification with that group, and as a result feel higher levels of self-acceptance, and lower levels of perceived estrangement from others (McKenna & Bargh, 1998). Baron and colleagues

(1996) found that the social corroboration that comes from associating with others who concur with extreme opinions works to intensify the individual's confidence and belief extremity about that issue.

Ward and Hudson (2000) have suggested that pedophilic offenders gravitate toward environments (e.g. other individuals with similar attitudes and beliefs) that support their own lifestyles and belief systems. These communities allow individuals with deviant interests to contact others who share their deviant ideology, thus reinforcing their beliefs (Durkin & Bryant, 1999; Malesky & Ennis, 2004).

Interactions between individual (I), sociocultural (SC), and situational (S) factors

The relevance of the three main factors that can be used to explain multiple perpetrator sexual offending has been described individually above. These three factors are likely to interact in various ways that would further increase the likelihood of sexual violence by multiple offenders.

Internalization of sociocultural factors (I x SC)

This level of interaction refers to the extent to which an individual will internalize sociocultural norms, values, beliefs and myths to shape their individual attitudes, beliefs and cognitions. When individuals are immersed in a sociocultural context that is conducive to rape (e.g. those accepting male dominance and hypermasculinity) inevitably some people will internalize some of these sociocultural factors (Henry *et al.*, 2004). It is hypothesized that these distorted attitudes (e.g. men are entitled to have sex with women) increase the likelihood of many types of multiple perpetrator sexual offences.

Cognition

Cognitive distortions are offence-supportive statements (Gannon *et al.*, 2007). They can take the form of beliefs, self-statements, or assumptions that are used to deny, justify, minimize, or rationalize behavior. Neutralization is a similar sociological concept describing the process used to disavow deviant behavior and present oneself as normal, attempting to dispute a deviant identity and normalize law-breaking behavior (De Young, 1988). Neutralizations are conceptualized as stigma-reducing strategies to lessen the expected legal and public reaction to the behavior. These often contain similar content to cognitive distortions. Distorted sexual thoughts or attitudes are widely thought to influence sexual offending (Abel *et al.*, 1989; De Young 1988; Hanson & Harris, 2000; Hayashino *et al.*, 1995; Murphy, 1990; Stermac & Segal, 1989; Thornton, 2002).

Implicit theories are clusters of beliefs that are unified under an underlying schema (Gannon & Polaschek, 2006; Ward & Keenan, 1999). These implicit theories guide how one interprets their social world and are thought to develop during childhood to help people make sense of unusual occurrences in their lives, such as abuse (Ward & Keenan, 1999). For those with child victims the implicit theories that have been identified are 'children as sexual beings' (i.e. children are inherently sexual and enjoy and seek out sex), 'nature of harm' (i.e. only extreme violence results in harm and sex with children is not inherently harmful), 'dangerous world' (i.e. *all* individuals, including children are hostile and rejecting and must be dominated or all adults are hostile and rejecting but children are safe and accepting), 'uncontrollability' (i.e. sexual urges are perceived as out of an individual's control or other outside factors, such as stress or alcohol are responsible), and 'entitlement' (i.e. some individuals are inherently superior and entitled to behave however they like) (Ward & Keenan, 1999). Similarly, in those with adult victims, the 'dangerous world' and 'uncontrollability' implicit theories have been identified in addition to the 'women are dangerous' (i.e. hostile attitudes towards women) and 'women as sexual objects' implicit theories (Beech *et al.*, 2006; Polaschek & Gannon, 2004).

The multi-factorial model hypothesizes that individuals holding offence-supportive implicit theories are likely to be influenced by their sociocultural context. This could explain how some individuals could commit a sexual offence, including sexual offences in groups. Whilst these cognitions have been identified as pertinent to offenders committing individual sexual offences, research has not investigated the relationship with multiple perpetrator sexual offences. It is possible that individuals who hold these cognitions seek each other, or that such cognitions held by one or more individuals in a group could influence others in that group, if relevant group processes such as deindividuation are at work.

Group processes (I X S)

There are a number of ways in which a given situation can exert an influence on an individual. Social psychological explanations can help describe how individuals behave in very different ways when they find themselves in group situations (see Viki & Abrams, Chapter 1). The powerful influence of group processes can increase an individual's susceptibility to multiple perpetrator offences (Henry *et al.*, 2004). By its very definition, multiple perpetrator sexual offending involves more than one person and thus would constitute a social process. Theories of group behavior (e.g. social comparison, social dominance, deindividuation, conformity, and groupthink) are useful in understanding the phenomenon of multiple perpetrator sexual offending because they specifically pertain to the ways individuals interact in a given situation. Although there are many theories explaining group behavior, space precludes a detailed description of these. Thus only those deemed most pertinent in explaining multiple perpetrator sexual offending will be highlighted here for consideration.

Social comparison

It is suggested (see Schultz, 1967) that groups are formed to meet individual's interpersonal needs for inclusion (e.g. to belong), control (e.g. to dominate), and affection (e.g. friendship). In explaining how the needs for inclusion and affection are met in groups, social comparison theory posits that we look to others for support of our beliefs. This may be the case in some multiple perpetrator sexual offences in which individuals do not want to participate in sexual offending, but go along with it because they are trying to meet other needs (i.e. inclusion, control, and affection) in these groups. If such support is there, the beliefs acquire a 'social reality' resulting in high levels of confidence in the beliefs, and in turn, can lead to extreme behaviors (Baron & Kerr, 2003). In the face of disagreement, the group first tries to bring the dissenting others around to the group's way of thinking, but failing this, the non-conforming group members will be rejected (Festinger, 1954). A clear example of this is provided by Bourgois (1996) who describes an individual partaking in a street gang multiple perpetrator rape to gain acceptance from the group. Some individuals reported not wanting to, but taking part in rapes in war situations because they feared for their own safety if they were to refuse (Price, 2001). Similar pressures have been reported by some individuals in fraternities (Sanday, 2007). This theory accounts for how the group members come to take part in the sexual offence and how the sexual behavior by the group is maintained. This theory could be used to explain how multiple perpetrator offences occur in a variety of contexts.

Social dominance

In terms of understanding the next interpersonal need met by groups as described by Schultz (1967), namely the need for control, social dominance theory proves useful. This theory specifies that intergroup relations are primarily derived from perceived social hierarchies referred to as 'stratification systems' (Sidanius & Pratto, 1999). These stratification systems can be based on age, gender, and socially constructed hierarchies such as ethnicity, social class, religion, and nation (Sidanius & Pratto, 1999). Thus, this theory could explain how in some contexts, one group will attempt to exert control over others that they view as lower on the hierarchy. Specifically, some people may engage in multiple perpetrator sexual offending in order to exert or maintain their perceived higher status in the hierarchy. In some cases, this attempt to exert control could be manifested in multiple perpetrator sexual offending. Social hierarchies based on age are relevant in multiple perpetrator offences against children as they involve disproportionate power over younger people. In terms of gender hierarchies, offending contexts by street gangs and fraternities are relevant as they highlight women's disproportionate lack of social and political power in these settings. The socially constructed hierarchies such as those based on ethnicity or religion are directly relevant to group sexual aggression in war.

Conformity

Conformity refers to individuals changing their attitudes, statements, or behavior to be consistent with a group norm (Baron & Kerr, 2003). Normative social influences affecting conformity are based on group-controlled rewards and punishments (Baron & Kerr, 2003). Compliance is a type of normative social influence in which the individual's actual attitudes have not changed, but they bring their behavior and verbal expressions in line with the group (Baron & Kerr, 2003). This can occur in multiple perpetrator sexual offending when individuals go along with offences that they would not have initiated on their own, because they do not want to lose the perceived rewards they get from the group, or the punishment if they were to choose not to comply. Examples where this may be seen are in street gangs, fraternity members, and in day care abuse. Conformity most commonly occurs when the group needs to come to a unanimous consensus and those who deviate are likely to be punished (e.g. in war, residential care) or rejected (e.g. fraternities) (Baron & Kerr, 2003). This would also be the case in gangs as the individual would not want to lose the support or respect of their fellow gang members.

Obedience to authority

Obedience to authority describes the actions of individuals when complying with the orders of perceived superiors or leaders (Milgram, 2005). This would occur in multiple perpetrator sexual offences when there is clearly someone in an authority position in the group. For instance, this has direct relevance to multiple perpetrator rape in war as in some cases rape is used as a military policy (Buss, 1998). Milgram notes 'behaviour that is unthinkable in an individual who is acting on his own may be executed without hesitation when carried out under orders' (2005: xvii). This highlights the importance of the interaction with individual characteristics such as leadership qualities and the group.

Social corroboration

Social corroboration occurs in groups containing others who provide support for shared attitudes or choices, resulting in the individual experiencing heightened confidence in their attitudes or choices (Baron & Kerr, 2003). This can result then, in increased confidence in extreme views such as acceptance of pedophilia observed amongst those who are members of pedophilic support groups. This is because individuals who hold extreme views must be confident in the face of beliefs that may entail potential ridicule (Baron *et al.*, 1996), or even scorn in the case of pedophilic sexual interest. There is also evidence to support increases in confidence about the validity of a position after having one's opinion corroborated (Baron *et al.*, 1996). Beliefs and attitudes supportive of multiple perpetrator sexual offending are clearly not generally accepted in society thus this theory is relevant to individuals who hold such positions. As well as being relevant to those who offend in pedophile organizations, this could play a role for those involved in child sex rings, and abuse in day care centers.

Deindividuation

Deindividuation is a group process which occurs when someone loses their sense of individuality and becomes submerged in a group (Goldstein, 2002). Zimbardo (2007: 305) states that:

> Deindividuation creates a unique psychological state in which behaviour comes under the control of immediate situational demands and biological, hormonal urges. Action replaces thought, seeking immediate pleasure dominates delaying gratification and mindfully restrained decisions give way to mindless emotional responses. A state of arousal is often a precursor to and consequence of deindividuation.

This explains why individuals in crowds are less self-conscious, more impulsive and more willing to engage in anti-social behavior (Baron & Kerr, 2003). Indeed, according to Zajonc (1965) when people are around others, they are more physically excited and motivated. This has direct relevance to explaining why individuals in groups may engage in multiple perpetrator sexual offences in that they are more willing to go along with the group as they lose their sense of individuality.

As a result of perpetrators feeling anonymous, the process of deindividuation also allows them to act without accountability, responsibility, and self-monitoring (Zimbardo, 2007). Furthermore, the more individuals who engage in a deviant act, such as a multiple perpetrator sexual offence, the greater the sense that they experience diffusion of responsibility for their role as any one individual feels less responsible for their actions due to collective responsibility (Baron & Kerr, 2003). Thus involvement in group aggression such as multiple perpetrator sexual offences can result in individuals absolving themselves of guilt by attributing primary responsibility to others (Baron & Kerr, 2003). Aggressive behaviors have been found to escalate in groups in comparison to individual task performance, which has been linked to the process of deindividuation (Goldstein, 2002). For example, evidence suggests that group-administered aggression (in the form of shocks) exceeds individual-administered aggression in terms of pace and intensity of shocks (Jaffe & Yinon, 1979; Jaffe *et al.*, 1981). Deindividuation was noted as relevant to their offending by several youths who committed a multiple perpetrator offence together (Etgar & Prager, 2009). In their treatment group, they reported that 'aggression towards women served as a way to strengthen their masculinity and simultaneously 'divide and distribute' the responsibility amongst everyone present' (Etgar & Prager, 2009: 304). Deindividuation would be relevant in all the group offending contexts discussed here.

Groupthink

Groupthink is a phenomenon that occurs in groups in which there is strong pressure to conform. Due to efforts to minimize conflict within such groups and hesitation to critically evaluate options and offer alternatives, poor decision making results (Janis, 1982). It works to promote self-censorship, stifle dissent, and lead to exaggerated feelings of moral correctness and superiority (Baron & Kerr, 2003). It can be triggered by conditions such as directive leadership style, intense group cohesion, similarity of ideology, pressure for unanimity, insecure member self-esteem, and group insulation from critics (Janis, 1982). These conditions combine to suppress dissent so much so that members agree to policies or norms that are not well-considered, resulting in poor decision making (Janis, 1982). Thus some may go along for multiple perpetrator sexual offences for the reasons outlined here. Considering these points, groupthink may be most relevant to multiple perpetrator sexual offending in street gangs, fraternities, war, and explain why employees in residential homes may partake in or turn a blind eye to, the abuse of children.

Subcultural context (S x SC)

The subcultural context is thought to represent the interaction between wider sociocultural factors and specific situational contexts. For instance, Wood (2005) describes sociocultural practices in South Africa in which sexual violence against women is deemed culturally acceptable. She also describes subcultures such as *tsotsis* (i.e. disaffected young men who survive by their wits and criminal means, embody a sort of 'streetwise' style, and represent a sexual risk to females deemed to have 'disrespected' them) in which these attitudes are exacerbated. Thus, cultural practices at a societal level can prime young men (in this instance) to sexually offend in groups, which can be exacerbated given a situation conducive to this behavior. The presence of both sociocultural and situational factors together increases the probability of an multiple perpetrator sexual offence taking place.

Once groups are formed, group norms are established (Goldstein, 2002). Group norms are the behaviors, attitudes, and perceptions of what is approved and expected of group members, which have powerful effects on the thoughts and actions of group members (Baron & Kerr, 2003). Settings in which multiple perpetrator sexual occurs, such as fraternities and war, have established group norms that allow multiple perpetrator sexual offences to occur. These can be generated through a number of the other factors discussed in this chapter (e.g. rape myths). The text below describes how a subculture emphasizing male bonding is likely to occur in some sociocultural contexts and given a specific situation. Two specific subcultures will be used to illustrate how sociocultural beliefs may be endorsed in fraternities or by the military during war time which may increase the chances of sexual offences being carried out by these groups in specific contexts.

Male bonding

Male bonding is achieved through a force, link, or affectionate tie that serves the purpose of unifying men (Curry, 1991). Male bonds are derived from doing things together and involve less intimacy and disclosure relative to female bonding

(Sherrod, 1987). Some male bonding activities involve negativity towards females in various forms such as sexist joking (Curry, 1991; Lyman, 1987). Brownmiller (1975) suggests that male bonding is facilitated through sexual activity which also provides a basis for competition and status within male peer groups and generates group solidarity. The institutional bonding of men, such as that which occurs in the military, is often accomplished through the exclusion of women and an ideological emphasis on men's superiority to women (Flood, 2008). Rape is not uncommon in battle to assert masculinity and as a means of male bonding (Brownmiller, 1975). The behavior of a specific subculture can promote male dominance and bonding via participating in the group rape and humiliation of the victim and/or by watching the assault (Holstrom & Burgess, 1980; Ullman, 1999).

Specific subcultures

It is argued that fraternities create a subculture in which the use of coercion in interactions with women is normative and that the mechanisms to keep this behavior in check are minimal or absent (Martin & Hummer, 1989). Sanday (2007) describes the occurrence of multiple perpetrator rapes that occur in fraternities. She explains that this often occurs when the victim and perpetrators consume large amounts of alcohol and drugs, followed by some situations in which the victim consents to sex with one individual, but is then sexually assaulted by a number of men who later enter the room. Alternatively, a situation can occur in which the victim loses consciousness and then awakens to find that she is being sexually assaulted by multiple members of the fraternity. Humphrey and Kahn (2000) note the need to distinguish between fraternities which have a sociocultural context supportive of rape, and those that do not. They found some fraternities had higher levels of sexual aggression, male peer support for sexual assault, and higher levels of hostility towards women than others. Evidence suggests that even when men who do not typically hold such attitudes attend parties at these 'riskier' fraternities, they adopt the sociocultural norms of the fraternity while they are there (Boswell & Spade, 1996). Thus, it is suggested that this type of sexual aggressive behavior can be learned in this setting, as opposed to being a characteristic of the individual prior to them living in a fraternity (Boeringer *et al.*, 1991).

It is possible that some people come into a group setting or situation with beliefs common to a rape culture already entrenched, but it may also be the case that individuals adopt the beliefs of that rape culture once they come into the situation. Either way, a subcultural context is created in which the individuals of the group normalize rape myths, increasing the likelihood that multiple perpetrator sexual offences will be accepted and carried out by the group.

The very nature of multiple perpetrator sexual offending warrants an understanding of the effects of the group on the individual's behavior and it is clear from the above discussion that theories of group behavior can partly explain why sexual offending in groups may occur. Despite this, little research to date has considered this phenomenon. Such understanding is necessary if a comprehensive approach to the assessment, prevention, and intervention of this type of offending behavior is to be achieved.

Conclusions

Together, the above sources of information highlight the complexity of multiple perpetrator sexual offending and that some types of this behavior are better understood and researched (e.g. war, fraternities) than others (e.g. sex rings and daycares). This chapter compliments the work of Harkins and Dixon (2010), and together these works are the first to consider how multiple perpetrator sexual offences may be generally conceptualized.

It is evident that theories of group behavior are relevant to all subcategories of multiple perpetrator sexual offences, and as this level of analysis is commonly not considered in the assessment of offending behavior, it is important to highlight the contribution that such factors can have upon an individual's behavior. For instance, it is possible that the different individuals involved in committing multiple perpetrator sexual offences will pose different levels of risk for future offending. In particular, those who demonstrate deviant sexual interests and leadership traits, for instance, would likely pose a higher risk than those who are do not hold deviant interests, but are easily influenced in group situations. Future work is needed to illuminate the relationship between the factors outlined here and future (lone and multiple perpetrator) sexual offending.

These factors outlined in our model would also have an impact on appropriate treatment targets for individuals who perpetrate sexual offences in groups. For some, their treatment needs would be similar to those addressed in traditional sexual offender treatment programs (e.g. deviant sexual interest, offence-supportive attitudes). However for others, the best chance of reducing their likelihood of future-offending may be achieved through work directed at minimizing their susceptibility to group influence. Appropriate treatment efforts should also be implemented alongside advances in our understanding of how the factors outlined in the multi-factorial model relate to increased risk.

As highlighted, many problems with definitional issues currently exist hampering further research and understanding in this area. Clarification and consistency in the use of terminology amongst practitioners and researchers will aid clarity in this area and allow robust research to be carried out. For example, additional research is needed to examine the potential differences between perpetrators who offend in smaller groups relative to larger ones.

In conclusion, this chapter demonstrates the need to conduct more work in this area. Specifically, research that examines the contribution of psychological theory to our understanding of this phenomenon is needed. Viewing multiple perpetrator sexual offences through the group aggression literature will increase our understanding of the nature, purpose, and maintenance of such sexually aggressive groups, which will aid the success of much needed prevention and intervention efforts.

References

Abel, G.G., Blanchard, G.T. & Becker, J. (1978). An integrated treatment program for rapists. In R. Rada (ed.), *Clinical Aspects of the Rapist* (pp. 161–214). New York: Grune & Stratton.

Abel, G.G., Gore, D.K., Holland, C.L., Camp, N., Becker, J.V., and Rathner, J. (1989). The measurement of the cognitive distortions of child molesters. *Annals of Sex Research, 2*, 135–153. DOI: 10.1177/107906328900200202

Amir, M. (1971). *Patterns in Forcible Rape*. Chicago, IL: University of Chicago Press.

Baron, R.S. and Kerr, N.L. (2003). *Group Processes, Group Decision, Group Action* (2nd edn). Berkshire: Open University Press.

Baron, R.S., Hoppe, S., Kao, C.F., Brunsman, B., Linneweh, B., and Rogers, D. (1996). Social corroboration and opinion extremity. *Journal of Experimental and Social Psychology, 32*, 537–560.

Baron, L., Strauss, M.A., and Jaffee, D. (1988). Legitimate violence, violent attitudes, and rape: a test of cultural spillover effect. In R.A. Prentky, and V.L. Quinsey (eds), *Human Sexual Aggression: Current Perspectives. Annals of the New York Academy of Science, vol. 528* (pp. 79–110). New York: New York Academy of Sciences. DOI: 10.1111/j.1749-6632.1988.tb50853.x.

Beech, A.R., Ward, T., and Fisher, D. (2006). The identification of sexual and violent motivations in men who assault women: implications for treatment. *Journal of Interpersonal Violence, 21*, 1635–1653. DOI: 10.1177/0886260506294242.

Beech, A.R., Elliot, I.A., Birgden, A., and Findlater, D. (2008). The internet and child sexual offending: a criminological review. *Aggression and Violent Behavior, 13*, 216–228. DOI: 10.1016/j.avb.2008.03.007.

Biljeveld, C.C.J.H., Weerman, F.M., Looije, D. and Hendriks, J. (2007). Group sex offending by juveniles: coercive sex as group activity. *European Journal of Criminology, 4*, 5–31. DOI: 10.1177/1477370807071728.

Blanchard, W.H. (1959). The group process in gang rape. *The Journal of Social Psychology, 49*, 259–266.

Boeringer, S.B., Shehan, C.L., and Akers, R.L. (1991). Social contexts and social learning theory in sexual coercion and aggression: assessing the contribution of fraternity membership. *Family Relations, 40*, 58–64.

Boswell, A.A., and Spade, J.Z. (1996). Fraternities and collegiate rape culture: why are some fraternities more dangerous places for women? *Gender and Society, 10*, 133–147. DOI: 10.1177/089124396010002003.

Bourgois, P. (1996). In search of masculinity: violence, respect and sexuality among Puerto Rican crack dealers in East Harlem. *British Journal of Criminology, 36*, (3) 412–427.

Bronfenbrenner, U. (1979). *The Ecology of Human Development: Experiments by Nature and Design*. Cambridge, MA: Harvard University Press.

Browning, C. (2001). *Ordinary Men: Reserve Police Battalion 11 and the Final Solution in Poland*. London: Penguin.

Brownmiller, S. (1975). *Against Our Will: Men, Women and Rape*. London: Penguin Books.

Burgess, A.W. (1984). *Child Pornography and Sex Rings*. Toronto: Lexington Books.

Burgess, A.W. and Grant, C.A. (1988). *Children Traumatized in Sex Rings*. Arlington, VA: National Center for Missing and Exploited Children.

Burt, M. (1980). Cultural myths and supports for rape. *Journal of Personality and Social Psychology, 38,* 217 Burgess, A.W. and Grant, C.A. (1988). *Children Traumatized in Sex Rings* 230. DOI: 10.1037/0022-3514.38.2.217.

Buss, D.E. (1998). Women at the border: rape and nationalism in international law. *Feminist Legal Studies, 6,* 171–203.

Burt, M.R. (1980). Cultural myths and supports for rape. *Journal of Personality and Social Psychology, 38,* 217–230.

Cicchetti, D., and Lynch, M. (1993). Toward an ecological/transactional model of community violence and child maltreatment: consequences for children's development. *Psychiatry: Interpersonal and Biological Processes, 56* (1), 96–118.

Conradie, H. (2001). The structure and functioning of child pornography. *Crime Research in South Africa, 4.* Retrieved from http://www.crisa.org.za/downloads/cp.pdf (accessed 26 April 2009).

Curry, T.J. (1991). Fraternal bonding in the locker room: a profeminist analysis of talk about competition and women. *Sociology of Sport Journal, 8* (2), 119–135.

De Young, M. (1988). The indignant page: techniques of neutralization in the publications of pedophile organizations. *Child Abuse and Neglect, 12,* 583–591. DOI: 10.1016/0145-2134(88)90076-2.

Durkin, K.F. and Bryant, C.D. (1999). Propagandizing pederasty: a thematic analysis of the on-line exculpatory accounts of unrepentant pedophiles. *Deviant Behavior: An Interdisciplinary Journal, 20,* 103–127. DOI: 10.1080%2F016396299266524.

Dutton, D.G. (2006*). Rethinking Domestic Violence.* Vancouver: UCB Press.

Etgar, T., and Prager, K.G. (2009). Advantages of group therapy for adolescent participants in the same gang rape. *Journal of Child Sexual Abuse, 18,* 302–319. DOI: 10.1080/10538710902881329.

Festinger, L. (1954). A theory of social comparison processes. *Human Relations, 7,* 117–140. DOI: 10.1177/001872675400700202.

Finkelhor, D., Williams, L.M., and Burns, N. (1988). *Nursery Crimes: Sexual Abuse in Day Care.* London: Sage.

Flood, M. (2008). Men, sex, and homosociality: how bonds between men shape their sexual relations with women. *Men and Masculinities, 10,* 339–359. DOI: 10.1177/1097184X06287761.

Franklin, K. (2004). Enacting masculinity: antigay violence and group rape as participatory theatre. *Sexuality Research and Social Policy, 1,* 25–40. DOI: 10.1525/srsp.2004.1.2.25.

Gannon, T.A., and Polaschek, D.L.L. (2006). Cognitive distortions in child molesters: a re-examination of key theories and research. *Clinical Psychology Review, 26,* 1000–1019. DOI: 10.1016/j.cpr.2005.11.010.

Gannon, T.A., Ward, T., and Collie, R, (2007). Cognitive distortions in child molesters: theoretical and research developments over the past two decades. *Aggression and Violent Behavior 12,* 402–416. DOI: 10.1016/j.avb.2006.09.005.

Goffman, E. (1961). *Asylums.* Harmondsworth: Penguin.

Goldstein, A.P. (2002). *The Psychology of Group Aggression.* Chichester: Wiley.

Green, L. (2001). Analysing the sexual abuse of children by workers in residential care homes: characteristics, dynamics and contributory factors. *Journal of Sexual Aggression, 7,* 5–25.DOI: 10.1080/13552600108416164.

Green, L. and Parkin. W. (1999) Sexuality, sexual abuse and children's homes: oppression or protection. In The Violence Against Children's Study Group, *Children, Child Abuse and Child Protection: Placing Children Centrally.* Chichester: Wiley.

Groth, A.N. and Birnbaum, H.J. (1990). *Men who Rape: The Psychology of the Offender.* London: Plenum Press.

Hanson, R. K. and Bussière, M. T. (1998). Predicting relapse: a meta-analysis of sexual offender recidivism studies. *Journal of Consulting and Clinical Psychology, 66,* 348–362.DOI: 10.1037/0022-006X.66.2.348.

Hanson, R.K. and Harris, A.J.R. (2000). Where should we intervene? Dynamic predictors of sexual offence recidivism. *Criminal Justice and Behavior, 27,* 6–35.DOI: 10.1177/0093854800027001002.

Hanson, R.K. and Morton-Bourgon, K. (2005). The characteristics of persistent sexual offenders: a meta-analysis of recidivism studies. *Journal of Consulting and Clinical Psychology, 73,* 1154–1163. DOI: 10.1177/F0093854800027001002.

Harkins, L. and Dixon, L. (2010). Sexual offending in groups: an evaluation. *Aggression and Violent Behavior, 15,* 87–99. DOI: 10.1016/j.avb.2009.08.006.

Hayashino, D. S., Wurtele, S. K., and Klebe, K. J. (1995). Child molesters: an examination of cognitive factors. *Journal of Interpersonal Violence, 10,* 106–116. DOI: 10.1177/088626095010001007.

Henry, N., Ward, T., and Hirshberg, M. (2004). A multi-factorial model of wartime rape. *Aggression and Violent Behavior, 9,* 535–562. DOI: 10.1016/S1359-1789%2803%2900048-X.

Holmstrom, L. L. and Burgess, A. W. (1980). Sexual behavior of assailants during reported rapes. *Archives of Sexual Behavior, 9,* 427–439. DOI: 10.1007/BF02115942.

Horvath, M.A.H. and Kelly, L. (2009). Multiple perpetrator rape: naming an offence and initial research findings. *Journal of Sexual Aggression, 15,* 83–96. DOI: 10.1080/13552600802653818.

Humphrey, S.E. and Kahn, A.S. (2000). Fraternities, athletic teams, and rape: importance of identification with a risky group. *Journal of Interpersonal Violence, 15,* 1313–1322. DOI: 10.1177/088626000015012005.

Hunter, J.A., Hazelwood, R.R. and Slesinger, D. (2000). Juvenile-perpetrated sex crimes: patterns of offending and predictors of violence. *Journal of Family Violence, 15,* 81–93. DOI: 10.1023/A:1007553504805.

Jaffe, Y. and Yinon, Y. (1979). Retaliatory aggression in individuals and groups. *European Journal of Social Psychology, 9,* 177–186. DOI: 10.1002/ejsp.2420090206.

Jaffe, Y., Shapiro, N., and Yinon, Y. (1981). Aggression and its escalation. *Journal of Cross-Cultural Psychology, 12,* 21–36. DOI: 10.1177/0022022181121002.

Janis, I.L. (1982). *Groupthink* (2nd edn). Boston: Houghton-Mifflin. DOI: 10.1080/09515088808572934.

Kanin, E.J. (1967). Reference groups and sex conduct norm violations. *The Sociological Quarterly, 8,* 495–504. DOI: 10.1111/j.1533-8525.1967.tb01085.x.

Kanin, E.J. (1969). Dyadic aspects of male aggression. *The Journal of Sex Research, 5,* 12–28. DOI: 10.1080/00224496909550593.

Koss, M.P. (1993). Rape: scope, impact, intervention, and public policy responses. *American Psychologist, 48,* 1062–1069. DOI: 10.1037/0003-066X.48.10.1062.

La Fontaine, J.S. (1993). Defining organized sexual abuse. *Child Abuse Review, 2,* 223–231. DOI: 10.1002/car.2380020404.

Levine, S. and Koenig, J. (eds) (1983) *Why Men Rape.* London: W.H. Allen.

Lonsway, K.A. and Fitzgerald, L.F. (1994). Rape myths: in review. *Psychology of Women Quarterly, 18,* 133–164. DOI: 10.1111/j.1471-6402.1994.tb00448.x.

Loseke, D.R., Gelles, R.J. and Cavanaugh, M.M. (2005). Section I: controversies in conceptualisation. In D.R. Loseke, R.J. Gelles, and M.M. Cavanaugh (eds), *Current Controversies on Family Violence* (pp. 1–4). Thousand Oaks: Sage.

Lyman, P. (1987). The fraternal bond as a joking relationship: a case study on the role of sexist jokes in male group bonding. In M.S. Kimmel (ed.), *Changing Men: New Directions in Research on Men and Masculinities* (pp. 148–163). Beverly Hills: Sage.

Malamuth, N.M., Sockloskie, R.S., Koss, M.P., and Tanaka, J.S. (1991). Characteristics of aggressors against women: testing a model using a national sample of college students. *Journal of Consulting and Clinical Psychology, 59*, 670–681.

Malesky, L.A. and Ennis, L. (2004). Supportive distortions: analysis of posts on a pedophile internet message board. *Journal of Addictions and Offender Counseling, 24*, 94–100.

Marshall, W.L. and Barbaree, H.E. (1990). An integrated theory of the etiology of sexual offending. In W.L. Marshall, D.R. Laws, and H.E. Barbaree (eds), *Handbook of Sexual Assault: Issues, Theories, and Treatment of the Offender* (pp. 257–275). New York: Plenum.

Martin, P.Y. and Hummer, R.A. (1989). Fraternities and rape on campus. *Gender and Society, 3*, 457–473. DOI: 10.1177/089124389003004004.

McKenna, K.Y.A. and Bargh, J.A. (1998). Coming out in the age of the internet: identity 'de-marginalization' through virtual group identification. *Journal of Personality and Social Psychology, 75*, 681–694. DOI: 10.1037/0022-3514.75.3.681.

Milgram, S. (2005). *Obedience to Authority: An Experimental View*. London: Pinter and Martin.

Murphy, W.D. (1990). Assessment and modification of cognitive distortions in sex offenders. In W.L. Marshall, D.R. Laws, and H.E. Barbaree (eds), *Handbook of Sexual Assault: Issues, Theories, and Treatment of the Offender*. New York: Plenum Press.

Polaschek, D.L.L. and Gannon, T.A. (2004). The implicit theories of rapists: what convicted offenders tell us. *Sexual Abuse: A Journal of Research and Treatment, 16,* 299–314. DOI: 10.1177/107906320401600404.

Porter, L.E. and Alison, L.J. (2001). A partially ordered scale of influence in violent group behavior: an example from gang rape. *Small Group Research, 32*, 475–497. DOI: 10.1177/104649640103200405.

Porter, L.E. and Alison, L.J. (2006). Leadership and hierarchies in criminal groups: scaling degrees of leader behaviour in group robbery. *Legal and Criminological Psychology, 11*, 245–265. DOI: 10.1348/135532505X68692.

Price, L.S. (2001). Finding the man in the soldier-rapist: some reflections on comprehension and accountability. *Women's Studies International Forum, 24*, 211–227. DOI: 10.1016/S0277-5395(01)00157-1.

Quinsey, V.L., Rice, M.E., and Harris, G.T. (1995). Actuarial prediction of sexual recidivism. *Journal of Interpersonal Violence, 10*, 85–105. DOI: 10.1177/088626095010001006.

Russell, D.E.H. and Finkelhor, D. (1984). The gender gap among perpetrators of child sexual abuse. In D.E.H. Russell (ed.), *Sexual Exploitation: Rape, Child Sexual Abuse, and Workplace Harassment* (pp. 215–231). Beverly Hills, CA: Sage.

Sanday, P.G. (2007). *Fraternity Gang Rape: Sex, Brotherhood, and Privilege on campus* (2nd edn). New York: New York University Press.

Schultz, W.C. (1967). *FIRO*. New York: Holt, Rinehard, & Winston.

Schrag, C. (1954). Leadership among prison inmates. *American Sociological Review, 19*, 37–42. DOI: 10.2307/2087477.

Sherrod, D. (1987). The bonds of men: problems and possibilities in close male relationships. In H. Brod (ed.), *The Making of Masculinities: The New Men's Studies* (pp. 213–239). Boston: Allen & Unwin.

Sindanius, J. and Pratto, F. (1999). *Social Dominance: An Intergroup Theory of Hierarchy and Oppression.* Cambridge, UK: Cambridge University Press.

Smuts, B. (1996). Male aggression against women: an evolutionary perspective. In D.M. Buss and N.M. Malamuth (eds), *Sex, Power Conflict: Evolutionary and Feminist Perspectives* (pp. 231–268). New York: Oxford University Press.

Stermac, L.E. and Segal, Z.V. (1989). Adult sexual contact with children: an examination of cognitive factors. *Behavior Therapy, 20,* 573–584. DOI: 10.1016/S0005-7894(89)80135-2.

Thrasher, F.M. (1927). *The Gang: A Study of 1313 Gangs in Chicago.* Chicago: University of Chicago Press.

't-Hart-Kerkhoffs, L.A., Vermeiren, R.R.J.M., Jansen, L.M.C., and Doreleijers, T.A.H. (2010). Juvenile group sex offenders: a comparison of group leaders and followers. *Journal of Interpersonal Violence,* 1–18.

Thornton, D. (2002). Constructing and testing a framework for dynamic risk assessment. *Sexual Abuse: A Journal of Research and Treatment, 141,* 139–153. DOI: 10.1177/107906320201400205.

Ullman, S.E. (1999). A comparison of gang and individual rape incidents. *Violence and Victims, 14,* 123–133.

Ward, T. and Hudson, S. (2000). A self-regulation model of relapse prevention. In D.R. Laws, S.M. Hudson, and T. Ward (eds), *Remaking Relapse Prevention with Sex Offenders* (pp. 79–102). Thousand Oaks, CA: Sage.

Ward, T. and Keenan, T. (1999). Child molesters' implicit theories. *Journal of Interpersonal Violence,* 14, 821–838. DOI: 10.1177/088626099014008003.

Ward, T., Polaschek, D., and Beech, A.R. (2006). *Theories of Sexual Offending.* Chichester: Wiley.

White, J.W. and Koss, M.P. (1993). Adolescent sexual aggression within heterosexual relationships: prevalence, characteristics, and causes. In H.E. Barbaree, W.L. Marshall, and S.M. Hudson (eds), *The Juvenile Sex Offender (*pp. 182–202). New York: Guilford Press.

White, J.W. and Kowalski, R.M. (1998). Male violence toward women: an integrated perspective. In R.G. Geen, and E. Donnerstein (eds), *Human Aggression: Theories, Research, and Implications for Social Policy* (pp. 203–226). San Diego: Academic Press.

Wood, K. (2005). Contextualizing group rape in post-aparteid South Africa. *Culture, Health, and Sexuality,* 7, 303–317. DOI: 10.1080/13691050500100724.

Woodhams, J. (2004). Characteristics of juvenile sex offending against strangers: findings from a non-clinical study. *Aggressive Behavior, 30,* 243–253. DOI: 10.1002/ab.20053.

Woodhams, J., Cooke, C., Harkins, L., and Da Silva, T. (2012) Leadership in multiple perpetrator rape. *Journal of Interpersonal Violence, 27*(4), 728–752.

Wright, R. and West, D.J. (1981). Rape: a comparison of group offences and lone assaults. *Medicine, Science and the Law, 21,* 25–30.

Zajonc, R.B. (1965). Social facilitation. *Science, 149,* 269–274. DOI: 10.1126/science.149.3681.269.

Zimbardo, P. (2007). *The Lucifer Effect: How Good People Turn Evil.* London: Rider.

Part 2
Criminal networks

5 The role of group processes in terrorism

Margaret A. Wilson, Emma Bradford and Lucy Lemanski, Department of Applied Psychology, University of Liverpool, UK

In order to deter or reduce terrorism, it is vital to understand terrorist motivations and the group processes that underpin terrorist movements. Gaining this understanding is no easy feat; the majority of primary data available for evaluation has been gained from interviews with terrorist actors, some of which have been conducted under conditions of significant power imbalance. Many researchers do not even have access to primary data sources and instead have to work with secondary data such as published autobiographical accounts. This dilution of information makes it difficult to study terrorism in the same way as we can other, more common and easily accessible crimes.

Researchers have argued that there are a number of different factors which influence an individual's involvement in terrorism (e.g. Alonso, 2006; Horgan, 2005). Explanations for what lures people into terrorism, what sustains their involvement and what finally motivates them to leave have ranged from the psychological to the social, but the dominant theme is the role of group processes. In this respect, researchers have drawn parallels between terrorist actors and other criminal subgroups, for example, street gangs. Whilst there are some obvious parallels that can be drawn between gangs and terrorist organizations (e.g. groups of individuals who operate in extra-legal environments) there are other similarities involved in the initial motivations to join these types of group, and the forces involved in maintaining their membership, and these will be considered later in this chapter.

As a whole, individuals involved in terrorism are relatively heterogeneous in terms of their age, sex, education, social economic status, and so forth (Silke, 2003). Early psychological research on terrorism focused on finding common psychological deficiencies amongst terrorists that could offer explanation for their commission of violent crimes. However, the failure of such 'psychiatric profiles' meant that other explanations for their behavior needed to be pursued. More recent research has acknowledged that there is no exclusive pathway that leads to terrorism (e.g. McCauley & Moskalenko, 2008), and the sheer diversity of terrorist groups and their activities means that it would be extremely unlikely that one explanation could fit all.

Nevertheless, persistent research efforts have uncovered a number of relatively common denominators among terrorist actors. These factors are neither necessary nor sufficient to draw individuals into terrorism. However, their prevalence and the need for new ways of looking at the terrorist problem warrants their further consideration. For instance, Borum (2004) summarizes the motivational forces behind terrorist acts as perceived injustice, identity and the need for belonging. This chapter will review the evidence for these positions, along with competing theories that have been considered in the history of terrorism research and will examine how group psychology influences group membership in terms of recruitment, maintenance and exit from terrorism.

Lone actors and organizational diversity

Before considering the group processes surrounding terrorism, it is worth looking briefly at the notion of whether terrorism is always a group phenomenon. The answer to this is 'no'. There have been examples of terrorist action conducted by so called 'lone wolves' or 'lone actors'. For these individuals, their behavior and commitment to a cause are not influenced by group dynamics. Examples of this type of 'lone wolf' actor include John Allen Muhammad, a.k.a. the 'Washington Sniper', and Ted Kaczynski, the 'Unabomber'. However, despite not being involved with well-known terrorist groups, these individuals have been linked to larger social movements (McCauley & Moskalenko, 2008).

One suggestion that has been offered to explain lone terrorists is that they are more likely than terrorist group members to suffer from some form of psychopathology (McCauley & Moskalenko, 2008). As such, members of terrorist organizations are less likely to enroll these individuals as their erratic behavior may pose a threat to the cause (Horgan, 2003; McCauley & Moskalenko, 2008; Silke, 2003). In these cases then, it might be reasonable to assume that lone actor terrorists' actions are a manifestation of a clinical disorder and as such are not representative of the largely non-clinical terrorist population. Since they are often not as successful as their group counterparts, this might be a function of increased man-power, resources, expertise, etc., enabled by 'team work'. Alternatively, it may be more than the availability of 'collective resources' that drives the disaffected to join up with like-minded others.

Aside from those who truly act alone, there has been some debate about the kind of groups or organizational structures within which terrorist actors operate. A person can be a member of a group or organization at a number of different levels at the same time. For instance, they may be a member of: a close-knit cell, the larger terrorist organization and indeed the wider disaffected community. For each form of membership different group processes are likely to operate (Taylor, 2010).

It is also worth considering that different terrorist organizations work within different forms of organizational structure, including some that operate a 'franchise' style 'flat' structure with activists engaged in essentially independent campaigns under the same umbrella ideology. These are sometimes referred to as 'leaderless resistance' (Silke, 2003). Thus, terrorist organizations range in structure from extremely hierarchical groups who adhere to strict role distinctions, to more disordered groups who fit an anarchical model. The variety of group structures seen from one organization to the next suggests that we should examine common themes of group membership rather than aspects specific to groups of a particular structure if we want to gain a generalized understanding of why individuals join terrorist groups.

Individual motivators for involvement in terrorism

The 'terrorist personality'

Early research into terrorism focused on searching for a 'terrorist profile', that would facilitate the identification of actual or potential terrorists. Whilst some focused on demographic factors, many sought personality or personality disordered explanations. The notion of terrorism being the manifestation of psychopathology or deviant personality types appeals to people's logic. Individuals like to distance themselves from others who have the capacity to cause widespread pain and suffering and they can create this distance by labeling the actor as psychologically different from one's self, and in some way, abnormal. For example, Ferracuti and Bruno (1981: 206) studied Italian terrorists and concluded that:

> a general psychiatric explanation of terrorism is impossible. To define all terrorists as mentally ill would be an easy way to solve the problem, simply by invoking evil spirits in order to exclude from normality those from whom we want to be as different as possible.

These types of belief are not empirically supported but they do show a certain level of a logic. For instance, a seeming lack of empathy towards victims offers a distinct parallel between aspects of terrorist violence and psychopathic behavior (Horgan, 2003). However, this apparent lack of remorse may actually be the result of successful rationalization of their behavior in terms of a legitimate pursuit of a political cause or justified retaliation (Lyons & Harbinson, 1979).

In fact, reviews of the early literature on terrorist personality all agreed that there is no evidence that terrorist populations differ in their psychological make-up at all (Crenshaw, 1981; Horgan, 2003). As Crenshaw (1981: 390) states, 'what limited data we have on individual terrorists … suggest that the outstanding common characteristic of terrorists is their normality'. However, McCauley (1991: 132) emphasized that this 'is not to say that there is no pathology among terrorists, but the rate of diagnosable pathology, at least, does not differ significantly from control groups of the same age and background'. In this respect, terrorism research parallels research on gangs. Membership in both types of organization appears to be driven more by rational forces than by psychopathology (see also Wood & Alleyne, Chapter 2).

Perceived injustice and revenge

When individuals share the grievances of a terrorist group, they may see their enrolment with the organization as a rational step which is comparable to joining the armed forces. Post and colleagues (2003) summarized these feelings with a quote from a Palestinian terrorist who said, 'Enlistment was for me the natural and done thing … In a way, it can be compared to a young Israeli from a nationalist Zionist family who wants to fulfill himself through army service' (p. 182). Within certain communities, failure to join terrorist organizations has even been regarded as abnormal in the context of the perceived suffering of an oppressed population. It is understandable that people may take such views since in many conflicts, 'terrorists' are viewed as 'freedom fighters' and sometimes even heroes – a definitional distinction that many authors have stressed. The debate on what actually constitutes terrorism is too lengthy to repeat here, but suffice it to say that it is determined by elements of the act, rather than elements of the actor (see for example, Wilson & Lemanski, 2010a).

Accounts of terrorist involvement as a defense of the community relate to Borum's (2004) concept of 'perceived injustice', and closely related to perceptions of injustice is the concept of revenge. Silke (2003) claims that understanding the psychology of vengeance is one of the most important keys to appreciating why some people choose to engage in terrorism, since the desire for vengeance represents a 'darker side' to people's strong sense of justice (p. 39). Although destructive vengeance may seem irrational, revenge does fulfill certain goals. It is not only associated with the redress of perceived injustice, but also the restoration of self-worth (of the individual originally targeted) and the deterrence of potential future injustice (Kim & Smith, 1993, as cited in Silke, 2003).

In terms of terrorism, Silke (2003) observes that the backgrounds of terrorist actors are often filled with encounters with security forces or rival organizations, in which family or friends have been harassed, attacked or killed. Such pivotal events can act as a catalyst, resulting in a powerful desire for vengeance and responses such as enrolment in a terrorist organization – even in the absence of prior sympathy or ideological identification with the relevant campaign (Silke, 2003). The same may often be true of suicide bombers (e.g. see Akhmedova & Speckhart, 2006) and highlights the importance that counter terrorism (CT) efforts should not actually make things worse by adopting 'heavy handed' techniques.

However, Alonso's (2006) study of IRA and ETA recruits placed an emphasis on factors other than the cause as determining people's decision to join. Although motivations were often multiple and inter-connected, including feelings of frustration and revenge, they also included relations formed via social networks (e.g. family and friends), the promise of excitement and adventure and social status and acceptance as part of the group. Although these group processes alone cannot account for the motivation to join a terrorist group, they do point to more social psychological theories for group membership (discussed later in this chapter) and draw some obvious parallels with research on gang membership.

Rationality and ideology

So far in this chapter, we have explored and rejected the role of mental disorder as a common explanation for individual involvement in terrorism. Instead, we have begun to consider other motivations (e.g. revenge) in order to provide a more cogent account of terrorist enrolment. Although vengeance might, at the outset, seem like an emotionally driven retaliation to perceived wrongdoing, Silke (2003) has demonstrated how even the most expressive of reactions can have a logical, goal-directed value. So, terrorism research has turned to the rational actor model in order to understand motivations. The rational actor model is the prevalent way of understanding terrorism in contemporary theory. The model holds that there must be subjective utility in terrorists' actions, (i.e. that the expected benefits of involvement will outweigh the costs; e.g. Crenshaw, 1988, 1990; Gambill, 1998; McCormick, 2003). The instrumental function of terrorism is to bring about political or societal change – a purpose that is integral to the definition of terrorism – and while no one can condone terrorist action, those involved in a particular conflict may believe that the greater benefit is worth the cost.

Although an ideological commitment is frequently cited as one of the most important elements of becoming involved in terrorist organizations, one controversial finding is that, across a number of different terrorist organizations, many activists do not have a very clear understanding of the political purpose or ideological goals underpinning their group's action (e.g. Alonso, 2006; Bloom, 2007 as cited in Abrahms 2008; White, 1992). For instance, Abrahms (2008) cites one study where, of the 1,100 terrorists interviewed, individuals were ten times more likely to report that they enrolled in the terror organization due to friendship bonds than because of the ideology of the group, a finding we will return to later in this chapter. The advantages offered to those enlisting in a terrorist group are well recognized, and include benefits such as respect, status and protection (e.g. Silke, 2003), which is also analogous with gang membership findings (see Wood & Alleyne, Chapter 2).

For some, the reason for joining a terrorist group may be more instrumental; the allure of the group is through the economic resources it can provide to them or their families. Families of terrorists who are wounded, killed or captured may receive economic aid and material assistance from the organization (Post *et al.*, 2003). Of course, different terrorist organizations have differential amounts of resources and so some groups are able to offer their members immediate financial recompense on their recruitment whilst others can only promise rewards that accompany victory (Weinstein, 2005). The allocation of 'death benefits' and posthumous family care in instances of martyrdom (e.g. Hoffman, 2006) demonstrates a clear benefit of group membership that would not occur following lone action since lone actor martyrdom would only serve to financially jeopardize their families by removing a source of income. Consequently, the benefits of group membership in terrorism may not only benefit the individual, but his/her family too.

Whilst financial support can clearly be seen as a 'rational', or instrumental motivator, it is far from prevalent and yet is all too often used to explain the 'inexplicable'. Media representations of the causes of terrorism frequently focus on educational and financial deprivation. However, taken as a whole, research has shown that there is no relationship between economic deprivation and involvement in terrorism (Krueger & Malečková, 2003). As such, whilst some individuals might be influenced by economic incentives, monetary factors alone do not offer a sufficient explanation for engagement in terrorist action.

Force and persuasion

Whatever the reason people choose to become members of terrorist groups, be it revenge, ideology, material gain or some other factor, in the large majority of cases, individuals actively volunteer for membership. They weigh up the pros and cons of offers to join or actively solicit membership of a chosen organization. Whilst this is true in most instances, on occasion some terrorist groups have actively coerced individuals to join their organization. For instance, the UDA in Northern Ireland has been reported to use threats and intimidation to force membership (Silke, 2003). This type of coercive recruitment is said to be more common in loyalist (pro-state) groups who as such have to compete for recruits with official State security forces (Bruce, 1992). Since they are unable to offer rewards or incentives equivalent to that offered by legitimate security forces, these groups have, on occasion, resorted to forceful means of recruitment. Clearly, in such cases it is not the idea of the 'group' which attracts individuals to join, but the threat of reprisals from the group if membership is not taken up.

Even if an individual wants to join a terrorist group, it is the group that gets the final say in terms of who they allow to join. Most terrorist organizations give lengthy consideration to candidates and conduct thorough background checks on all potential recruits (e.g. McKeown, 2000). Becoming a member often involves active participation on the part of the would-be member. Some even require successful completion of criminal acts designed to test an individual's commitment (Silke, 2003). It has been suggested that 'severe' costs associated with initiation can also inhibit *departure,* even from legitimate organizations (Hirschman, 1970). Applied to terrorism research, this idea might help explain why some organizations require recruits to commit an illegal act as a form of initiation. Not only will committing a crime act as a declaration of commitment, it will also help sustain their involvement (Crenshaw, 1988) since such 'bridge-burning acts' can generate feelings of intense guilt which act to prevent the new recruit's return to society and strengthen their bonds with group members who will be their only source of support and reassurance (Barkun, 1974).

Persuasion and charismatic leaders

So far, a common theme in the explanations for terrorist action has been the apparent need for the *observer* to rationalize why people would get involved; they must be forced, disturbed, deprived or desperate. While these things are true in certain cases, they are not the primary explanations. Other over-used beliefs that are often applied to the issue of terrorist groups are that recruits are persuaded into the group by 'charismatic leaders' and/or 'brainwashing.'

Concepts of 'charismatic leadership' emphasize persuasive influences that engender not only emotional states in the follower (e.g. emotional attachment to the leader, emotional and motivational arousal), but also boost the valence of the group's mission, as well as intrinsic motivation within devotees (Shamir *et al.*, 1993: 577). In a review of the literature, Walter and Bruch (2009) set out a number of behaviors that are believed to typify charismatic leadership. Charismatic leaders tend to: act as a role model for their followers; demonstrate a sense of power and confidence; make bold and unconventional choices; cultivate the agreement of shared goals in the group; and motivate followers in order to accomplish group aspirations.

These 'visionary' type theories propose that leaders 'transform the needs, values, preferences and aspirations of followers from self-interests to collective interests' (Shamir *et al.*, 1993: 577), acquiring intensely committed followers who are willing to make considerable personal sacrifices for the benefit of the mission. Instead of focusing on defining the *nature* of the influence, Shamir *et al.* (1993) advance a motivational theory that describes the *process* by which profound transformational influence in followers is accomplished, proposing that charismatic leaders engage followers' 'self-concepts'.

It has therefore become a popular belief that the persona of charismatic leaders can have a significant impact on organizational situations. However, many scholars remain skeptical of how much influence is really attributable to the charismatic persona of leaders, believing instead that individuals are prone to give too much credit to the impact of leaders in complex circumstances that are difficult to comprehend (Shamir *et al.*, 1993). Further, empirical evidence that the persona of a single individual can so directly influence prospective extremist recruits is entirely lacking. Crenshaw (2006) observes that individuals are more often attracted to terrorist organizations by social influence and group processes, specifically as opposed to the persuasiveness of a leader, factors that will be considered in more depth later in this chapter.

Rather than the qualities of the leaders themselves, Gordijn and Stapel (2008) propose that it is the nature of environmental *circumstance* that renders individuals more *susceptible* to the persuasiveness of charismatic leaders. Specifically, they found that environments of terror and political unrest are particularly conducive to inspiring faith in, and persuasion by charismatic leaders, as susceptibility is inflated due to the growing need for 'vision'.

The concept of susceptibility to terrorist recruitment leads us to the similarly oft cited, and correspondingly unsubstantiated notion of 'brainwashing'. Of the little empirical research that has been conducted into the vulnerability of individuals targeted for recruitment, scholars have found that 'psychographic' and 'state' variables (i.e. emotional/physical distress, cultural disillusionment, lack of intrinsic religious belief/value system, family dysfunction, susceptibility and dependent personality traits) appear to be the most important in defining the success or failure of attempted enrolment (see Gerwehr & Daly, 2006).

However, Silke (2006) makes use of historical examples in order to demonstrate that sensationalist theories describing suicide terrorism as the result of 'madness, brainwashing, coercion and fanaticism' (p. 45) are meaningless when considered against other explanations that adopt far greater significance. For example, he draws on the case of the Japanese kamikaze of World War II, whose suicide missions were regarded with 'horror, incredulity, and dread' (p. 45) at the time. It is clear now that the kamikaze campaigns were in fact highly successful. Silke demonstrates the rationality behind kamikaze missions by simply pointing out that they caused twice as much damage (to Allied shipping in the Philippines, 1944) compared to traditional air-raid missions, despite the fact that many more conventional raids were executed. The post-WWII US Strategic Bombing Survey describes the Japanese kamikaze campaign as 'effective [and] *supremely practical* under the circumstances' (cited in Silke, 2006: 45; emphasis added by Silke). Silke concludes his report by stating that '[I]t is possible, if indeed not probable, that history will provide a similar assessment of the campaigns of suicide terrorism we face today' (2006: 45).

Persuasion and the internet

For the potential terrorist, the advent of the internet offers an additional source of persuasive influence. The internet provides an extremely large and international pool from which terrorist organizations are able to select and draw in 'rank and file' candidates (Silke, 2003). Freiburger and Crane (2008) cite research that found that by 2000, many terrorist organizations had established an internet presence represented by their own websites (Weimann, 2004). Freiburger and Crane (2008) claim that the internet provides an environment that is particularly conducive to the needs of terrorist organizations, as it requires few skills to use, is lacking in regulation, and provides terror groups with a worldwide, international audience. As such, terrorist groups can not only send information rapidly, anonymously, at little cost (Lachow & Richardson, 2007; Weimann, 2004; Whine 1999) but they can do so with minimal risks. It is therefore unsurprising that terrorist groups have embraced the use of the internet for propaganda distribution, recruitment, training and planning (Freiburger & Crane, 2008).

Freiburger and Crane (2008) state that the internet has allowed terrorist organizations to reach individuals who are both unfamiliar with their country of origin as well as feeling different to those in their new country, and are therefore left unable to identify with either, rendering them particularly susceptible to online recruitment. Freiburger and Crane describe how such individuals can lack relationships which native peers possess; instead of dealing with their feelings of isolation alone, such individuals are able – via the internet – to seek social support systems and share their feelings with others in similar positions.

Indeed, more general research has shown that online communities can be particularly influential for certain types of group. For example, McKenna and Bargh (2000) found that internet users with perceived stigmatized identities were more likely to 'come out' to their family and friends in the real-world if they were involved in a virtual support group (Freiburger & Crane, 2008). This study demonstrates how participation in a virtual group can influence 'real-life' behaviors and supports the idea that the internet might have similar effects on young people suffering feelings of marginalization, who seek support in terror organizations (Freiburger & Crane, 2008). The internet therefore provides an easy way for individuals to 'meet' like-minded others, and to gain a sense of belonging to a group even though many members may never meet face to face.

The importance of 'belonging' to a group is heavily intertwined in theories of social identity and group processes, which researchers have successfully applied to terrorist enlistment and continued membership. The social benefits to be gained from enrolment in a terrorist organization (or indeed any group) will be considered in detail shortly. First, however, we will consider how persuasion can emerge from group processes in terms of group polarization.

Group polarization, persuasion and extremist views

Bringing the processes of leadership and online persuasion together, the development of 'group polarization' is the process by which discussion between like-minded individuals leads to their holding more extreme positions than they held prior to the discussion (see Viki and Abrams, Chapter 1, for a more in-depth discussion). In brief, Stoner (1961, 1968) compared individual and group responses to risk-taking behavior. Individual pre-deliberation views were recorded and participants were then asked to come to a unanimous group decision. Post-deliberation views were also recorded and the extremity of each of these responses was compared. Both the group and individual post-deliberation views were found to show an increase in risk-taking. Stoner labeled this phenomenon the 'risky shift'; group dynamics causing a significant shift in private and public opinion towards risk taking. Further, it has been shown that polarisation is heightened if members of the group have a shared identity, show a high degree of solidarity, and if they are connected by affective ties. As we have already mentioned, all of these aspects are common in terrorist groups and as such, members will be particularly suseptable to 'risky shift'.

Sunstein (1999) states that the social comparison explanation for group polarization relies upon the premise that individuals want to have positive self-perceptions and be favorably perceived by other members. So, when they have heard the beliefs of others, people tend to adjust their own beliefs in the direction of the 'dominant' opinion. Sunstein's (1999) second explanation for group polarization further emphasizes the role of persuasion, and is based on a 'common sense intuition' that all personal beliefs on a particular issue are (at least in part) dependent on which group arguments appear to be most convincing. Thus, in the context of terrorist groups, the beliefs of group members are likely to already be skewed in one direction; the direction that encouraged them to become group members in the first place, and so there will be a disproportionate number of arguments in support of that track. The consequence of discussion therefore, will be that participants shift even further towards their initial beliefs due to a limited argument pool.

Sunstein (1999) observes that these circumstances are clearly relevant to the possible effects of group deliberation online. The covert nature of terrorism induces isolation from others' norms and beliefs, which serves to enhance the impact of the group as the sole social influence to which members are exposed. As such, members receive no 'normalizing' influences or competing opinions, reducing the perceptibility of flaws in arguments, thereby removing the capability for critical evaluation of competition (Sunstein, 1999).

Interpersonal and social factors in terrorist groups

The pathway into terrorism is a complex one which is all too often attributed to factors such as radical political commitment, brainwashing, the allure of charismatic leaders, or forms of psychopathy. However, the reality is that there are many reasons why people become members of terrorist groups; potential rewards can go beyond the political or ideological and are often based in the fulfillment of more basic psychological and material needs. As already noted, the benefits of group membership afforded to the potential terrorist include, but are not limited to, the fulfillment of individual needs (e.g. to belong to a group, excitement), social needs (e.g. to increase their social standing and their reputation) and material/financial needs. The following sections will explore what the group itself can offer the potential terrorist.

Social identity and terrorist groups

During interview, terrorists often report that their membership of a terrorist group provided them with a sense of belonging that was otherwise absent from their lives (Alonso, 2006). Furthermore, the opportunity to formalize a social identity and develop social relationships has been noted as influencing a new recruit's involvement in terrorist organizations more than any political or ideological agendas (see for example, Alonso, 2006 on recruits to ETA and the IRA).

Relevant to this discussion is Social Identity Theory (see also Viki & Abrams, Chapter 1) which involves our self-perceptions of our various roles in different social groups that we identify with. Group memberships are said to shape an individual's self-concept, and influence the way they treat others. Ludwick (2008) applies Social Identity Theory (SIT) directly to the terrorist arena and elaborates on the ways that it works. At the cognitive level, joining a group identifies the person with their motivations and sustained identity is derived from taking part in (often legitimate) activities such as marches and protests. The membership carries an emotional component where the person may view themselves as contributing positive action in support of a repressed community. SIT holds that with increased association with the 'in-group', comes an increased negative perception of the 'out-group', a feature used to explain the ability of terrorist group members to 'distance' the 'other', against whom the fight is directed.

Drawing on these notions, Ludwick (2008) sets out how collective violence can emerge from a series of factors. He states that violence is more likely where there is greater 'cultural distance', that is, differences in aspects of the 'out-group's' social and religious practices, along with functional independence, (e.g. a lack of reliance on the services or support of the 'out-group' within the community). These two factors, when combined with close 'relational distance' (i.e. in their daily interaction), and a perception of social or financial inequality can serve to increase the likelihood of collective violence.

Social status and terrorist groups

As previously discussed, in many conflicts membership of a terrorist organization affords people a level of respect from the wider community. A Palestinian terrorist stated that: 'Recruits were treated with great respect. A youngster who belonged to Hamas or Fatah was regarded more highly than one who didn't belong to a group and got better treatment than unaffiliated kids' (Post *et al.*, 2003: 178). This view of terrorists as courageous and honorable has been documented in research looking at different organizations. Members of the IRA even alluded to sexual advantages that can be gained from membership: 'there is no shortage of women willing to give more than the time of day to IRA volunteers' (Collins & McGovern, 1997: 165). The glorification of terrorism and terrorist actions can be seen throughout communities in which terrorism is rife (e.g. 'martyr of the month' paintings that depict suicide bombers in Paradise; Horgan, 2008).

Research on gang members has shown that they value the importance of social status significantly more than non-gang peers (Alleyne & Wood, 2010) and a desire for social status that they would otherwise lack is also considered to be a motivating factor for involvement in terrorist organizations (Alonso, 2006). Research on gangs has shown that gang members tend to come from socially marginal or economically disadvantaged groups with unstable community structures. As such, potential gang members find themselves of a social standing which affords them few legitimate sources for positive self-validation and self-definition. By joining a gang, individuals have the opportunity to attain a level of 'success'. The gang also provides members with a sense of both individual power and protection that is otherwise missing for them and can provide structure in an otherwise unstructured existence. Similarly, terrorist groups can offer individuals a sense of community and structure whereby members may view engagement in terrorist activities as being the most accessible avenue for 'success' and stability.

Family, friends and terrorist groups

With respect to deviant behavior, research has shown that the 'family' and parental support can serve a protective function for young individuals (e.g. Crosnoe *et al.*, 2002). In accordance with this, studies have revealed that many gang members have unstable or absent family networks and as such it has been argued that the gang offers them the emotional support, loyalty, understanding and recognition that they are otherwise deprived of (Vigil, 1988, as cited in Rubel & Turner, 2000).

In terrorism research, many terrorist group members have also been found to come from economically and/or politically impotent families where the father figure was either absent or estranged (Stahelski, 2004). Wasmund (1982; cited in Crenshaw, 1986) argues that terrorist groups function as a familial substitute for many members. Furthermore, research shows that some terrorist recruits are individuals who have experienced difficulty in forming consistent group identities in a variety of legitimate social forums (e.g. school, work; Stahelski, 2004). However, the reliability of this partial profile of terrorists as coming from inadequate/deficient social and economic backgrounds is questionable; as mentioned earlier, economic and educational deprivation is *not* correlated with terrorist involvement across all causes or cultures (Krueger & Malečková, 2003).

The role of the family is a strong factor in terrorist groups, and in terms of promoting the decision to join, as long ago as 1982, Wasmund (cited in Crenshaw, 1986) noted a significant number of sibling and romantic pairs involved in terrorism. Friends, partners and relatives have often been found to be pivotal in recruitment and retention to terrorist groups. In fact, research has often shown that 'friendship and kinship bonds predate ideological commitment' (Crenshaw, 2000: 156). Studies on a wide variety of terrorist organizations (including al-Qaida, Fatah, Hamas, Hezbollah, Islamic Jihad, Palestinian and Turkish organizations) have found that the primary factor which influences terrorist group membership is having a friend or relative already involved in the organization. This observation is consistent with conclusions drawn by previous research which looked at the role of family and friends in European-based terrorist organizations (e.g. ETA, the IRA, Italian and German right-wing and Marxist terrorist groups) and contemporary research on Guantanamo Bay detainees which showed that knowing an al-Qaida member was a significantly better predictor of terrorism enrolment than believing in the jihad (Abrahms, 2008).

McCauley and Moskalenko (2008) suggest that it is pre-established loyalty or 'love' for existing terrorist members that draws many individuals into terrorist movements: 'love often determines who will join. The pull of romantic and comradely love can be as strong as politics in moving individuals into an underground group' (McCauley & Moskalenko, 2008: 421). These group affiliations are likely to be further strengthened after recruitment as shared goals and mutual threats act to increase group solidarity and cohesion, which in turn facilitate group maintenance by reducing the likelihood of disbanding (McCauley & Moskalenko, 2008). The presence of existing social affiliations can also effect recruitment in a top-down manner: organizations require the utmost loyalty from members and have to trust them to not go to the authorities and divulge information on covert operations. As a result, trusted friends and family members often represent the most reliable source of new recruits (McCauley & Moskalenko, 2008).

Maintaining membership

Once recruited, the commission of violent crimes through radical terrorist action has the potential for negative psychological repercussions on those directly involved as well as those involved by association. However, group processes can serve protective functions against psychological trauma. For instance, membership in a terrorist group can help individuals cope with any guilt they might feel as a result of their actions. As previously mentioned, the group generates and promotes its own standards and norms in a secluded environment in which violence against the enemy is portrayed as morally acceptable. For instance, with reference to the IRA, Alonso (2006) finds that long-established historical myths and legends, along with extreme customs and habits that sanction the use of violence against political opponents are used by terrorist organizations 'in order to make those means appear morally and politically justifiable' (p. 193). There are a number of psychosocial features of terrorist organizations that can lead to the internalization of group standards, values and morals. As previously discussed, the clandestine nature of terrorist organizations reduces members' exposure to competing views and renders them less able to detect potential flaws in an argument or give it objective consideration (Sunstein, 1999).

Despite this, some individuals might still feel guilt for their actions, and if they feel stress as a result of this guilt, the clandestine nature of terrorist organizations ensures that the only people that members can turn to is other members of the group (Crenshaw, 1986). The end result is that members might find it increasingly difficult to leave the group because they become dependent on the group to provide them with support and reassurance. If they do choose to leave they would not only have to face the legal and social reprimands of the outside world, but they would also have to deal with their guilt alone (Crenshaw, 1986).

The group increases its ability to act as a buffer to negative psychological repercussions of violent action by providing its members with a certain degree of detachment from their actions. When operating as a group, shared action can lead to both the diffusion of responsibility and the displacement of responsibility (Bandura, 1986). Diffusion of responsibility is a psychological process that occurs under group conditions. It represents a degree of moral disengagement from one's actions which can result in the deactivation of regulatory self-restraint against harmful behaviors (Bandura, 1986; Bandura *et al.*, 1996). Diffusion of responsibility can also occur when individuals are assigned to fragmentary jobs which, in isolation appear relatively innocuous (e.g. ordering fertilizer via the internet), but in reality represent a vital contribution in the commission of a terrorist attack (e.g. the detonation of a fertilizer bomb that kills dozens of people). By making only partial contributions, members are able to psychologically distance themselves from the often devastating outcome of the group effort and are able to attribute blame to other actors along the chain of events (Bandura, 2003).

Displacement of responsibility, on the other hand, occurs when committing acts under the instruction of an authority. It is the process by which actors assign responsibility to those that have instructed them, thereby reducing feelings of personal responsibility (Bandura, 1986; Bandura *et al.* 1996). Bandura argued that '[i]n terrorism sponsored by states or governments in exile, functionaries view themselves as patriots fulfilling nationalistic duties rather than as freelancing criminals' (2003: 130). Both displacement and diffusion of responsibility ultimately act to protect individuals psychologically from the consequences of their actions and thus represent another protective aspect of group membership that can facilitate excessively violent action. Soldiers in combat are more or less isolated from the outside world, aside from their fellow soldiers. Members of terrorist organizations, like soldiers, live an isolated existence which is compounded by the extremely stressful and dangerous conditions in which they operate. In these scenarios, an extreme interdependence between group members results in extreme group cohesion, which in turn increases pressure for both behavioral compliance and for the internalization of group standards, values and morals (McCauley & Moskalenko, 2008).

In addition to group polarization forces, which can cause individuals to internalize beliefs that justify violent action, threats of rejection can also lead to superficial obedience and conformity. Research into non-violent cults has shown that members do not want to be rejected by their cult group, especially if they have invested in the group by sacrificing their former life (including friendships, family and possessions etc.). Rusbult's (1983) 'Investment Model' explains relationship commitment in terms of satisfaction with the relationship, quality of alternatives, and investment. The latter represents the amount of resources that have been invested in a relationship, albeit time, wealth, energy etc. It is believed that investment enhances commitment to a relationship because as investment increases, the cost of ending the relationship also increases, thus 'serving as a powerful psychological inducement to persist' (p. 359). When applied to terrorism, this theory would suggest that the more an individual invests in an organization, the more committed they will be, and the less likely they will be to exit (Wilson & Lemanski, 2010b).

By severing all ties with the outside world, non-violent cult members are totally dependent on their group which makes the threat of rejection more ominous (Stahelski, 2004). The threat posed by violent cults and terrorist groups to dissidents and deserters is even more tangible (Stahelski, 2004). Groups try to prevent members exiting the group by defining voluntary exit as betrayal, and can even discourage dissent and departure with force (Crenshaw, 1988). As a result, even if a member has not internalized the core beliefs and values of the group, they may still engage in extreme behavior consistent with group goals as a result of obedience/conformity to avoid violent retribution.

Similarly to cult groups, residual group affiliations or established identities from a potential recruit's mainstream life (e.g. family, friends) can inhibit total commitment to the cause (Stahelski, 2004). As such, like youth gangs and non-political cults and sects, terrorist organizations are isolated subcultures with their own sets of values and norms. The clandestine nature of terrorist groups isolates individuals from the outside world and from other social groups which acts to increase the strength of relationships between its members as the group becomes an individual's only source of social contact, trust and reassurance (Crenshaw, 1981). With no normalizing influence, members will find the depersonalization of victims increasingly easy and can get distorted views of the actual threat posed by the 'enemy'. If members are told that the enemy is overly hostile, they can justify more violent acts (Crenshaw, 1986). Furthermore, the extreme danger that group members perceive the outside world as posing stimulates their need for reassurance. This need is satisfied by the group and thus strong effective ties develop and an individual's desire to leave the group lessens (Crenshaw, 1986).

Conclusions

In summary, since the routes into terrorism vary so greatly, most researchers now consider it fruitless to search for a definitive *cause* for terrorism, and have agreed that the best that can be hoped for is to identify some of the factors that predispose individuals to engage in terrorist behaviors. Even with these in mind, we are still unable to account for why, from a very large number of people with the same factors in place, only a very small number will eventually find themselves involved in terrorist action (Horgan, 2008). Nonetheless, in this review, we have demonstrated that group processes play a key role in attracting terrorist recruits and maintaining their on-going membership.

With so many potential routes into terrorism there can be no one way to prevent terrorist recruitment. However, it is clear that Borum's (2004) summary of the causes of terrorism being perceived injustice, identity and the need for belonging finds considerable support.

The strong familial and friendship bonds between those recruited into a wide range of terrorist organizations worldwide has led to research using Social Network Analysis (SNA) (e.g. Ressler, 2006) which provides a useful tool for understanding interpersonal and intergroup connections. These techniques allow for social relations or 'links' between known terrorists or suspects to be identified, traced, and monitored.

Wilson and Lemanski (2010a) draw comparisons between terrorist actors and 'regular' offenders and conclude that while there are very important differences in motivation, there are also some strong similarities with regards to 'pathways into crime'. With this in mind, they suggest that terrorism research might well turn to the 'What Works' (after McGuire 1985; 2000) literature on the rehabilitation of non-terrorist offenders.

With respect to counter terrorism (CT) responses, many Western governments picked up on the idea that marginalized Muslim communities may be vulnerable to terrorist recruitment. However, identifying such 'at-risk' groups in the US, UK, and mainland Europe may well have resulted in further marginalization, serving to reinforce communities' feelings of not being accepted, and revealed increasing anger that there had been no interest in the problems experienced by Muslim communities (e.g. in terms of health, education and housing) until the community was branded as a 'threat' (see for example, Neville-Jones, 2011).

We also know that at the opposite extreme, where communities in conflict are vulnerable to terrorist recruitment, heavy handed military interventions and insensitive handling by law enforcement personnel have been shown to exacerbate the problem, leading to the recruitment of more people by increasing feelings of injustice. Perhaps one of the most important areas for terrorism research in the future will be the role of group processes; in reconciliation, reduction of prejudice, and in promoting co-operation in working together for positive change.

References

Abrahms, M. (2008). What terrorists really want: terrorist motives and counterterrorism strategy. *International Security, 32 (4)*, 78–105. DOI: 10.1162/isec.2008.32.4.78.

Akhmedova, K. and Speckhart, A. (2006) A multi-causal analysis of the genesis of suicide terrorism. In J. Victoroff (ed.), *Tangled Roots: Social and Psychological Factors in the Genesis of Terrorism*. Amsterdam: IOS Press.

Alleyne, E. and Wood, J.L. (2010). Gang involvement: psychological and behavioral characteristics of gang members, peripheral youth, and nongang youth. *Aggressive Behavior, 36*, 423–436. DOI: 10.1002/ab.20360.

Alonso, R. (2006). Individual motivations for joining terrorist organizations: a comparative study on members of ETA and IRA. In J. Victoroff (ed.), *Tangled Roots: Social and Psychological Factors in the Genesis of Terrorism* (pp. 187–202). Amsterdam: IOS Press.

Bandura, A. (1986). *Social Foundations of Thought and Action: A Socialcognitive Theory*. Englewood Cliffs, NJ: Prentice-Hall.

Bandura, A. (2003). Role of mechanisms of selective moral disengagement in terrorism and counterterrorism. In F.M. Moghaddam and A.J. Marsella (eds), *Understanding Terrorism* (pp. 121–150). Washington, DC: APA.

Bandura, A., Barbaranelli, C., Caprara, G.V. and Pastorelli, C. (1996). Mechanisms of moral disengagement in the exercise of moral agency. *Journal of Personality and Social Psychology, 71*, 364–374. DOI: 10.1037/0022-3514.71.2.364.

Barkun, M. (1974). *Disaster and the Millenium*. New Haven: Yale U.P.

Borum, R. (2004). *Psychology of Terrorism*. Tampa FL: University of South Florida.

Bruce, S. (1992). *The Red Hand: Protestant Paramilitaries in Northern Ireland*. Oxford: Oxford University Press.

Collins, E. and McGovern, M. (1997). *Killing Rage*. London: Granta Books.

Crenshaw, M. (1981). The causes of terrorism. *Comparative Politics, 13 (4)*, 379–399.

Crenshaw, M. (1986). The psychology of political terrorism. In M. Hermann (ed.), *Political Psychology: Contemporary Problems and Issues* (pp. 379–413). London: Josey-Bass.

Crenshaw, M. (1988). Theories of terrorism: instrumental and organizational approaches. In D.C. Rapoport (ed.), *Inside Terrorist Organizations* (pp. 13–30). New York: Columbia University Press.

Crenshaw, M. (1990). The logic of terrorism: terrorist behavior as a product of strategic choice. In W. Reich (ed.), *Origins of Terrorism: Psychologies, Ideologies, Theologies, States of Mind* (pp. 7–24). New York: Cambridge University Press.

Crenshaw, M. (2000). The psychology of terrorism: an agenda for the 21st century. *Political Psychology, 21* (2), 405–420. DOI: 10.1111/0162-895X.00195.

Crenshaw, M. (2006). Have motivations for terrorism changed? In J. Victoroff (ed.), *Tangled Roots: Social and Psychological Factors in the Genesis of Terrorism*. Amsterdam: IOS Press.

Crosnoe, R., Erickson, K.G. and Dornbusch, S.M. (2002). Protective functions of family relationships and school factors on the deviant behavior of adolescent boys and girls: reducing the impact of risky friendships. *Youth and Society, 33*, 515–544. DOI: 10.1177/0044118X02033004002.

Ferracuti, F. and Bruno, F. (1981). Psychiatric aspects of terrorism in Italy. In I.L. Barak-Glantz and R. Huff (eds), *The Mad, the Bad and the Different: Essays in Honor of Simon Dinitz*. Lexington, Mass.: Heath.

Freiburger, T. and Crane, J. (2008). A systematic examination of terrorist use of the internet. *International Journal of Cyber Criminology, 2(1)*, 309–319. Retrieved from http://www.cybercrimejournal.com/tinaijccjan2008.pdf (accessed 30 March 2012).

Gambill, G.C. (1998). The balance of terror: war by other means in the contemporary Middle East. *Journal of Palestine Studies, 28(1)*, 51–66.

Gerwehr, S. and Daly, S. (2006). Al-Qaida: terrorist selection and recruitment. In D. Kamien (ed.), *The McGraw-Hill Homeland Security Handbook* (pp. 73–89). New York: McGraw-Hill.

Gordijn, E.H. and Stapel, D.A. (2008). When controversial leaders with charisma are effective: the influence of terror on the need for vision and impact of mixed attitudinal messages. *European Journal of Social Psychology, 38*, 389–411. DOI: 10.1002/ejsp.411.

Hirschman, A. (1970). *Exit, Voice, and Loyalty: Responses to Decline in Firms, Organizations, and States*. Cambridge, MA: Harvard University Press.

Hoffman, B. (2006). *Inside Terrorism – Rev. and expanded ed.* New York: Columbia University Press.

Horgan, J. (2003). The search for the terrorist personality. In A. Silke (Ed.), *Terrorists, Victims and Society* (pp. 3–27). West Sussex, UK: John Wiley & Sons Ltd.

Horgan, J. (2005). *The Psychology of Terrorism*. London: Routledge.

Horgan, J. (2008). From profiles to pathways and roots to routes: perspectives from psychology on radicalization into terrorism. *The ANNALS of the American Academy of Political and Social Science, 618*, 80–94. DOI:10.1177/0002716208317539.

Krueger, A.B. and Malečková, J. (2003) Education, poverty and terrorism: is there a causal connection? *Journal of Economic Perspectives*, 17, 119–144. DOI: 10.1257/089533003772034925.

Lachow, I. and Richardson, C. (2007). Terrorist use of the internet: the real story. *JFQ: Joint Force Quarterly, 45*, 100–103. Retrieved from http://handle.dtic.mil/100.2/ADA518156 (accessed 30 March 2012).

Ludwick, K. (2008). *Closing the Gap: Measuring the Social Identity of Terrorists*. Retrieved from Naval Postgraduate School: http://handle.dtic.mil/100.2/ADA488713 (accessed 8 March 20110.

Lyons, H.A. and Harbinson, H.J. (1979). A comparison of political and non-political murderers in Northern Ireland, 1974–1984. *Medicine, Science and the Law, 26*, 193–198.

McCauley, C.R. (1991). Terrorism, research and public policy: an overview. *Terrorism and Political Violence, 3 (1)*, 124–144. DOI: 10.1080/09546559108427097.

McCauley, C. and Moskalenko, S. (2008). Mechanisms of political radicalization: pathways toward terrorism. *Terrorism and Political Violence, 20*, 415–433. DOI: 10.1080/09546550802073367.

McCormick, G.H. (2003). Terrorist decision making. *Annual Review of Political Science*, 6, 473–507. DOI: 10.1146/annurev.polisci.6.121901.085601.

McGuire, J. (2000). *What Works: Reducing Reoffending. Guidelines from Research and Practice*. Chichester, England: John Wiley and Sons. First published in 1985.

McKenna, K.Y.A. and Bargh, J.A. (2000). Plan 9 from cyberspace: the implications of the internet for personality and social psychology. *Personality and Social Psychology Review, 4*, 57–75. DOI: 10.1207/S15327957PSPR0401_6.

McKeown, L. (2000). Taking up arms. In M. Smyth and M. Fay (eds), *Personal Accounts from Northern Ireland's Troubles* (pp. 51–62). London: Pluto Press.

Neville-Jones, P. (2011) A new approach to counter-radicalization. Paper presented at the *Council on Foreign Relations*, New York. 1 April 2011.

Post, J.M., Sprinzak, E. and Denny, L.M. (2003). The terrorists in their own words. Interviews with 35 incarcerated Middle Eastern terrorists. *Terrorism and Political Violence, 15 (1)*, 171–184. DOI: 10.1080/09546550312331293007.

Ressler, S. (2006). Social network analysis as an approach to combat terrorism: past, present, and future research. *The Journal of Naval Postgraduate School Center for Homeland Defense and Security, 2 (2)*, 1–10. Retrieved from http://www.hsaj.org (accessed 30 March 2012).

Rubel, N.M. and Turner, W.L. (2000). A systemic analysis of the dynamics and organization of urban street gangs. *The American Journal of Family Therapy, 28*, 117–132. DOI: 10.1080/019261800261707.

Rusbult, C. (1983). A longitudinal test of the investment model: the development (and deterioration) of satisfaction and commitment in heterosexual involvements. *Journal of Personality and Social Psychology, 45*, 172–186. DOI: 10.1037/0022-3514.45.1.101.

Shamir, B., House, R.J. and Arthur, B.A. (1993). The motivational effects of charismatic leadership: a self-concept based theory. *Organization Science, 4(4)*, 577–594. DOI: 10.1287/orsc.4.4.577

Silke, A. (2003). Becoming a terrorist. In A. Silke (ed.), *Terrorists, Victims and Society* (pp. 29–53). West Sussex, UK: John Wiley & Sons Ltd.

Silke, A. (2006). *Terrorists, Victims and Society* (2nd edn). Chichester: Wiley.

Stahelski, A. (2004). *Terrorists Are Made, Not Born: Creating Terrorists Using Social Psychological Conditioning*. Retrieved from Homeland Security: http://www.homelandsecurity.org/journal/Articles/stahelski.html (accessed 8 March 2011).

Stoner, J.A.F. (1961). *A Comparison of Individual and Group Decisions Involving Risk*. In R Brown (ed.), *Social Psychology*. New York: Free Press.

Stoner, J.A.F. (1968). Risky and cautious shifts in group decisions: the influence of widely held values. *Journal of Experimental Social Psychology, 4*, 442–459. DOI: 10.1016/0022-1031(68)90069-3.

Sunstein, C.R. (1999). *The Law of Group Polarization*. Retrieved from The Chicago Working Paper Series: http://www.law.uchicago.edu/Publications/Working/index.html (accessed 8 March 2011).

Taylor, M. (2010). Is Terrorism a group phenomenon? *Aggression and Violent Behavior, 15*, 121–129. DOI: 10.1016/j.avb.2009.09.001.

Walter, F. and Bruch, H. (2009). An affective events model of charismatic leadership behavior: a review, theoretical integration, and research agenda. *Journal of Management, 35*, 1428–1452. DOI: 10.1177/0149206309342468.

Weimann, G. (2004). *www.terror.net: How Modern Terrorism Uses the Internet*. Washington D.C.: United States Institute of Peace.

Weinstein, J. (2005). Resources and the information problem in rebel recruitment. *Journal of Conflict Resolution, 49*, 598–624. DOI: 10.1177/0022002705277802.

Whine, M. (1999). Cyberspace: a new medium for communications, command and control by extremists. *Studies in Conflict and Terrorism, 22(3)*, 231–245.

White, R.W. (1992). Political violence by the nonaggrieved. In D. dellaPorta (ed.), *International Social Movement Research Volume 4* (pp. 83<n> 92). Greenwich, Conn.: Jai Press.

Wilson, M.A. and Lemanski, L. (2010a). The forensic psychology of terrorism. In J. Adler and J. Gray (eds) *Forensic Psychology; Concepts, Debates and Practice. Second Edition*. Abingdon, Oxon: Willan Publishing.

Wilson M.A. and Lemanski, L. (2010b) *Key Dimensions in Understanding Terrorist Bomb Attacks*. Final Report to Human Factors/Behavioral Sciences Division, Science and Technology Directorate, U.S. Department of Homeland Security.

6 Organized crime

Criminal organizations or organized criminals?

Vincent Egan, School of Psychology, University of Leicester, and Stephen Lock, Head of Group Business Protection, Old Mutual plc

Introduction

There are over 150 definitions of 'organized crime' (von Lampe, 2011). Most consistently these definitions allude to an actively structured and hierarchical criminal syndicate that provides resources that cannot be obtained legitimately or are sought without government regulation (for example, the illegal dumping of toxic material, or the importing of cigarettes without duty). The ambiguity of definitions combined with the lack of reliability and validity information for these competing interpretations handicaps effective risk assessment (Zoutendijk, 2010). 'Organized crime' is quite different from disorganized crime of the kind typically considered by forensic and clinical psychologists. This is because organized crime serves illicit human wants, rather than reflects human idiosyncrasies. Human qualities like impulsivity, ignorance and intoxication are cardinal to day-to-day individual offenders (Egan, 2011), and such characteristics have correspondingly typical developmental trajectories that are increasingly well understood. The crimes such persons commit often reflect disorganized minds – impulsive offences committed with little consideration of the intent, act, or consequences until after the event. This is not the case for persons involved in organized crime; many organized crime offenders do not have judicial contacts before adulthood, though they may then have considerable numbers of serious judicial contacts subsequently (van Koppen *et al.*, 2010; Bauwens & Egan, 2011). This late-onset pattern is antithetical to the general nature of criminal offending demographics, which peaks in late adolescence and young adulthood.

One could mischievously argue that organized crime is in some respects the dark side of capitalism and free enterprise, in which products – sex, drugs, untaxed items, unlicensed movement across international boundaries, the right to dump toxic chemicals without red tape or eco-laws – are provided by an organization who take the considerable commercial and custodial risk to provide this service. Such activities are clearly highly lucrative, and the amounts made by apparently organized criminal organizations are spectacular (Glenny, 2009); in 2012 the head of the United Nations Office on Drugs and Crime suggested crime generates around $2.1 trillion in global annual proceeds. This is approximately 3.6 percent of the world's gross domestic product, and makes criminal enterprise one of the top 20 global economic forces (Associated Press, April 23rd, 2012). Once the money has been gathered – classically in stained used notes transferred across national boundaries in suitcases, but increasingly via electronic exchanges – it has to be laundered so can be legitimately banked invested in legal and conventional ventures. The Columbian *Cali* cartel (which controlled 90 per cent of the world cocaine market in the 1990s) solved supply-line problems in the acquisition of the precursor chemicals for synthesising the drug by establishing a pharmacy chain of 400 shops (*'Drogas La Rebaja'*) in the 1980s, making such purchases unremarkable. This chain of shops was not closed until 2004. The cartel also established banks and radio stations. Each of these large operations was a legitimate business with employees unaware of their ultimate owners. Some of the Columbian state was also deeply associated with the cartel (Allum & Siebert, 2003).

These are matters that often apparently go beyond the individual and the small group – typically the subject of psychology – to large social networks and even geo-political levels. There is a strong argument for saying that 'narcostates' (nations which make a significant amount of their capital by the production of narcotics, such as the UK when it sold opium produced in India to China during the Victorian era, or the similar trade now driven by the Taliban in Afghanistan) show that organized crime can even operate at the national level, or overlap with terrorist organizations. The current disorder in Mexico's border area with the USA is caused by the conflict between two criminal cartels competing for the right to supply recreational drugs north of the border (Vulliamy, 2010). This violence is of such a magnitude that the Mexican Army is unable to contain the warring factions, and the police have apparently lost control of the situation (Carrroll, 2010). Many times what seems to be libertine choice (such as taking recreational drugs) is superseded by a moral concern if one becomes aware of the context; does one continue to use a resource provided by organized crime if one thus becomes complicit in a chain of events that leads to criminal violence sufficient to destroy actual societies or harm that you would not commit yourself?

Psychology is not generally in a position to change society at these macro-levels, although it may have relevance in reducing an individual's desire for unhealthy pleasures or irresponsible responses to regulation. This is because persons can be made more thoughtful about the consequences of their choices, and much 'criminal' thinking reflects thoughtlessness rather than callousness (Egan *et al.*, 2000). Nevertheless, there are aspects of psychological, sociological, criminological and economic research and thought that can usefully inform a better understanding of organized crime. The current chapter seeks to review aspects of the psychological, sociological and economic literature on organized crime to provide a means by which one might have a more structured grasp of the field. It also provides a broad overview of how an understanding of money laundering investigation can reveal the operations of organized criminal networks.

Some context

Much of what people think about organized crime reflects the dramatic constructions in films and novels that contribute to myths somewhat distant to the reality. Just as much alleged organized terrorism is somewhat *ad-hoc* and reflects groups of likeminded alienated persons who loosely know one another, and can contribute to one another's operations, the same follows for organized crime; ENRON and its disgraced directors is closer to the myth of organized crime than the loose trans-national criminal syndicates that often occur in reality. The pyramidic hierarchical structure of the stereotyped criminal organization is also often more informal and horizontal in structure; even if some persons in the criminal organization have been to business school and keep records (Venkatesh, 2009), it is imprudent for professional criminals (i.e. persons who make their living from criminal activity) to follow transparent methodologies. Informality and horizontal linkages are helpful, as they optimize the possibility that nobody knows too much about their peers, should they be identified by law enforcement agencies.

The complicity of states, organizations, groups and individuals in what can be called 'organized crime' is another way in which some of the assumptions about huge and pernicious criminal organizations sometimes break down. In poor or developing communities with cultures of honor and patronage, the process of achieving a goal often involves having to bribe a person to sign a form and to show deference to powerful local persons in the community. What may seem like extortion if one views the behavior from the perspective of the state, can be little more than competing bands of brigands predating upon some communities and defending others that prefer to keep established law enforcement as far from their lives as possible, and their wants free of state ordinance (Ruggerio, 2010). It is only as a society becomes more lawful and an increasing majority of the community is in agreement with such laws that communities reduce their support for brigandage. Though states are ostensibly above the messy realities of people's lives, as conflicts emerge between different nations in how they operate, a degree of complicity also emerges; peasants producing the base materials for the West's desire for recreational drugs from Afghanistan or Central America have livelihoods and local markets, and no alternatively lucrative cash crop (Blackman, 2010). Thus it is that one part of a nation state may declare a 'war on drugs' whilst another sees the sale of drugs as a clandestine means of subsidising counter-revolutionary activities. Elsewhere, international laws strictly opposing flagrant commercial piracy may be less enthusiastically enforced when another nation with whom trading is sought, has no intention of actually enforcing copyright. In practice, *realpolitik* general supersedes well-intentioned policy.

Moral panics also have a role in understanding aspects of organized crime. A moral panic occurs at times when aspects of a society cannot cope with major changes happening in other parts of that society. This inability to control changes in social morals makes elements within the society fearful and exaggerated in their concerns and even legislature. One could argue that crimes sometimes reflect moral standards imposed by religious or political values incompatible with the secularisation or democratising of societies. The public often choose to follow behaviors that are illegal or 'immoral' if they do not believe what they are doing is either. During the 1920s and early 1930s, the passing of the Volstead Act led to the Prohibition of alcohol in the USA. This made millions of people criminals for doing something that was culturally normal for them, and also facilitated the consolidation of criminal organizations into the framework of society as millions purchased bootleg liquor or used 'speakeasies'. Many would argue that the 40-year 'war on drugs' has been similarly unsuccessful; drug use is more common, proportionately cheaper, and moralizing about such recreational activity does not seem to be effective as a way of changing behavior (Mena & Hobbs, 2010). Whilst strong positions have been established by governments and international committees firmly stating their unwillingness to consider more flexible laws that might bring in much tax revenue and remove markets from gangsters, the criminal cartels that import the products in obvious demand have continued to thrive.

A major contemporary concern is 'people trafficking'. This can reflect persons from war or deprived zones being smuggled into a nation illegally (and who then often work in the black economy for cash-in-hand). Camps of destitute migrants at the coastal ports of northern France awaiting some way of entering the UK speaks eloquently of both how desperate they are, often having paid thousands of pounds to get as far as they have, and how attractive the UK remains to non-Britons. 'Snakehead' gangs bringing in Chinese illegal immigrants exemplify this process, and also the way that trafficked persons may become part of a nation's economy by doing cash-in-hand labour, for example harvesting fields or trawling for shellfish (which lead to the death of a number of illegal Chinese migrant workers in the UK in 2004). Many of the foreign women working in the UK sex industry's brothels, massage parlours and private flats are allegedly trafficked. Investigations of these women have often found that rather than being trafficked, the women are economic migrants, reasoning that they can earn more for the sale of the same basic product as they would have sold in their host nation (Augustín, 2007). A final way complicity occurs between networks of criminal gangs and people who don't perceive themselves to be criminal is the provision of licit materials and services without duty or legislation. Governments make a large amount of their revenue from taxes on alcohol, cigarettes and petrol, so whosoever is supplying these is competing against the Government's market. A related industry is in the production of fake goods (designer clothes, handbags and shoes) that disrupt a commercial brand, or the distribution of illegal digital materials, for example pirate DVDs.

Naylor (2002) regards these facets of the underground economy in terms of predatory, market-based and commercial criminal endeavours; domains involving force and violence (e.g. the settlement of disputes that cannot be dealt with through normal legal channels) are predatory; market-based endeavours involve the supply of products not available legally; and commercial endeavours provide products and services for less cost or without regulations the State has set. Naylor sees these services in terms of parallel markets. For as long as the State regulates pleasures (gambling, dancing, performing live music, let alone more exotic delights) many people will question why the State is correct to dictate such terms, resent apparently petty regulations limiting their choices, and thus crime becomes paradoxically embedded in the community through the actions of preventative regulations seeking to defend State markets and revenues.

Social groups, networks, and organized crime

Many criminal organizations are somewhat homogenous. This homogeneity reflects boundaries within societies of many kinds: physical locale, blood kinship, social status and class, religion and language. These forms of intimacy far exceed the closeness of men held in prison together, prison being, for many offenders, a time of considerable paranoia regarding criminal rivals, potential informers and ongoing dominance hierarchy issues (Kimmett *et al.*, 2003). Each of the homogenous attributes described above limits a dominant society from being able to enter the network, or move significantly within that network due to intentional, informal and intimidated loyalty; if one is unable to speak Turkish, one's ability to understand communications within the main criminal groups involved in the distribution of heroin within London will be greatly hindered (Covey, 2010). This homogenous form has lent itself to researching such groups using methods closer to sociology, for example participant observation and ethnography, and less quantitative approaches.

Another way to approach criminal organizations is to use the models and principles used in social and occupational psychology generally (Gottschalk, 2008). Structural models have been commonly used to conceptualise criminal networks, but these terms have often been used descriptively when they can be operationalized far more precisely. A social network comprises individuals ('nodes') that are connected ('tied, linked or edged') to other nodes on some attribute, and are a means of defining how persons within groups relate to other persons (Wasserman & Faust, 1994). Law enforcement intelligence observing 'persons of interest' can use this information to quantify the positions of persons linked to others, whether this is face-to-face social contacts, telephone calls or emails (though like all criminal investigation, is somewhat dependent on the quality of the source information and case-linkage to start with (Woodhams *et al.*, 2007)). Scott (1991) describes some key terms thus; a *point* in the network is an individual, group or entity within the network being examined; a *line* is a connection between two points; two points which are directly connected without intermediates are *adjacent*; any route that can go from a point to another through intervening points is a *path*; the *length* of the path is the number of lines that must be followed along a path (like the map of the London Underground, distances are defined in stops, not in material distance); and the *geodesic* between point X and point Y is the shortest path out of all possibilities. A particularly clear summary of this field is provided by McAndrew (2000), who explains that the lines between points can have *direction* reflecting the flow of some quality (command, product, finance), and that a line between two points may have *intensity* reflecting the frequency of traffic; more frequent communications would mean more activity (and thus intensity) on that line. This does not reflect the nature of that communication; a particular communication may be rarely given (e.g. an assassination or the delivery details for a large shipment of 'product') but be far more important than day-to-day operational communications.

Having established this terminology for describing the connections between points, it is possible to infer further properties of a network, which potentially inform target prioritisation. *Centrality* in a network can be contrasted with peripheralization, and the dimension by which each point can be rated on such a continuum. Points can be defined by their *degree* – how much they relate to other points in the network. Another relevant construct is *betweeness*, which is how much a point falls on the geodesic relative to other pairs of points (McAndrew, 2000.). The point closest to the geodesic is likely to be closest to the information flowing through a system; the more geodesics the point falls on, the greater the betweenness score. *Closeness* can also be calculated from such information; by examining all the geodesics in a system one can identify the length of the geodesic paths from a given point to all other points, and the shorter the total of these, the closer the point will be to the others in the network. As suggested above, the meaning of information in a system is critical, and the psychology underlying the dynamics between individuals can lead to asymmetries of data flow along with re-routing following changes of state in points due to dynamic processes (for example the competing efforts of a law enforcement agency to disrupt the action of a criminal network). To define this process, Stephenson and Zelen (1989) proposed the idea of *information centrality*, which compares geodesics and prioritises those with more degrees and shorter paths, until one can identify the point which has the optimum number of connections in the network. From this work has emerged concepts such as people having six degrees of separation from a stranger, and the idea that most persons have stable social relationships with no more than about 150 individuals (Dunbar, 1998; though others believe this value is between 230 and 290, e.g. Russell *et al.*, 1987).

It is easy to see how this ostensibly formal mathematical-sounding approach may relate to an understanding of criminal networks. Coles (2001) in particular has been very positive regarding how this methodology can examine successful criminal networks. This observation reiterates what seems to be a theme in the study of organized crime; that crimes are organized rather than the criminals themselves. The hierarchical models purported to liaise between sophisticated criminal networks are rarely found outside fiction, although the Apalachin meeting of 1957 (where over 100 senior Italian, Canadian and American mafia met to resolve a series of disputes) certainly occurred. However, this event was not necessarily driven by criminality alone. Using information on 800 US mafia members active in the 1950s and 1960s obtained by the Federal Bureau of Narcotics, Mastrobuoni and Patacchini (2010) found many of the criminal links between apparent gangsters was dependent on family ties, community roots and history, as well as their legal and illegal activities. As with any social hierarchy, there is both vertical and horizontal organization, with greater connections potentially producing more possibilities, but also greater risk of disruption. Mastrobuoni and Pattachini found that persons with the most connections in the network were linked by kinship, violence and mafia culture. Within the group there was evidence of strategic endogamy in which the partners of female children born to parents higher in the hierarchy were more likely to become subsequent leaders within the group. These constructs explained a third of the overall variance in the criminal ranking of the persons in the cohort. Underlying many of these relationships were assortative processes; whether it was for specific offences, or legitimate occupations, there were highly significant associations between individuals; persons who ran casinos knew other casino owners as much as persons who committed fraud offences knew one another. This observation sustains into contemporary analyses of criminal networks, which also show individuals in criminal networks linked together with one another by means of direct and indirect contacts.

A study of the social networks behind black market labour in the Swedish building trade illustrates the similarities and differences in types of criminal social network (Heber, 2009). Heber found that there were two key roles required to facilitate illegal immigrants being employed; a 'fixer' and a 'criminal entrepreneur'. Fixers are knowledgeable about different types of economic crime, whereas the criminal entrepreneur operates as a link between the client and their requirement. A study of data held by the Swedish Register of Suspected Offenders found a degree of overlap between fixer and criminal entrepreneur economic crime networks. Fixers have larger networks than criminal entrepreneurs, have contacts in their networks who are suspected of larger numbers of offences, commit offences more frequently with others and also have larger numbers of suspected co-offenders, as compared to criminal entrepreneurs. Criminal entrepreneurs tend to know their suspected co-offenders for longer periods of time than fixers. In the Swedish context, fixers appear to specialize in fraud and forgery offences, whereas criminal entrepreneurs have a greater number of motoring offences, smuggling and drug offences. In both cases, the social networks are very male-dominated and predominantly comprise older men compared to traditional offenders, both types typically having been suspected of committing offences with the same co-offenders over time, with more transient parts of the social network being more peripheral to the organization but also committing more general offences, few of which are violent. All parties were tax avoiders.

Knowing they may not be able to destroy such criminal organizations, law enforcement agencies sometimes instead seek to find the best ways to disrupt their operation. Morselli (2010) examined the more vulnerable and strategic positions in criminal networks, using the example of recreational drugs distributed by a branch of the Canadian Hells Angels. He used measures of centrality to define the importance of persons in the network, for example direct centrality (the number of direct contacts surrounding a person), and betweenness centrality (where a person's importance as a mediator is inferred by the number of indirect relationships they mediate). It was found that the person's position in the criminal network influences who gets arrested; higher centrality made it more likely that people would be arrested, whereas there was minimal correlation for the betweenness of persons and actually being arrested. Persons mediating the network ('middle men' who act as brokers and link active elements together) were less likely to be members of the Hells Angels themselves, and moved between different groups. The strategies used by criminal-justice professions to disrupt criminal organizations need a good grasp of the dynamics of the organization's current network, and target strategically important rather than visible but relatively petty persons in a hypothetical criminal organization. This view suggests 'zero tolerance' strategies to enforce drug misuse may fill the legal system with low-level offenders whilst leaving the peripheral (but key) importers and overall executives of the network (who may be involved in a variety of other criminal endeavours) untouched.

Cultures of violence and cultures of honor

Although one perspective on organized crime is the 'unofficial businessman' model, some organized criminal groups are notoriously violent. With access to weapons, potentially huge losses if their markets are disrupted or taken over by other groups, and a greater loyalty to the group, it is unsurprising that this is so. Cultures of honor, histories of extreme official and unofficial violence, and arbitrary, consequence-free brutality by the State and powerful individuals help one to understand why this may be the case, and why it perpetuates, particularly from persons who have lived in war zones or persistently unstable regions. Many nations are riven by internecine ethnic conflicts maintained by grievance thinking that governments can only bluntly control. Ancient codes of extreme violence justify the violent behavior of contemporary Nigerian, Albanian and Chinese organized crime groups (Steenkamp, 2005; Arsovoka & Craig, 2006).

Groups of this kind thrive on an overt criminal identity in which outsiderdom is celebrated, and their aggression, callousness and loyalty to antisocial norms reaffirms who they are. An example is the Russian Mafia, which emerged out of the *Vorovskoy Mir* ('thieves community') who functioned as a distinct subculture within the urban centres and prisons of Tsarist Russia (Volkov, 2002). Criminals who appropriated their imagery (for example, elaborate tattoos that form a hard-to-fake statement of commitment for whatever subculture one aspires connection to) but were not actually committed to the values of the *Vorovskoy Mir* could be killed (this usefully initiating a more committed aspirant to the valued group who would be invited to commit the killing). In Communist times, the *Vorovskoy Mir* were central to the black market upon which much of Russia depended, and their provision of products blocked by a repressive and inefficient authoritarian state led them to be viewed as a necessary evil (Finckenauer & Waring, 2001). In this respect, the Russian mafia differ little from any generic criminal group's 'economic' function, and the community's partial acceptance (and complicity with) of their role.

When Communism collapsed under the accumulation of its own contradictions (something of an irony for Marxists who thought that it was this process that would lead to the demise of capitalism), the Russian Mafia were well situated materially, financially and socially to survive the change of regime. Russia is itself a series of nations, and when persons could be imprisoned in gulags thousands of miles from home, dominance hierarchies of prisoners would lead to the most powerful and connected (but temporarily incarcerated) to network with each other (see also Griffin *et al.*, Chapter 7, for a discussion of networks in prison), forming affiliations probably not so dissimilar to those formed by academics meeting their counterparts at national and international conferences. These links have links themselves, and thus social networks are made, with each network having its own potential speciality; drugs from those places notorious for growing them, and arms from nations with more flexible attitudes to their sale. When local cultural traditions support immediate and even ultimate violence, these values are inevitably also instantiated within the social groups of the community. Should such groups come up competitively against similar groups who are less quick to respond with violence, a differential advantage will ensue for the more lethal group – at least until law enforcement or criminal homeostasis restates itself (or the other criminal group becomes as violent itself). Some nations are arguably more vulnerable to organized crime and terror than others, and this is a dynamic process reflecting development and democratic governance. Berry *et al.* (2003) argue that these phenomena are driven by official corruption, incomplete or weak legislation, poor enforcement of existing, laws, non-transparent financial institutions, unfavourable economic conditions, lack of respect for the rule of law in society and poorly guarded national borders. Lavezzi (2008) argues that it is for such reasons that Sicily was particularly affected by organized crime, as traditional and territorial specificity, small companies, a largely unskilled workforce dependent upon specific materials and a large state bureaucracy optimise typical organized crime activities (e.g. extortion, tax avoidance, enforcing cartels),

On top of these cultural and historical processes are cultures of violence that express aggressively masculine values with biological and evolutionary roots. Wolfgang and Ferracuti (1967) describe cultures of violence as those in which participants are trained for violence, carry weapons and explicitly express willingness to engage in violence or use it to retaliate, and a lack of guilt about such conduct. The culture of Pathan tribesmen and their patronage of the flourishing open arms market in Darra Adam Khel in north-west Pakistan exemplifies well such a culture (Gilmour, 2009). The degree to which the person seeks recourse to violence under provocation indicates the degree to which violent values are upheld. Whilst these values may be common in the particular society, they are most common between adolescence and early middle age. This reflects the broad demographics of violence globally, which are associated with 'young male syndrome' (Daly & Wilson, 1985), in which risk-taking, youth, intra-sexual displays and the discounting of consequences are cardinal.

These behaviors arguably have an evolutionary basis, in that they are particularly necessary for those males who have a competitive disadvantage (relative to other males who are higher in intelligence or other skills that enable them to create an identity and form legitimate relationships; Duntley & Shakelford, 2008). A learning process supposedly underpins cultures of violence, the formation of attitudes that support the use of violence and this is typically explained by criminologists by reference to 'differential association' processes (see also Wood & Alleyne, Chapter 2). A meta-analysis by Pratt *et al.* (2010) found that whilst there is good evidence for the influence of antisocial attitudes and the preference for antisocial peers in offenders, 'differential reinforcement' and 'modelling and imitation' had only weak effect sizes. It is these assortative and evolutionary processes that perhaps provide what Wolfgang and Ferracuti do not: an explanation of what underlies the 'culture of violence'. Ellison (1991) extended this model to incorporate the differentially greater violence in the southern USA, reconstruing the culture of violence to one of honor and reputation, in which no insult is accepted, but a strong culture of social decorum mostly precludes such insults in the first place. A culture of honor may lead to vengeance and have the function of acting as a deterrent against violent or criminal threat in an under-developed society (Shackelford, 2005). Thus it is that the violence of an apparently organized criminal group may simply reflect the society from which the group emerged (Cottino, 1999).

Working with these theoretical underpinnings, it is easy to see why organized crime can sometimes be very violent, and that the dynamics of their activities and inter-relations with similar groups can be somewhat Shakespearian. But it is not the groups themselves that are violent, so much as the elements within them; strategically, violence is unhelpful for a group that seeks to work unobtrusively making money, as the attention of law enforcement will interfere with any informal business plan, and perhaps expose processes and mechanisms that generally work constructively. Junior members of the hierarchy may be more aggressive, and older and more experienced persons will discourage unproductive displays of violence.

Organized crime in contemporary financial services

The thinking criminal prefers to acquire resources without drawing the attention of law enforcement agencies, and traditional organized crime's reputation for violence and aggression is the antithesis of such a strategy. Money largely moves around the world electronically rather than physically, and stealing this money requires a means by which to break into the networks which circulate this financial information and the bodies which try to ensure that the networks are secure. The final section of this chapter addresses this fast-moving and critical topic.

Cybercrime is a constant in our daily lives, and as individuals we expend much time and effort protecting ourselves as well as having to decide whether an official looking e-mail is legitimate or a nefarious attempt to get us to disclose confidential information that will enable a remote criminal to have access to our personal financial details (a process known as '*phishing*'). Organized criminals continually target financial services firms to steal money and, more recently, to steal identity data. However, much of the daily front-end assault on firms comes from individual criminals loosely linked to organized crime networks – often because they are paying organized criminals for access to expertise, technology or data to facilitate fraud. This is particularly true in the cybercrime context where we can see something of a mirror image of mainstream capitalism. Major organized criminals invest capital in 'infrastructure projects' (i.e. projects that facilitate cybercrimes) to sell to entrepreneurial individual criminals (Choo, 2008). These lower-tier criminals display considerable entrepreneurship in their dealings with each other as they seek to exploit the opportunities provided – or perhaps franchised – by their organized colleagues. However, it is also apparent that much of this mutual empowerment (albeit for financial gain) is around networks of individual entrepreneurial criminals rather than traditional organized crime groups. In the early 2000s the main body of opinion held that, in the virtual world, most criminal activities were initiated by individuals or small networks of individual criminals. This changed relatively quickly; by the mid 2000s organized crime groups were exploiting new opportunities offered by the internet beyond simply pornography and counterfeit goods (Moore *et al.*, 2009). Williams (2011) believes that most organized crime will continue to operate in the real world rather than the cyberworld, and most cybercrime will be perpetrated by individuals rather than criminal organizations, conceding that the degree of overlap between the two is likely to increase considerably as life becomes ever more internet-based.

This anticipated overlap has proved prescient, and the inter-relationship between skilled computer programmers and criminal entrepreneurs can be seen clearly in the world of stolen personal and financial information (where not only credit card details and compromised bank accounts, but also addresses, phone numbers, social security numbers, full names and dates of birth are acquired). This data has a monetary value because it can be used to gain access to bank accounts and credit cards, or to perpetrate identity fraud to establish new lines of credit. Stolen data is retailed in the criminal underworld and is driving a range of new illegal activities, including crimeware distribution and the hacking of corporate customer and card databases (e.g., Albert Gonzalez – aka 'soupnazi' – who stole 130 million card records from Heartland Payment Systems: Suddath, 2009).

These criminal activities are backed up by a fully fledged infrastructure of malicious code writers and hackers, specialist web hosts and leased networks of thousands of compromised computers which carry out automated attacks online, to access and steal personal data. As this underground economy has grown in sophistication, 'service providers' have also emerged to offer payment card verification number generators. The European Police organization Europol takes the view that this criminal infrastructure represents a break from the traditional organized crime gangs. Cybercriminal groups often have no obvious leadership, dividing labour according to technical abilities, with most members only knowing each other online. Online forums are essential tools for the digital underground economy to recruit and make introductions across borders, enabling criminals to swarm together to work on specific projects. These forums are also where crimeware components are advertised and budding cybercriminals learn their trade through tutorials. The technology skills required mean that those involved in cybercrime rarely fit the traditional profile of transnational organized crime groups. These cybercriminals are usually young, highly skilled individuals, under the age of 25, and are often recruited from universities (Rogers, 2010). This social world is shown in the dialogue presented at Figure 6.1.

The criminal website 'DarkMarket', which was infiltrated and taken down by law enforcement, is a good example of this model (widely covered in UK and overseas papers (e.g. Davis, 2010). At the time, DarkMarket was the top English language cybercrime site in the world and effectively a global one-stop shop for cybercrime and banking fraud. Table 6.1 gives an example of the services it offered.

The site also featured 'breaking news' style updates on the latest compromised material available, and criminals could even buy banner adverts to promote their wares. Payment for services was undertaken via electronic purse accounts (WebMoney, or E-Gold) supported by electronic cash cards sometimes supported via more traditional transfers (e.g. via international cash transfer systems). Considerable money was exchanged – for example, one buyer spent £250,000 on stolen personal information in just six weeks.

As with some of the more notorious paedophile electronic networks, membership to sell on DarkMarket was strictly by invitation. To be accepted, criminals had to present details of 100 compromised cards free of charge: 50 to one reviewer, 50 to another. Reviewers would test the cards and write an online review of customer satisfaction in a similar fashion to eBay customers. Those that delivered useable cards were recommended for acceptance. Once vetted, its vendors and buyers traded everything from card details, obtained through computer hacking, phishing and ATM skimming devices, to viruses with which buyers could extort money by threatening company websites; the reader might wish to consider the implications for an online gambling website of a denial of service attack in the 30 minutes running up to the Grand National. The ramifications of such activity on legitimate business are already being considered (Smith *et al.*, 2011).

Table 6.1 DarkMarket services offered (all prices US$).

• Dumps data from magnetic stripes on batches of 10 cards	Standard cards: $50. Gold/platinum: $80. Corporate: $180.
• Card verification values information needed for online transactions.	$3-$10 depending on quality.
• Full information/change of billing information needed for opening or taking over account details.	$150 for account with $10,000 balance. $300 for one with $20,000 balance.
• Skimmer device to read card data.	Up to $7,000.
• Bank logins	2% of available balance.
• Hire of botnet software robots used in spam attacks.	$50 a day.
• Credit card images both sides of card.	$30 each.
• Embossed card blanks	$50 each.
• Holograms	$5 per 100.

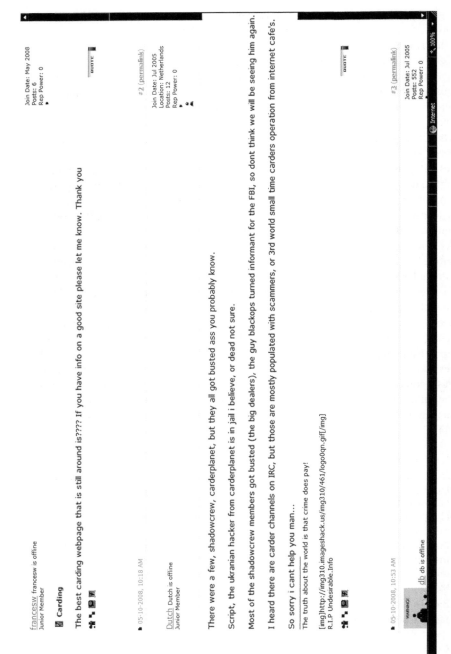

Figure 6.1 Extract from mail exchanges between budding fraudsters – note individualistic nature of their intercourse and complaints suggesting that law enforcement activity having some element of effectiveness.

Within DarkMarket, honor amongst thieves was paramount – in distinct contrast to some areas of organized crime. DarkMarket was fastidious in banning 'rippers' who would cheat other criminals. It operated an 'escrow' service, with payments and goods exchanged through a third party and an arbitration service resolved disputes. This contrasts with traditional organized crime networks, that punish 'ripping' physically and with apparent enthusiasm. DarkMarket also introduced a degree of 'product regulation' to help keep a low profile by banning any trade in firearms, drugs or counterfeit currency, which again differentiated it from the activities of traditional organized crime.

The inter-relationships and organization emerging between different types of criminals can also be seen in the context of money laundering. Organized criminals need to be able to launder significant cash sums. Schneider (2008) suggested that this rose from 595 billion USD in 2001 to 790 billion USD in 2006; (five years on, the amount must now be in the trillions) acquired domestically in such a way as to facilitate the continuation of illicit international trade (drugs, people trafficking, fraud, counterfeiting, etc.). The logistics of carrying large sums of cash across borders and increasing legally enforced scrutiny by UK banks and building societies has led such criminals to look beyond the UK banking system and identify other service providers to meet this need. As per the world of fraud, there is a relationship between organized criminals and local criminal entrepreneurs in the shape of money services businesses (MSBs). These businesses have often been set up to provide basic cash and foreign exchange services to specific ethnic groups (sometimes referred to as underground banking, hawala etc.). There have been a number of court cases in the past 10 years involving MSBs and organized criminals, particularly in relation to moving the proceeds of drugs trafficking and duty evasion (Regina versus Ramzan & Others (2006); Regina versus Liaquat Ali and others (2005). These have usually involved a prosaic and straightforward process; the cash is collected by the MSB which deposits it under its name into a UK high street bank.

A recent widely reported case highlighted a variant on this methodology was 'Operation Eaglewood' (Davies & Dodd, 2011) that also involved organized crime usage of MSBs. In this case, criminals were channelling the proceeds from drug trafficking into a London taxi firm. Staff from the taxi firm would bag up the money and change the cash into €500 notes at a local MSB. The cash amounts varied from day to day, but the scale of the activity was significant, and each week over £1m was exchanged. From the criminal perspective, €500 notes are considerably easier to transport than other forms of currency. For instance, £1m in £50 notes is made up of 20,000 individual notes and weighs 50kg; the same in €500 is 2,300 notes and weighs little more than 2kg. A subsidiary outcome of this case and further research by the UK Serious Organized Crime Agency (SOCA) led to the withdrawal of the €500 note from UK banknote wholesaling. SOCA's research found that over 90 per cent of €500 notes provided by note wholesalers (c €600m) were used by small independent MSBs to launder money on behalf of organized criminals (Sefton, 2010; Doyle, 2010).

The other outcome of note from the case was a 10-year custodial sentence handed out to the MSB's Money Laundering Reporting Officer (MLRO),

Jean Claude Frigieri. MSBs are required by law to appoint such officers to ensure that they comply with UK anti-money laundering legislation, and to ensure that reports of suspicions of client money laundering are reported to the UK SOCA. Frigieri had no previous convictions, but the 10-year custodial sentence he received reflected his personal involvement in the physical transfer of cash and the high standards of propriety expected of MLROs whether of large banks or small MSBs. This example and other cases highlight how organized criminals reach beyond their own traditional networks to identify individual criminals or possibly to subvert individual entrepreneurs. This does not necessarily mean that the individual criminals become part of the organized crime group. Rather, they provide an outsourced service that, from the organized criminal perspective, has the advantage that it can be shut down and moved quickly – and flexibility and opacity to criminal investigators are vital to an effective organized criminal group.

As is thus apparent, financial crime now requires a more intelligent offender adept at finding a way between security technology, and the checks and balances implemented by regulatory agencies. The rational models they present reflect a very different population to that embedded in national and cultural history, and one which likewise requires a different model of policing to that hitherto used by the State, along with a rather greater number of skilled staff to detect, investigate and prosecute such offences (Swire, 2009). One core means by which such offenders and the groups they represent can be identified is an awareness of the networks that physically or virtually link individuals to each other, and following the money which is being moved.

Conclusions

This chapter has sought to discuss organized crime in the context of general psychological processes. It firstly examined the social context in which organized crime emerges, and the day-to-day cultural and social influences on its establishment. These are not readily addressable by psychology, which tends to focus on individuals. It then discussed how an established psychological method – that of the formal analysis of social networks – can be applied to criminal groups to provide law enforcement agencies with strategies for understanding the relationship between different elements, and selecting targets to disrupt. The nature of the violence used by organized criminal organizations was then discussed, and it was argued that differential use of violence reflects the underlying ethnic culture of the group, for example, 'cultures of honor' which, when in a disordered society, can become 'cultures of violence'. We then considered the behavior underlying organized financial crime, and how this can be operationalised and managed. We explained how organized criminal network members can be highly interdependent even if they don't know one another. While organized crime groups are in some respects unlike more conventional criminal groups, for example imprisoned gang members (Egan & Beadman, 2011; see also Griffin *et al.*, Chapter 7), the recourse to violence and internecine conflicts by more central and visible parts of the network reflects the underlying disposition of some key elements, and it is this potential for force (or its delegation) that reminds one that organized criminals are not simply businessmen providing a clandestine need.

It is not that organized crime does not exist; it clearly does. However the extent and structure of organized crime has been sometimes exaggerated by overly formal models that assume pyramidic structures which are more apposite to legal (but sometimes criminal groups) than individuals who work with like-minded others to organize criminal activity. Professional criminals, unlike their more spontaneous criminal peers, are not stupid, and it would be surprising if they did not use modes of thinking and technology which many other thinking individuals use in their working and personal lives. Albanese's question 'do criminals organize around opportunities for crime, or do criminal opportunities create new offenders?' (Albanese, 2000: 409) remains apt. Our lives become ever more regulated, and for those who object to such regulation, some rebellion is to be expected. This gap between what is wanted and what is allowed will inevitably lead to organized criminals seeking to exploit this market, and for the regulators to try and keep such exploitation under some control. Intelligent criminals will place themselves at the periphery of such organizations, and profit from the risks taken by the less shrewd or more desperate. The detection of these more intelligent persons requires a shift in strategy whereby the behavior of the organization can be increasingly monitored, and easy but minor targets are eschewed for more substantial members of the group.

Acknowledgement

Thanks to Stephanie Chan and Rupert Egan for their support in the preparation of this chapter.

References

Albanese, J.S. (2000). The causes of organized crime. *Journal of Contemporary Criminal Justice, 16*, 409 –423. DOI: 1043986200016004004.

Associated Press. (2012). UN official: crime generates revenues in the trillions of dollars each year. The Washington Post, Washing DC, USA: retrieved from http://www. washingtonpost.com/un-0official-says-up-tp-24-million-are-human-trafficking-victims-at-any-given-time/2012/04/23/glQAuBTabT_story.html (accessed April 25th, 2012).

Allum, F. and Siebert, R. (2003). *Organized Crime and the Challenge to Democracy.* London: Routledge

Arsovska, J. and Craig, M. (2006). 'Honorable' behavior and the conceptualisation of violence in ethnic-based organized crime groups: an examination of the Albanian Kanun and the code of the Chinese triads. *Global Crime, 7*, 214–246. DOI: 10.1080/17440570601014479.

Augustín, L.M. (2007). *Sex at the Margins: Migration, Labour Markets and the Rescue Industry.* Plymouth, UK; Zed Books.

Bauwens, A. and Egan, V. (2011). Are white-collar criminals a homogeneous or heterogeneous group? *Home Team Journal* (Singapore Ministry of Home Affairs), 3, 91–101.

Berry, L., Curtis, G.E., Gibbs, J.N., Hudson, R.A., Karacan, T., Kollars, N. and Miró, R. (2003). *Nations Hospitable to Organized Crime and Terrorism*. Federal Research Division, Library of Congress, Washington, D.C. Retrieved from: http://www.loc.gov/rr/frd/pdf-files/Nats_Hospitable.pdf (accessed 10 April 2012).

Blackman, S. (2010). Drug war politics: governing culture through prohibition, intoxicants as customary practice and the challenge of drug normalisation. *Sociology Compass, 4*, 841–855. DOI: 10.1111/j.1751-9020.2010.00324.x.

Carroll, R. (2010). Mexican drug war: the new killing fields. *The Guardian*, 3 September 2010. Retrieved from http://www.guardian.co.uk/world/2010/sep/03/mexico-drug-war-killing-fields (accessed 4 January 2011).

Choo, K.-K.R. (2008). Organized crime groups in cyberspace: a typology. *Trends in Organized Crime. 11*, 270–295. DOI: 10.1007/s12117-008-9038-9.

Coles, N. (2001). 'It's not what you know – it's who you know that counts': analysing serious crime groups as social networks. *British Journal of Criminology, 41*, 580–594. DOI: 10.1093/bjc/41.4.580.

Cottino, A. (1999). Sicilian cultures of violence: the interconnections between organized crime and local society. *Crime, Law and Social Change, 32*, 103–113. DOI: 10.1023/A:1008389424861.

Covey, H.C. (2010). *Street Gangs throughout the World*. Springfield, Illinois; Charles C. Thomas Publisher.

Daly, M. and Wilson, M. (1985). Competitiveness, risk taking, and violence: the young male syndrome. *Ethology and Sociobiology, 6*, 59–73. DOI: 10.1016/0162-3095 (85)90041-X.

Davis, C. (2010). Welcome to DarkMarket – global one-stop shop for cybercrime and banking fraud. *The Guardian*, 10 January. Retrieved from http://www.guardian.co.uk/technology/2010/jan/14/darkmarket-online-fraud-trial-wembley (accessed 10 April 2012).

Davies, C., & Dodd, V. (2011). Police smash 'one-stop shop' for London gangsters. *The Guardian*, 5 January. Retrieved from http://www.guardian.co.uk/world/2011/jan/05/police-smash-london-drug-gangster-syndicate (accessed 10 April 2012).

Doyle, J. (2010). 'Currency of the criminal': Britain axes 500 euro note overorganized crime fears. *Daily Mail*, 13 May. Retrieved from http://www.dailymail.co.uk/news/article-1277892/Britain-axes-500-euro-note-organized-crime-fears.html (accessed 10 April 2012).

Duntley, J.D. and Shackelford, T.K. (2008). Darwinian foundations of crime and law. *Aggression and Violent Behavior, 13*, 373–382. DOI: 10.1016/j.avb.2008.06.002.

Dunbar, R. (1998). *Grooming, Gossip, and the Evolution of Language*. Cambridge, Mass., USA; Harvard University Press.

Egan, V. (2011). Individual differences and antisocial behavior. In *Handbook of Individual Differences* (pp. 512–537). Chichester, UK: Wiley. DOI: 10.1002/9781405184359.

Egan, V. and Beadman, M. (2011). Personality and gang embeddedness. *Personality and Individual Differences Home Team Journal* (Singapore Ministry of Home Affairs), 3, 91–101.

Egan, V., McMurran, M., Richardson, C. and Blair, M. (2000), Criminal cognitions and personality: what does the PICTS really measure? *Criminal Behavior and Mental Health, 10*, 170–184. DOI: 10.1002/cbm.355.

Ellison, C.G. (1991). An eye for an eye? A note on the southern subculture of violence thesis. *Social Forces, 69*, 1223–1239. Retrieved from http://www.jstor.org/stable/2579310 (accessed 10 April 2012).

Finckenauer, J.O. and Waring, E. (2001). Challenging the Russian Mafia mystique. *National Institute of Justice Journal*, 2–7. Retrieved from http://nij.ncjrs.gov/App/ publications/Pub_search.aspx?searchtype=basic&category=99&location=top&P SID=32 (accessed 10 April 2012).

Gilmour, B. (2009). *Warrior Poets: Guns, Movie-making and the Wild West of Pakistan.* Sydney, Australia: Pier 9, Murdoch Books.

Glenny, M. (2009). *McMafia: Seriously Organized Crime.* London, UK: Vintage.

Gottschalk, P. (2008). Managing criminal organizations. *International Journal of Police Science and Management, 10*, 289–301. DOI: 10.1350/ijps.2008.10.3.85.

Heber, A. (2009). Networks of organized black market labour in the building trade. *Trends in Organized Crime, 12*, 122–144. DOI: 10.1007/s12117-008-9060-y.

Kimmett, E., O'Donnell, I. and Martin, C. (2003). *Prison Violence: The Dynamics of Conflict, Fear and Power.* Cullompton, Devon: Willan.

Lavezzi, A.M. (2008). Economic structure and vulnerability to organized crime: evidence from Sicily. *Global Crime, 9*, 198–220. DOI: 10.1080/17440570802254312.

Mastrobuoni, G. and Patacchini, E. (2010). *Understanding Organized Crime Networks: Evidence Based on Federal Bureau of Narcotics Secret Files on the American Mafia.* Carlo Alberto Notebooks, 152. Retrieved from http://econ.arizona.edu/docs/Seminar_ Papers/Fall%2010_Mastrobuoni.pdf (accessed 10 April 2012).

McAndrew, D. (2000). The structural analysis of criminal networks. In D. Canter and L. Allison (2000) *The Social Psychology of Crime: Groups, Teams and Networks* (pp. 53–94). Aldershot, UK: Dartmouth-Ashgate.

Mena, F. and Hobbs, D. (2010). Narcophobia: drugs prohibition and the generation of human rights abuses. *Trends in Organized Crime, 13*, 60–74. DOI: 10.1007/ s12117-009-9087-8.

Moore, T., Clayton, R. and Anderson, R. (2009). The economics of online crime. *The Journal of Economic Perspectives, 23*, 3–20. DOI: 10.1257/jep.23.3.3.

Morselli, C. (2010). Assessing vulnerable and strategic positions in a criminal network. *Journal of Contemporary Criminal Justice*, 26, 382–392. DOI: 10.1177/ 1043986210377105.

Naylor, T.R. (2002). *Wages of Crime: Black Markets, Illegal Finance, and the Underworld Economy.* Ithica, USA: Cornell University Press.

Pratt, T.C., Cullen, F.T., Sellers C.S., Winfree, Jr., L.T., Madensen, T.D., Daigle, L.E., Fearn N.E. and Gau, J.M. (2010). Empirical status of social learning theory: a meta-analysis. *Justice Quarterly, 27*, 765–802. DOI: 10.1080/07418820903379610.

Regina versus Liaquat Ali and others. (2005). *Judge's Summing Up.* Case number 2003 03958, 04027, 04111 C1; 2004 06347, 07 June 2005. Retrieved from http://www.bailii. org/ew/cases/EWCA/Crim/2005/87.html (accessed 22 June 2011).

Regina versus Ramzan and others. (2006). *Judge's Summing Up.* Case number: 200204128 C4, 21 July 2006. Retrieved from www.ccrc.gov.uk/CCRC_Uploads/RAMZAN_ AMER.DOC (accessed 22 June 2011).

Rogers, M.K. (2010). The psyche of cybercriminals: a psycho-social perspective. *Cybercrimes: A Multidisciplinary Analysis, 5*, 217–235. DOI: 10.1007/978-3-642-13547-7_14.

Ruggiero, V. (2010). *Organized Crime: Between the Informal and the Formal Economy.* Working Papers Series, no. 4, July, Global Consortium on Security Transformation. Retrieved from http://www.securitytransformation.org/gc_publications.php (accessed 10 April 2012).

Russell, B.H., Shelley, G.A. and Killworth, P. (1987). How much of a network does the GSS and RSW dredge up? *Social Networks, 9,* 49–63. Retrieved from http://www. elsevier.com/wps/find/journaldescription.cws_home/505596/description (accessed 10 April 2012).

Schneider, F.G. (2008). Money laundering and financial means of organized crime: some preliminary empirical findings. *Paolo Baffi Centre Research Paper No. 2008–17.* Available at SSRN: http://ssrn.com/abstract=1136149 (accessed 10 April 2012).

Scott, J.P. (1991). *Social Network Analysis: A Handbook.* London, UK: Sage.

Sefton, E. (2010). Crime-friendly 500 euro note withdrawn in Britain. *The First Post,* 13 May. Retrieved from http://www.thefirstpost.co.uk/63313,business,crime-friendly-500-euro-note-withdrawn-in-britain-1000-swiss-franc (accessed 10 April 2012).

Shackelford, T.K. (2005). An evolutionary psychological perspective on cultures of honor. *Evolutionary Psychology, 3,* 381–391. Retrieved from http://www.epjournal.net/ (accessed 10 April 2012).

Smith, K.T., Smith, M. and Smith, J.L. (2011). Case studies of cybercrime and its impact on marketing activity and shareholder value. *Academy of Marketing Studies Journal.* Available at SSRN: http://ssrn.com/abstract=1724815 (accessed 10 April 2012).

Steenkamp, C. (2005). The legacy of war: conceptualizing a 'culture of violence' to explain violence after peace accords. *The Round Table: The Commonwealth Journal of International Affairs, 94,* 253–267. DOI: 10.1080/00358530500082775.

Stephenson, K. and Zelen, M. (1989). Rethinking centrality: methods and applications. *Social Networks, 11,* 1–37. DOI: 10.1016/0378-8733(89)90016-6.

Suddath, C. (2009). Master hacker Albert Gonzalez. *Time,* 19 August. Retrieved from http://www.time.com/time/business/article/0,8599,1917345,00.html (accessed 10 April 2012).

Swire, P. (2009). No Cop on the beat: underenforcement in E-commerce and cybercrime. *Journal of Telecommunications & High Technology Law, 7,* 107–126. Retrieved from http://www.jthtl.org/ (accessed 10 April 2012).

van Koppen, V.M., de Poot, C.J. and Blokland, A.A. (2010). Comparing criminal careers of organized crime offenders and general offenders. *European Journal of Criminology, 7,* 356–374. DOI: 10.1177/1477370810373730.

Venkatesh, S. (2009). *Gang Leader for a Day.* London, UK: Penguin.

Volkov, V. (2002). *Violent Entrepreneurs: The Use of Force in the Making of Russian Capitalism.* Ithaca, NY: Cornell University Press.

Von Lampe, K. (2011). Definitions of organized crime. Retrieved from http://www. organized-crime.de/OCDEF1.htm (accessed 4 January 2011).

Vulliamy, E. (2010). *Amexica: War Along the Borderline.* London, UK: Bodley Head.

Wasserman, S. and Faust, K. (1994). *Social Network Analysis: Methods and Applications.* Cambridge, UK: Cambridge University Press.

Williams, P. (2011). Organized crime and cybercrime: synergies, trends, and responses. Retrieved from http://www.iwar.org.uk/ecoespionage/resources/transnational-crime/ gj07.htm (accessed 22 June 2011).

Wolfgang, M. E. and Ferracuti, F. (1967). *The Subculture of Violence: Towards an Integrated theory in Criminology.* London: Tavistock Publications.

Woodhams, J., Hollin, C.R. and Bull, R. (2007). The psychology of linking crimes: a review of the evidence. *Legal and Criminological Psychology, 12,* 233–24. DOI: 10.1348/135532506X118631.

Zoutendijk, A. (2010). Organized crime threat assessments: a critical review. *Crime, Law & Social Change, 54,* 63–86. DOI: 10.1007/s10611-010-9244-7.

7 Surviving and thriving

The growth, influence and administrative control of prison gangs.

Marie L. Griffin, David Pyrooz and Scott H. Decker, School of Criminology & Criminal Justice, Arizona State University

When presented with an environment designed to highlight the deprivation of most social comforts and intended to house a population of individuals who value predatory behavior and use of force as a means of establishing status, the development of prison-based criminal groups seems inevitable. As noted by Jacobs (1974), the 'gang thing' is the most significant reality behind the walls (p. 399). Understanding the formation of prison gangs and the nature of gang activities has been a focus of penal scholars and correctional practitioners for some time. This chapter draws on such research to examine the development and role of gangs as distinct prisoner groups within correctional systems.

Given the capacity of the U.S. prison system and legislators' apparent willingness to incarcerate individuals for long periods of time, it should not be surprising that most prison gang research has been conducted in the United States. As such, much of the discussion here focuses on the development and expansion of prison gangs as experienced within the United States penal system and the organizational responses to prison gang activity that often are specific to U.S. prisons. The extent to which similarities between the United States prison gang experience and that of other countries has been only briefly explored and remains an area in need of further research. Such cross-cultural studies could provide, however, additional insight into strategies that would more effectively identify, manage, and/or reduce prison gang activities regardless of the cultural context.

The formation of prison gangs

During the past decade, prison scholars have continued to explore the function and growth of prison gangs, refining measures and attempting to more clearly articulate the way in which prison groups inhabit and influence the prison environment. According to Camp and Camp (1985), a prison gang is a 'close-knit and disruptive group of inmates organized around common affiliation for the purpose of mutual caretaking, solidarity, and profit-making criminal activity' (p. 71). Prison gangs are hierarchical, self-perpetuating criminal groups whose members generally range in age from 20 to 40 years old, and are disproportionately involved in prison misconduct. Prison gangs are found primarily in men's prison facilities and operate through an established code of conduct. Gangs are often organized along racial and/or ethnic lines, and membership also may be influenced by religious and/or political beliefs, prior affiliation with a street gang, and/or geographic location. Members show intense loyalty to the group, espouse group values and norms that promote criminal behavior, and engage in both symbolic and instrumental forms of violence (Fleisher & Decker, 2001a; Griffin & Hepburn, 2006; Pyrooz *et al.*, 2011; Scott, 2001). For example, violent misconduct can be used as 'a means of self-help, self-defense, or social control by which inmates seek to establish social status, maintain public identities, or gain economic benefits' (Griffin & Hepburn, 2006: 420).

Two models have emerged to explain the development of prison culture, more broadly, and prison gangs, specifically. The *deprivation model* suggests that the prison environment (e.g. inmate code, violent misconduct, formation of gangs, etc.) is shaped by inmates' adaption to the 'pains of imprisonment' (Poole & Regoli, 1983; Sykes, 1958). Harsh conditions within prison, such as the loss of liberty, the lack of autonomy, the loss of safety and security, and the lack of heterosexual contact, force inmates to respond in often violent ways as a means of coping with such stressful living conditions. Faced with intense deprivations, inmates may join a prison gang as gang membership in prison functions in a manner similar to the outside in terms of providing a sense of safety, security, and access to contraband (Kalinich & Stojkovic, 1985; Scott, 2001). The deprivation model has been used to explore the overlapping influences of the prison environment and administrative control strategies finding that physical or social deprivations may be worsened as a result of variations in security level, inmate programs, staff-to-inmate ratio, staff training and turnover, and overcrowding. For example, Gover *et al.* (2000) found that stress among inmates is increased in those prisons with higher security levels that allow for little or no activity or treatment. As a result, inmates tend to exhibit poor coping mechanisms and increased aggressive behavior.

The second model developed to understand the process by which the prison environment develops is the *importation model*. This model argues that inmates bring with them into the prison setting the norms, values, and attitudes of the community from which they come. Such belief systems also are informed by race, gender, and class (Bosworth, 2010; Irwin, 1981; Irwin & Cressey, 1962). The prison environment, including gang formation, misconduct, and use of violence to solve disputes, is a reflection of their dysfunctional and often violent lives before entering prison. As such, inmates 'import' this subculture into institutions and use violence as a means to navigate the prison setting (Poole & Regoli, 1983). When discussing gang formation from this perspective, one would argue that 'prison gangs do not emerge due to indigenous conditions within the prison; rather, they emerge due to pre-institutional conditions that inmates bring with them (Pyrooz *et al.*, 2011: 15). Researchers and criminal justice practitioners have made use of this notion of importing individual level characteristics into the prison setting when examining how such characteristics can be used to predict behavior once incarcerated. For example, criminal history, prior incarceration, street gang membership, and substance abuse history are variables often used to calculate risk scores. Not surprisingly, studies have found that individual level factors such as a prior history of violence or prior gang involvement are consistent predictors of violent misconduct while in prison (Berg & DeLisi, 2006; Bottoms, 1999; Cunningham & Sorensen, 2007; DeLisi *et al.*, 2004; Griffin & Hepburn, 2006; Harer and Langan, 2001). Most correctional scholars agree that both the values and norms brought into the institution by individuals and the structural deprivations of the prison environment interact to influence the development of the prison culture (Goodstein & Wright, 1989; Jiang & Fisher-Giorlando, 2002; McCorkle *et al.*, 1995). As noted by Griffin and Hepburn (2006: 422),

> individual-level factors is an easily observed surrogate measure of the likelihood that the inmate is importing into the prison a set of attitudes, values, and personal experiences that will amplify the degree of risk-taking and aggressive behaviors that will occur in response to the deprivations of incarceration and the opportunities for personal gain.

More comprehensive models have begun to emerge that account for both of these realities. These models attempt to integrate both deprivation and importation frameworks to specify more clearly the way in which the organization and the individual interact (e.g. Gaes et al., 2002; Heubner et al, 2007; Hochstetler & DeLisi, 2005; Varano et al, 2011). A comprehensive and integrative theoretical framework is critical to understanding the nature of prison gang activities, prison gang involvement, the development of gang suppression strategies, as well as the impact of prison gang membership on successful re-entry into the community upon release from prison.

The development and expansion of prison gangs

It is important to understand the development and expansion of prison gangs within the broader context of changing penal ideologies and the resulting increased reliance on incarceration as a primary form of punishment in the United States (Garland, 2001; Pyrooz *et al.*, 2011; Travis, 2005). The U.S. custody prison population increased from 319,598 in 1980 to 1,524,513 in 2009, a nearly five-fold increase. In 2009, more than 7.2 million people in the United States were under some form of correctional supervision (Bureau of Justice Statistics, 2009). To house this growing population, a 'penal housing boom' began in the early 1980s. Reflecting the growing 'get tough' penal philosophy of the time, the architectural design of these new prisons focused more on 'maximum economic efficiency and order' rather than the rehabilitative campus-style institutions of the 1970s (Bosworth, 2010: 140). California was the leading builder of prisons during the 1980s, opening eight prisons in four years. With the rapid expansion of prison construction, especially between 1989 and 2005, much as a direct result of the War on Drugs, soaring U.S. incarceration rates provided increased opportunities for the growth of prison gangs (Useem & Piehl, 2008).

Prison gangs began to emerge in the 1950s and early 1960s in California, Washington, and parts of the Southwest (Fleisher, 2006; NIC, 1991). These gangs were typically based on race or ethnic identification and were a small part of the inmate population. Early prison gangs included the Gypsy Jokers, the Mexican Mafia, La Nuestra Familia, the Texas Syndicate, the Aryan Brotherhood, and the Black Guerilla Family (Camp & Camp, 1985; Hunt *et al.*, 1993; Irwin, 1980). Scholars have documented the emergence of prison gangs within these state systems, describing differing dynamics. For example, Crouch and Marquart (1989) explain the rise of powerful prison gangs within the Texas prison system as a result of the significant changes in administrative control structures in the wake of prison reform case *Ruiz v. Estelle* (1980). Jacobs (1974) details the powerful dynamic between street gang and prison gang membership in Stateville prison, arguing that the street gang members brought with them the norms and organization from the streets of Chicago. The increasingly high rate of incarceration of urban youth – largely minority and affiliated with a street gang – that began in the 1970s provided a foothold for street gangs to expand their influence in prison. The prison environment provided an opportunity to strengthen street and prison gang linkages through continued recruitment of gang members and sustained involvement of prisoners in street gang activities while incarcerated (Fleisher & Decker, 2001b; Seiter, 2001; Spergel, 1995; Venkatesh & Levitt, 2000).

Penal scholars also point to the impact of management strategies on the proliferation of prison gangs during this time. Some scholars attribute the increasing growth and strength of prison gangs in the 1970s and 1980s to the informal prison management strategy of engaging prison gang leaders in a type of reciprocal relationship. Rather than taking an approach of control through suppression, some administrators worked with prison gang leaders, rewarding them for their ability to control segments of the prison population and thus reduce the likelihood of violence and misconduct (Venkatesh & Levitt, 2000; see also Jacobs, 1974; Spergel, 1995). This reciprocity between keeper and kept was rather short-lived and proved to be a less than successful approach to maintaining control and security within the prison system. Instead, researchers argue that this gang management strategy resulted in increased gang power and control within correctional institutions, as well as escalated gang rivalries and concomitant violence (Camp & Camp, 1985). The influence of prison gangs also was often transported to other state and federal facilities by way of inmate transfers.

During the 1990s, a crackdown by local, state and federal law enforcement officials on violent crime targeted powerful street gang leaders in an effort to dismantle those organizations involved in gang-related violence and drug trafficking. As a result, a large number of gang members were sent to prison and while there, 'formed associations along ethnic lines during this time in an attempt to protect their operations, giving rise to large, influential prison gangs' (National Gang Intelligence Center, 2009:5). Today, researchers and correctional practitioners have begun to identify and document the influence of prison gangs not only within a particular prison system, but also at the regional and national levels. For example, national level prison gangs (e.g. La Eme) operate across multiple state prisons and may have members and/or associates in other foreign countries. They use these extensive networks to control drug distribution within prison systems and significantly influence drug distribution in local communities (National Gang Intelligence Center, 2009).

Prison gang/street gang overlap

The way in which prison gang activity and membership intersects or overlaps with street gang activity and membership has received little attention. As Irwin (1980) noted, inmates do not enter prison as a blank slate – they enter prison with individual, social, and cultural 'baggage', or predispositions, that interact with the prison environment. One such pre-incarceration characteristic is street gang membership. A recent study by Varano, Huebner and Bynum (2011) found that approximately one-third of inmates were affiliated with street gangs prior to prison admission. It is interesting to note that few studies specifically examine how street gang membership interacts with the prison environment. This is a critical gap in the corrections research given the implications for how criminologists understand and prison officials respond to the consequences of social organization in correctional settings.

In those instances where such issues have been explored, researchers recognize the reinforcing nature of the relationship between street gangs and prison gangs noting that prison serves not as a time away from the gang life for many prisoners, but as a time to become further enmeshed in this lifestyle (Trulson *et al.*, 2006). Jacobs' (1974) study of Stateville Penitentiary described an almost fluid movement of information and gang members between street and prison settings. The four gangs he observed in prison – Black P. Stones, Gangster Disciples, Vice Lords, and Latin Kings – all operated and maintained a prominent position in the street. When street gang members were admitted into prison, they integrated into their gang's prison arrangements thus reaping the benefits of their existing group membership. The former two gangs 'recruit[ed] vigorously' in an attempt to extend their ranks inside prison, while the latter two did not' (Jacobs, 1974: 399). Decker *et al.* (1998) conducted interviews in parole and prison settings with 85 gang members from the two most organized black and Latino gangs in Chicago and San Diego. Nearly every gang member reported that street and prison gangs maintained relationships which were, arguably, mutually beneficial. There was some variation, however, wherein the Chicago prison gangs influenced activities on the street while no influence was observed among San Diego gangs. More recently, Petersilia (2006) discussed the dominance of prison gangs over street gangs, noting that California's 'catch and release' parole policies that continuously move offenders between prison and the community 'clearly facilitates this linkage between street and prison gangs' (p. 33).

Correctional administrators also recognize the unique role the prison environment plays as a site for the continued socialization of gang members and the reification of their gang identity. As discussed by Jacobs (2001), prison 'provides an opportunity to perform in front of some of the gang's legendary leaders; rank and status are won and lost, criminal careers are shaped' (p. vi). In an effort to suppress gang activity inside and outside prison walls, prison administrators coordinate with local law enforcement officials to gather and disseminate gang-related intelligence (California Department of Corrections, 2008; National Institute of Corrections (NIC), 1991). Correctional agencies make use of databases to track prison and suspected prison gang members. Some agencies utilize these databases to record inmate affiliations using digitized photos of tattoos, scars or other identifying marks (Fleisher & Decker, 2001a). Many state departments of corrections have made accessible to the public extensive websites detailing the major prison gangs located within their facilities (e.g. Florida Department of Corrections; Arizona Department of Corrections). Such websites provide information regarding gender and racial makeup, gang origins, identifiers and symbols, prison allies and rivals, and the types of disruptive behaviors usually engaged in by these groups. Sharing these kinds of data between agencies is critical given that relationships between street gangs and prison gangs serve to strengthen both organizations. Reports suggest that once gang affiliated inmates are released back into their community they often 'resume their former street gang affiliations, acting as representatives of their prison gang to recruit street gang members who perform criminal acts on behalf of the prison gang' (National Gang Threat Assessment, 2005; see also NIC, 1991). Prison administrators and law enforcement officials believe that such coordinated efforts will improve their ability to recognize, respond, and eventually eradicate gang-related illicit activities that are strengthened by the intersection of prison and street gang networks.

The prevalence of prison gang members

Current estimates of prison gang membership vary widely. As will be discussed later in the chapter, significant debate exists regarding the identification of prison gangs, prison gang members, and prison gang-related violence and other misconduct. These issues of measurement and definition complicate what, on the surface, would appear to be straightforward accounting of inmate behavior. What does remain clear, however, is that 'the gang thing' continues to be the dominate subculture in prisons across the United States, representing an obvious threat to safe and secure operations of prison systems (Knox, 2005).

Assessing the prevalence of prison gang membership is difficult for several reasons. First, with the growing use of administrative sanctions for gang affiliation, prison gang members are increasingly wary of engaging in behaviors that designate their status within a prison gang. Prisoners are more secretive in their associations and are less likely to sport tattoos and other outside symbols of membership (Fischer, 2002; Spergel, 1995). In addition, the lack of a shared understanding of what is meant by prison gang membership and variation in data collection methods have done little to shed light on the scope of this problem. Conflicting statistics often are the result of surveys conducted during different time periods wherein definitions of what constitutes a prison gang member have changed (Trulson *et al.*, 2006). Inconsistent reports of prison gang activity and membership also reflect multiple understandings of what constitutes a 'prison gang member'. Some studies make distinctions based on the nature and level of gang involvement (i.e., leader, hard-core member, and marginal member – see also Wood & Alleyne, Chapter 2, for a discussion of street gang membership levels), while others differentiate involvement based on an administrative process of verification (e.g. suspected gang member, validated gang member) (Gaes *et al.*, 2002). Still other studies distinguish between those prisoners who are affiliated with certified prison gangs (security threat groups), other prison gangs, and/or street gangs (Griffin, 2007; Griffin & Hepburn, 2006; Huebner, 2003). As such, it often is difficult to examine prison gang trends within one facility or system over time, or make comparisons between prison systems. What is important to keep in mind, however, is that regardless of how prison gang affiliation is measured, the bulk of corrections research suggests that the majority of prisoners *are not* affiliated with prison gangs.

Arguably, wide-ranging estimates of gang membership fail to provide a coherent description of the gang problems faced by correctional institutions. Illustrating this potential for frustratingly conflicting statistics, estimates of prison gang membership have varied from as low as 3 per cent (Camp & Camp, 1985) to as high as 90 per cent (Lane, 1989). The National Gang Crime Research Center survey found that nearly one-quarter of state prisoners were gang members (Knox, 2005). Others estimated that street and prison-based gang members represented less than 5 per cent of all prison inmates, nationwide; this figure dropped to 1.2 per cent when considering only 'prison-based' gang members (Trulson *et al.* 2006). Not surprisingly, estimates on the prevalence of prison gang membership vary by state or region, with prisons in the Western part of the United States reporting a higher proportion of gang affiliated inmates (Ruddell, 2009). According to Trulson *et al.*, (2006), California and Texas had more than 5,000 gang members, while other state prison systems reported having fewer than 1,000 gang members. One study reported that approximately one-quarter of inmates released from Illinois prisons during 2000 were identified as gang members (Olson *et al.*, 2004). In Arizona, state correctional administrators estimated that only 5 per cent of the inmates in their facilities were validated members of security threat groups (Fischer, 2002). In California, less than 2 per cent of the total inmate population was identified as 'validated' gang members (Petersillia, 2006). Within the federal prison system, it was estimated that almost 12 per cent of the inmate population was involved in gang-related misconduct (Wells *et al.*, 2002). Perhaps the most recent and comprehensive survey of federal and state prison systems (representing nearly three-quarters of all prisoners in the United States) reported that approximately 12 per cent of inmates were validated security threat group members (Winterdyk & Ruddell, 2010). According to the survey, this represented a significant increase in the prevalence of security threat group members over the last five years. In addition, correctional administrators described these prison gangs as increasingly sophisticated and disruptive.

The impact of prison gang activity on prisons

Prison gang behavior is multifaceted and includes activities such as trafficking drugs and other contraband, theft of personal property, strong-arm robbery, extortion, gambling, loan-sharking, contract murder and prostitution. According to Seiter (2001), prison gangs have become extremely sophisticated – 'some have extensive membership and money available to them, they have clear and understood linkages to the street gang, and they plan and communicate in a way that would make a Fortune 500 company jealous' (p. iv). Researchers have noted the negative influence of prison gangs on the prison environment through their attempts to intimidate and compromise staff members, facilitate an extensive and often lucrative underground economy, and undermine rehabilitation programs through nonparticipation (Ruddell, 2009; Winterdyk & Ruddell, 2010). Given their composition along racial and ethnic lines, prison gangs also perpetuate racist attitudes, exacerbating existing racial/ethnic tensions (Ruddell, 2009). Underlying these actions, of course, is the use of violence by prison gang members as a means to achieve both symbolic and instrumental goals. Gang affiliated inmates use violence, or the threat of violence, to establish power, gain status, acquire goods and services, and resolve disputes. Inmates often join prison gangs for reasons of safety and security, but a growing body of research suggests that inmates who become affiliated with a gang increase their own risk of victimization and as gang affiliation increases within a facility, so does the rate of overall violence (Camp & Camp, 1985; Cunningham & Sorenson, 2007; Griffin & Hepburn, 2006; Huebner, 2003; Ruddell, 2009; Sorenson & Pilgrim, 2000).

Regardless of whether only a relatively small number of inmates actively participate in prison gangs, this small group poses significant problems for prison management and any attempts to maintain a safe and orderly environment (Griffin & Hepburn, 2006; Trulson *et al.*, 2006). As noted by Varano *et al.*, (2011), whether inside prison walls or on the streets, 'gangs can provide the motivation and opportunity for deviance' (p. 31). While estimates vary, and official reports often *underestimate* the extent and nature of misconduct on the part of gang affiliated inmates, a survey of prison administrators in thirty-three states concluded that prison gang members comprised only 3 per cent of the prison population, yet were responsible for at least half of the prison violence (Camp & Camp, 1985). Compared to non-gang affiliated inmates, those inmates involved with a prison gang were found to have an increased number of disciplinary offenses, fighting offenses, and drug offenses. This is supported by more recent studies that continue to attribute a disproportionate amount of prison misconduct to gang-affiliated inmates (Carlson, 2001; Gransky & Patterson, 1999; Ralph, 1997; Rivera *et al.*, 2003; Scott, 2001).

Placing an even finer point on this relationship between gang membership and prison misconduct, Gaes *et al.* (2002) examined the likelihood of misconduct in relation to the nature of the inmate's gang affiliation. Inmates with no gang affiliation were less likely than those inmates marginally affiliated with prison gangs to engage in violent misconduct; marginally affiliated gang members were, in turn, less likely than core gang members to engage in violent misconduct. This study also found a decrease in the likelihood of violent misconduct the longer an inmate was affiliated with a gang. This suggests that long-time gang affiliates may assume a greater leadership role within the gang, insulating themselves from direct involvement in gang misconduct and the actual exercise of violence by delegating these tasks to more junior gang members. In another study examining the relationship between gang affiliation and violence, Griffin & Hepburn (2006) found that prison gang affiliation increased the likelihood participation in violent behavior during the early years of incarceration, a time when misconduct rates are generally higher among all inmates regardless of gang affiliation. Even after controlling for individual risk factors (age, ethnicity, violent history, prior incarceration), newer inmates who were affiliated with a prison gang, compared to those who were not affiliated with a gang, were more likely to engage in violent behavior (cf. Wood & Alleyne, Chapter 2). These two studies, taken together, suggest that prison administrators are faced with having to deal with violence that is perhaps more opportunistic and instrumental since it is likely that newer gang members are involved in violent behavior in an attempt to establish themselves and gain status within the gang hierarchy.

It is not surprising, then, that given the instrumental and symbolic purposes of gang-related violence, the presence of gangs in prison increases the potential for significant disorder and violent misconduct. Prison gangs represent an alternate source of power and authority in the prison organization. Prison administrators are aware of the likelihood of gang-initiated violence impacting the general population and recognize this threat to the safety and security of both officers and non-gang affiliated inmates (Clear *et al.*, 2009). Supporting this contention is research linking gang membership with increased assaults on both staff and inmates (Huebner, 2003). In addition, studies have suggested that as gangs grow in size and strength, and as formal administrative controls within the prison weaken, the level of violent misconduct by non-affiliated inmates increases. In an attempt at self-protection, prisoners who possess no affiliation with a gang are forced to use violence or seek protection by affiliating with a gang (Reisig, 2002; Wooldredge, 1998). Prison gang activity, both violent and non-violent, contribute to a breakdown of formal social controls within the prison facilities, thus reducing the ability of the staff to effectively manage the prison population (Fleisher & Decker, 2001a; Kalinich & Stojkovic, 1985; Ralph, 1997). Petersilia (2006) describes this situation as 'cyclical and toxic' (p. 33). Some would argue that this is especially troubling since a basic premise of *administrative control theory* is the notion that the primary element of successful prison management are practices that center first on the control and order of all facets of the prison organization, and then on providing inmates earned benefits (DiIulio, 1987). Prison disorder will flourish in all areas of the prison (i.e. apathetic staff and disorderly inmates) in the face of weak management strategies that fail to promote strict control over policies governing the security and administration of a prison (Clear *et al.*, 2009; Griffin, 2009; Useem & Kimball, 1989). Studies examining the relationship between prison management and prison gangs have found that in those prisons with higher levels of gangs and gang affiliated inmates, the effectiveness of administrative controls is reduced (Fleisher & Decker, 2001a; Kalinich & Stojkovic, 1985; Ralph, 1997).

Prison gang activity outside the U.S.

Prison gang activity, both inside and outside prison walls, is not found only within the United States. Gangs have been documented in European cities since the early 1990s (Klein *et al.*, 2001; Decker and Pyrooz, 2010). The presence of gangs in European cities and communities suggests that these groups should be found in prisons and jails as well, given the over-representation of gang members in crime, as well as the nature of the relationship between gang membership and imprisonment in the U.S. There is, however, very little knowledge of the presence of prison gangs outside of England. While there are media reports of gangs in prisons in Columbia, Brazil, Russia and South Africa, there has been little research on these groups.

Similar to results in the U.S., Bennett and Holloway (2004) found that current English street gang members were more involved in robbery, drug-related offenses, and weapons offenses than former and non-gang members. Despite the fact that gang members were less than 15 per cent of their total sample, they accounted for 31 per cent of all reported offenses. These results are consistent with studies in the U.S. and suggest that increased criminal behavior on the part of gang members is related to a stronger representation in prison. Wood and colleagues have conducted a number of studies of the perceptions of prisoners and staff members in sixteen English prisons (Wood, 2006; Wood and Adler, 2001; Wood *et al.*, 2009; Wood *et al.*, 2010). Staff members reported that gang activity was highest in medium security institutions that housed males (Wood and Adler, 2001). From prisoners' perspectives, gang-related activity was viewed as more prevalent in male facilities compared to female facilities, but there was little difference seen in the level of gang-related activity across all male facilities (Wood 2006). Race and region of residence were important factors in determining gang affiliations, and drug possession and dealing were important activities for prisoners involved in gang-related activity.

Similar results have been found for Canadian gangs. This is not surprising given the presence of street gangs and the increased levels of involvement in crime and violence which their members display. In their study examining prisons located in Edmonton, Grekul and La Boucane-Benson (2008) report an over-representation of Aboriginal gang members. This reflects not only their involvement in crime and gangs, but also the research examining historic and contemporary factors that characterize life for Aboriginal youth in the province. Correctional Service of Canada (CSC) (2009) determined that there were few proven strategies to respond to these groups. Ironically, prison appears to facilitate gang membership as nearly half of all prison gang members reported no prior (street) affiliation before entering prison. Fear of violent attack was a primary motivation for joining a prison gang, a finding similar to the English and American settings.

Despite the growing body of literature, at both the national and international levels, there remain significant gaps in our knowledge of the relationship between misconduct by prison gang members and its impact on the prison environment. Similar to other areas of prison research, studies examining the nature and prevalence of prison gang activity face multiple obstacles. These problems stem primarily from a difficulty in documenting gang activity; a concern on the part of prison officials to allow gang research for security reasons; and the secretive nature of the population under examination (Fong & Buentello, 1991). Importantly, administrative efforts over the past decade to more effectively identify, suppress or otherwise manage prison gangs have resulted in increased interest on the part of scholars and policy makers to further explore the influence of these organized criminal groups on the prison environment.

The identification and suppression of prison gangs

As evidenced thus far, prison gangs present a serious and persistent threat to the safe and secure operation of correctional facilities. Over the years, prison administrators have implemented a variety of strategies aimed at eradicating or at least minimizing the negative influence of these disruptive groups, relying on various organizational, legal and legislative approaches (Trulson *et al.*, 2006). Again, some of the earliest strategies attempted to engage the leaders of prison gangs in a reciprocal relationship with the prison authorities. In exchange for controlling inmates and providing some semblance of order, inmate leaders were given added benefits and privileges (Jacobs, 1974; Davidson, 1974). In some institutions, notably in the Texas Department of Corrections, the administration employed the *official* use of powerful inmates to maintain order and control especially among more dangerous segments of the prison population (Marquart & Crouch, 1984). These 'elite' inmates were known as 'building tenders' or BTs and were given considerable privileges not available to regular inmates. This rather unique system was formally abolished in 1983 and, as mentioned previously, some argue that the power vacuum left by the dissolution of this system result in the rise of powerful gangs within Texas prisons (Crouch & Marquart, 1989).

With the expansion of prison gangs in the 1980s, prison administrators targeted more directly the 'collective misconduct' of prison gangs, attempting to suppress the power and authority of these groups through a variety of means. In many instances, gang affiliated inmates have been concentrated in specific prison units and gang leaders have been transferred to other prison systems (Decker, 2001; Pizarro & Stenius, 2004). It is not clear, however, how effective these strategies have been on suppressing the growth of prison gangs with many arguing that the transfer of prison gang leaders to other prison facilities has merely spread the influence of prison gangs (Fleisher & Decker, 2001a). It is also important to keep in mind that successful suppression efforts, in particular, can be costly. According to Trulson *et al.*, (2006) the efforts of the Texas prison system to disrupt gang activity and reduce violence and disorder required a significant investment in new facilities to provide secure cells and special housing areas for gang members.

In addition to segregation and dispersion, the most popular strategies currently used by prison administrators to suppress the growth and influence of prison gangs include altering the prison environment to help make inmates feel safer; increasing efforts to prosecute gang-affiliated inmates for crimes committed while in prison; and developing gang-free prisons (Petersilia, 2006). Providing effective correctional treatment to gang-affiliated inmates is another avenue by which prison administrators may be able to influence the gang-related misconduct. According to Di Placido *et al.* (2006), the implementation of 'correctional treatment that follows the risk, need and responsivity principles' (p. 93) appears to reduce the likelihood of major institutional misconduct among prison gang members. The problem with this approach of course, is that while gang affiliated inmates are among the most in need of correctional treatment and programming, the sanctions associated with gang affiliation and misconduct often preclude them from receiving such services (Griffin, 2007).

Essential to many of these more recent strategies to suppress prison gang influence is the need for prison administrators to accurately identify prison gangs and prison gang members. Unlike non-criminally involved prison groups, prison gangs espouse beliefs of 'loyalty, unity, identity, and reward of members' criminal or antisocial activity' (NIC, 1991: 2). Prison officials assess possible prison gangs in terms of the level and nature of organization, solidarity, and criminal activity. According to the National Institute of Corrections, the following four factors distinguish between inmate groups and prison gangs (NIC, 1991: 1–2):

•   Does the group have an organized leadership with a clear chain of command?
•   Does the group remain unified through good times and bad, and during conflict in the institution?
•   Does the group demonstrate its unity in obvious, recognizable ways?
•   Does the group engage in activities that are criminal or otherwise threatening to institution operations?

At both the federal and state levels, the development of a classification system has created a new 'language' or set of terms to describe those groups who pose the *greatest* threat to the safety and security of the prison institution. It is with this system of classification and documentation that specific prison gangs are *certified* as posing a significant threat to the prison institution – some states refer to these groups as Security Threat Groups (STGs) – and prisoners are *validated* as being members of these certified groups (Fischer, 2002). These formal processes allow administrators to apply additional sanctions (i.e. administrative segregation) since validated membership in a certified gang is a violation of prison policy (Griffin, 2007). According to this policy, mere validation – and not new instances of prison misconduct – can result in an inmate being sanctioned. Under this framework, not all 'traditional' prison gangs are certified and street-gangs generally are treated separately. According to the Arizona Department of Corrections (ADOC, 2011), one of many states that utilize this policy, a security threat group is:

Any organization, club, association or group of individuals, either formal or informal (including traditional prison gangs), that may have a common name or identifying symbol, and whose members engage in activities that include, but are not limited to planning, organizing, threatening, financing, soliciting, committing or attempting to commit unlawful acts that would violate the Department's written instructions, which detract from the safe and orderly operations of prisons.

Indicators or signs associated with a Security Threat Group often include the following (ADOC, 2011):

- Bylaws or a constitution that often incorporates a 'Blood In/Blood Out' rule – generally a slogan or oath that requires a prospective member to seriously assault or kill someone to become a member of the gang (blood in); the only way to leave the gang is either through natural death or by dying violently, perhaps at the hands of the gang (blood out)
- STG specific tattoos, logos, and other symbolism
- Art work and graffiti of STG specific symbols
- Rank structure, council system, or military type rank system
- Group includes leaders, members, probates, associates, wannabes, dropouts, debriefed members (defectors), and enemies
- Membership rosters
- The existence of a 'hit list'
- Establishment of 'missions' for members and/or probationary members to follow inside and/or outside of prison.

To provide some context as to the type and number of identified STGs across different correctional systems, ADOC (2011) has certified nine prison gangs as Security Threat Groups including: the Arizona Aryan Brotherhood, Border Brothers, 'New' Mexican Mafia, 'Old' Mexican Mafia, Grandel, Mau Mau, Warrior Society, Surenos, and Dine' Pride. The Texas Department of Criminal Justice recognizes twelve Security Threat Groups: Aryan Brotherhood of Texas, Aryan Circle, Barrio Azteca, Bloods, Crips, Hermanos De Pistoleros Latinos, Mexican Mafia, Partido Revolucionario Mexicanos, Raza Unida, Texas Chicano Brotherhood, Texas Mafia, and the Texas Syndicate. The Massachusetts Department of Corrections (2011) has designated approximately 52 Security Threat Groups with a total membership of 1,858. The Latin Kings, La Familia, and NETA represent the greatest threat accounting for approximately 40 per cent of the validated inmates in Massachusetts corrections system.

Once a prison gang has been certified as a Security Threat Group, prison administrators can begin targeting those inmates they believe to be likely STG members. Specific processes vary from one correctional system to another but generally follow a similar strategy. Prison systems usually have a dedicated gang intelligence unit responsible for investigating a suspected STG member and collecting evidence to construct an official validation packet (Fischer, 2002).

Evidence used in the certification process often includes 'self-proclaimed membership, gang-identifying tattoos, appearance on gang membership lists, possession of gang paraphernalia, and association with known gang members' (Griffin, 2009: 137). The policies of some correctional systems attach 'points' to particular gang criteria used to validate an inmate. In those instances, a certain number of points are necessary to officially identify an inmate as a member of an STG. For example, validation criteria and associated point values include: self admission (5 points); tattoos (7 points); symbolism (2 points); documents (5 points); publications (1 point); authorship (7 points); court records (9 points); group photos (2 points); association (2 points); contacts (2 points); verification from other agencies (8 points) (ADOC, 2011).

An inmate who has been validated as a member of a Security Threat Group faces possible administrative sanctions including restrictions on contact visits, frequency of visits, participation in academic or vocational programming, good time credits, and work opportunities. Validated members also may face restricted movement, placement in administrative segregation, and notification of state and local law enforcement agencies upon release (Massachusetts Department of Corrections, 2011). Inmates who have been validated as STG members usually have the opportunity to renounce or 'disassociate' their gang affiliation and participate in a debriefing process. Generally, those gang members who choose to renounce their affiliation and are debriefed are placed in protective segregation to ensure their own safety (Fischer, 2002). Validated inmates who refuse to renounce their gang membership often are placed in a super-maximum security unit where they stay for the remainder of their sentence.

Conclusion

Organized criminal gangs seem to always have been a part of the fabric of the prison system in America. As noted by Trulson *et al.* (2006: 27),

> Imprison a large batch of others, add a competitive market, and divisions will form. The bottom line is that gangs or other illicit inmate groupings have been and will be a part of the prison forever. Perhaps this is a natural response to the organization of prisons and other places where individuals believe they must group to compete, thrive, and survive.

Organizational response to these criminally involved groups has varied over time. Prison administrators have tried to co-opt inmate leaders to act as informal sources of social control. More recently, prison management has implemented more overt strategies of suppression to limit gang influence and minimize prison gang misconduct. Most agencies make use of multiple policies and interventions including intelligence gathering, staff training, the dissemination of data to multiple agencies, as well as the isolation and containment strategies discussed earlier. Few large scale evaluations, however, have examined the effectiveness or long term impact of these suppression strategies. What might work in one jurisdiction may do little to reduce the threat of gang activity and violence in another (Winterdyk & Ruddell, 2010). Borrowing from the more extensive body of research on street gangs, there must be some recognition of the importance of gang status and identity and with that the idea that some prison gang suppression strategies may very well act to establish or further enhance gang identity (Fleisher & Decker, 2001a; Griffin, 2007). With that in mind, it becomes clear that perhaps the most critical area of future prison research and evaluation is the intersecting influences of prison and street gangs. Sustained high rates of incarceration in the United States will certainly facilitate these dynamics as prisons continue to be the site of formation, growth and influence for criminal groups both inside and outside the prison walls.

References

Arizona Department of Corrections (2011). Security threat group unit. Retrieved from http://www.azcorrections.gov/adc/STG/Jeff_STG.aspx#terminology (accessed 18 March 2011).

Bennett, T. and Holloway, K. (2004). Gang membership, drugs, and crime in the UK. *British Journal of Criminology, 44*, 305–323. DOI: 10.1093/bjc/azh025.

Berg, M. and DeLisi, M. (2006). The correctional melting pot: race, ethnicity, citizenship, and prison violence. *Journal of Criminal Justice, 34,* 631–642. DOI: org/10.1016/j.jcrimjus.2006.09.016.

Bosworth, M. (2010). *Examining U.S. Imprisonment.* Thousand Oaks, CA: Sage Publishing.

Bottoms, T. (1999). Interpersonal violence and social order in prisons. In M. Tonry and J. Petersilia (eds), *Crime and Justice: A Review of Research: Vol. 26* (pp. 205–281). Chicago: University of Chicago Press.

Bureau of Justice Statistics (2009). *Correctional Surveys.* Washington, DC: Office of Justice Programs, U.S. Department of Justice.

California Department of Corrections and Rehabilitation (2008). *Operations Manual, Chapter 6, Classification.* Retrieved from http://www.cdcr.ca.gov/Regulations/Adult_Operations/docs/DOM/Ch_6_Printed_Final_DOM.pdf (accessed 1 January 2008).

Camp, G. M. and Camp, C. G. (1985). *Prison Gangs: Their Extent, Nature, and Impact on Prisons.* Washington: U.S. Department of Justice.

Carlson, P. M. (2001). Prison interventions: evolving strategies to control security threat groups. *Corrections Management Quarterly, 5*, 10–22.

Clear, T., Cole, G. and Reisig, M. (2009) *American Corrections*, 8th edn. Belmont, CA: Wadsworth Publishing Company.

Correctional Service of Canada. (2009). *Prison Gangs: A Review and Survey of Strategies.* West Ottawa, Ontario. Retrieved from http://www.csc-scc.gc.ca/text/rsrch/smmrs/rg/rg-b43/rg-b43-eng.shtml (accessed 10 April 2012).

Crouch, B. and Marquart, J. (1989). *Appeal to Justice: Litigated Reform of Texas Prisons.* Austin: University of Texas Press.

Cunningham, M. and Sorensen, J. (2007). Predictive factors for violent misconduct in close custody. *The Prison Journal, 87*, 241–253. DOI: 10.1177/0032885507303752.

Davidson, R.T. (1974). *Chicano Prisoners – The Key to San Quentin.* New York: Holt, Rinehart and Winston.

Decker, S. (2001). *From the Street to the Prison: Understanding and Responding to Gangs.* Richmond, Ky.: National Major Gang Task Force. American Correctional Association.

Decker, S. H. and Pyrooz, D.C. (2010). Gang violence worldwide: context, culture, and country. In *Small Arms Survey 2010: Gangs, Groups, and Guns* (pp. 128–155). Cambridge: Cambridge University Press.

Decker, S. H., Bynum, T. and Weisel, D. (1998). A tale of two cities: gangs as organized crime groups. *Justice Quarterly, 15*, 395–425. DOI: 10.1080/07418829800093821.

DeLisi, M., Berg, M. T. and Hochstetler, A. (2004). Gang members, career criminals and prison violence. Further specification of the importation model of inmate behavior. *Criminal Justice Studies, 17*, 369,en>383. DOI: 10.1080/14786010420003 14883.

DiIulio, J. (1987). *Governing Prisons: A Comparative Study of Correctional Management.* New York: Free Press.

Di Placido, C., Simon, T., Witte, T., Gu, D., and Wong, S. (2006). Treatment of gang members can reduce recidivism and institutional misconduct. *Law and Human Behavior, 30*, 93–114. DOI: 10.1007/s10979-006-9003-6.

Fischer, D.R. (2002). *Arizona Department of Corrections: Security Threat Group (STG) Program Evaluation, Final Report.* Retrieved from http://www.ncjrs.gov/pdffiles1/nij/grants/197045.pdf (accessed 23 February 2007).

Fleisher, M. (2006) Gang management in corrections. In P. Carlson and J.S. Garrett (eds) *Prison and Jail Administration: Practice and Theory* (2nd edn). Gaithersburg, MD: Aspen Publishing.

Fleisher, M. and Decker, S. (2001a). An overview of the challenge of prison gangs. *Corrections Management Quarterly, 5,* 1–9.

Fleisher, M. and Decker, S. (2001b). Going home, staying home: integrating prison gang members into the community. *Corrections Management Quarterly, 5,* 65–77.

Fong, R.S. and Buentello, S. (1991). The detection of prison gang development: an empirical assessment. *Federal Probation, 55,* 66–69.

Gaes, G. G., Wallace, S., Gilnam, E., Klein-Saffran, J., and Suppa, S. (2002). The influence of prison gang affiliation on violence and other prison misconduct. *The Prison Journal, 82*, 359–385. DOI: 10.1177/003288550208200304.

Garland, D. (2001) *The Culture of Control: Crime and Social Order in Contemporary Society.* New York: Oxford University Press.

Goodstein, L. and Wright, K. (1989). Inmate adjustment to prison. In L. Goodstein and D. MacKenzie (eds), *The American Prison: Issues in Research and Policy* (pp. 229–251). New York: Plenum.

Gover, A., MacKenzie, D. and Armstrong, G. (2000). Importation and deprivation explanations of juveniles'adjustment to correctional facilities. *International Journal of Offender Therapy and Comparative Criminology, 44*, 450–467. DOI: 10.1177/0306624 X00444004.

Gransky, L. and Patterson, M. (1999). A discussion of Illinois' 'gang-free' prison: evaluation results. *Corrections Management Quarterly, 3*, 30–42.

Grekul, J. and LaBoucane-Benson, P. (2008). Aboriginal gangs and their (dis)placement: contextualizing recruitment, membership and status. *Canadian Journal of Criminal Justice, 50*, 59–82.

Griffin, M. (2007). Prison gang policy and recidivism: short-term management benefits, long-term consequences. *Criminology & Public Policy, 6*, 223–230. DOI: 10.1111/j.1745-9133.2007.00430.x.

Griffin, M. (2009). Prison gangs and violence: an examination of origins, issues, and strategies for suppression and control. In N. Fearn and R. Ruddell (eds) *Understanding Correctional Violence* (pp.127–141). Richmond, KY: Newgate Press.

Griffin, M. and Hepburn, J. (2006). The effect of gang affiliation on violent misconduct among inmates during the early years of confinement. *Criminal Justice and Behavior, 33*, 419–448. DOI: 10.1177/0093854806288038.

Harer, M.D. and Langan, N.P. (2001). Gender differences in predictors of prison violence: assessing the predictive validity of a risk classification system. *Crime & Delinquency, 47*, 513–535. DOI: 10.1177/0011128701047004002.

Hochstetler, A. and DeLisi, M. (2005). Importation, deprivation, and varieties of serving time: an integrated lifestyle-exposure model of prison offending. *Journal of Criminal Justice, 33*, 257–266. DOI:10.1016/j.jcrimjus.2005.02.005.

Huebner, B.M. (2003). Administrative determinates of inmate violence. *Journal of Criminal Justice, 31*, 107–117. DOI: 10.1016/S0047-2352(02)00218-0.

Huebner, B.M., Varano, S.P. and Bynum T.S. (2007). Gangs, guns, and drugs: recidivism among serious, young offenders. *Criminology & Public Policy, 6*, 187–221. DOI: 10.1111/j.1745-9133.2007.00429.x.

Hunt, G., Riegel, S., Morales, T., and Waldorf, D. (1993). Changes in prison culture: prison gangs and the case of the 'Pepsi Generation'. *Social Problems, 40*, 398–409.

Irwin, J. (1980). *Prisons in Turmoil*. Boston: Little, Brown and Company.

Irwin, J. (1981). Sociological studies of the impact of long-term confinement. In D.A. Ward and K.F. Schoen (eds), *Confinement in Maximum Custody*. Lexington, MA: D.C. Heath.

Irwin, J. and Cressey, D.R. (1962) Thieves, convicts, and the inmate culture. *Social Problems, 10*, 142–155.

Jacobs, J. (1974). Street gangs behind bars. *Social Problems*, 21: 395–409.

Jacobs, J. (2001). Focusing on prison gangs. *Corrections Management Quarterly, 5*, vi–vii.

Jiang, S. and Fisher-Giorlando, M. (2002). Inmate misconduct: a test of the deprivation, importation, and situational models. *Prison Journal, 82*, 335–358. DOI: 10.1177/003288550208200303.

Kalinich, D., & Stojkovic, S. (1985). Contraband: the basis for legitimate power in a prison social system. *Criminal Justice and Behavior, 12*, 435–451. DOI: 10.1177/0093854885012004003.

Klein, M.W., Kerner, H.J., Maxson, C.L., and Weitekamp, E.G.M. (2001). *The Eurogang Paradox: Street Gangs and Youth Groups in the U.S. and Europe*. Dordrecht, the Netherlands: Kluwer.

Knox, G. (2005). *The problem of gangs and security threat groups (STGs) in American prisons today: Recent research findings from the 2004 Prison Gang Survey*. Retrieved from http://www.ngcrc.com/corr2006.html (accessed 20 February 2007).

Lane, M.P. (1989). Inmate gangs. *Corrections Today, 51*, 98–99.

Marquart, J.W. and Crouch, B.M. (1984) Co-opting the kept: using inmates for social control in a southern prison. *Justice Quarterly. 1(4)*, 491–509. DOI: 10.1080/07418828400088271.

Massachusetts Department of Corrections (2011). *List of Security Threat Groups*. Retrieved from http://www.mass.gov/?pageID=eopssubtopic&L=4&L0=Home&L1=Law+Enfor cement+%26+Criminal+Justice&L2=Prisons&L3=Security+Threat+Group+Informati on&sid=Eeops (accessed 18 March 2011).

McCorkle, R., Miethe,T., and Drass, K. (1995). The roots of prison violence: a test of the deprivation, management, and not-so-total institutional models. *Crime & Delinquency, 2*, 197–221. DOI: 10.1177/0011128795041003003.

National Gang Threat Assessment (2005). *The 2005 National Gang Threat Assessment*. Washington, DC: Office of Justice Programs, U.S. Department of Justice.

National Gang Intelligence Center. (2009). *National Gang Threat Assessment, 2009*. Washington, D.C.: National Gang Intelligence Center.

National Institute of Corrections (1991). *Management Strategies in Disturbances and with Gangs/Disruptive Groups*. Washington, DC: United States Department of Justice.

Olson, D., Dooley, B., and Kane, C. (2004). *The Relationship between Gang Membership and Inmate Recidivism*. Springfield: Illinois Criminal Justice Authority.

Petersilia, J. (2006). *Understanding California Corrections: A Policy Research Program Report*. Berkeley, CA: Regents of the University of California.

Pizarro, J. and Stenius, V. (2004). Supermax prisons: their rise, current practices, and effect on inmates. *The Prison Journal, 84*, 248–264. DOI: 10.1177/0032885504265080.

Poole, E. and Regoli, R. (1983). Violence in juvenile institutions. *Criminology, 21*, 213–232. DOI: 10.1016/S0047-2352(98)00033-6.

Pyrooz, D.C., Decker, S.H., and Fleisher, M. (2011). From the street to the prison, from the prison to the street: understanding and responding to prison gangs. *Journal of Aggression, Conflict, and Peace Research, 3*, 12–24. DOI: 10.5042/jacpr.2011.0018.

Ralph, P. (1997). From self-preservation to organized crime: the evolution of inmate gangs. In J. Marquart and J. Sorensen (eds), *Correctional Contexts: Contemporary and Classical Readings* (pp. 182–186). Los Angeles: Roxbury.

Reisig, M. (2002). Administrative control and inmate homicide. *Homicide Studies, 6*, 84–103. DOI: 10.1177/1088767902006001005.

Rivera, B., Cowles, E., and Dorman, L. (2003). An exploratory study of institutional change: personal control and environmental satisfaction in a gang-free prison. *The Prison Journal, 83*, 149–170. DOI: 10.1177/0032885503083002003.

Ruddell, R. (2009). Inmate perspectives on correctional violence. In N. Fearn and R. Ruddell (eds) *Understanding Correctional Violence* (pp. 197–215). Richmond, KY: Newgate Press.

Ruiz v. Estelle, 503 F. Supp. 1265 - Dist. Court, SD Texas 1980.

Scott, G. (2001). Broken windows behind bars: eradicating prison gangs through ecological hardening and symbolic cleansing. *Corrections Management Quarterly, 5*, 23–36.

Seiter, R. (2001). Winning a battle of wills: correctional administrators and prison gangs. *Corrections Management Quarterly, 5*, iv–v.

Sorenson, J. and Pilgrim, R. (2000). An actuarial risk assessment of violence posed by capital murder defendants. *Journal of Criminal Law & Criminology, 90*, 1251–1270.

Spergel, I.A. (1995). *The Youth Gang Problem: A Community Approach*. New York: Oxford University Press.

Sykes, G.M. (1958). *The Society of Captives*. Princeton, NJ: Princeton University Press.

Travis, J. (2005). *But They All Come Back: Facing the Challenges of Prisoner Reentry*. Washington, D.C.: The Urban Institute Press.

Trulson, C., Marquart, J., and S. Kawucha (2006). Gang suppression and institutional control. *Corrections Today, 68*, 26–30.

Useem, B. and Kimball, P. (1989). *States of Siege: U.S. Prison Riots, 1971–1986*. New York: Oxford University Press.

Useem, B. and Piehl, A. (2008) *Prison State: The Challenge of Mass Incarceration*. New York: Cambridge University Press.

Varano, S.P., Huebner, B.M., and Bynum, T.S. (2011). Correlates and consequences of pre-incarceration gang involvement among incarcerated youthful felons. *Journal of Criminal Justice, 39*, 30–38. DOI: 10.1016/j.jcrimjus.2010.10.001

Venkatesh, S. and Levitt, S. (2000). 'Are we family or a business?' History and disjuncture in the urban American street gang. *Theory and Society, 29*, 427–462. DOI: 10.1023/A:1007151703198.

Wells, J.B., Minor, K.I., Angel, E., Carter, L., and Cox, M. (2002). *A Study of Gangs and Security Threat Groups in America's Adult Prisons and Jails.* Indianapolis, IN: National Major Gang Task Force.

Winterdyk, J. and Ruddell, R. (2010). Managing prison gangs: results from a survey of U.S. prison systems. *Journal of Criminal Justice, 38*, 730–736. DOI: 10.1016/j.jcrimjus.2010.04.047

Wood, J. (2006). Gang activity in English prisons: the prisoners' perspective. *Psychology, Crime and Law, 12*, 605–617. DOI: 10.1080/10683160500337667.

Wood, J. and Adler, J. (2001). Gang activity in english prisons: the staff perspective. *Psychology, Crime and Law, 7*, 167–192. DOI: 10.1080/10683160108401793.

Wood, J., Moir, A., and James, M. (2009). Prisoners' gang-related activity: the importance of bullying and moral disengagement. *Psychology, Crime and Law, 15*, 569–581. DOI: 10.1080/10683160802427786.

Wood, J., Williams, G., and James, M. (2010). Incapacitation and imprisonment: prisoners' involvement in community-based crime. *Psychology Crime and Law, 16*, 601–614. DOI: 10.1080/10683160902971071.

Wooldredge, J. (1998). Inmate lifestyles and opportunities for victimization. *Journal of Research in Crime and Delinquency, 35*, 480–502. DOI: 10.1177/0022427898035004006.

Part 3

Group relevance in the treatment of offenders

8 Features of treatment delivery and group processes that maximize the effects of offender programs

W. L. Marshall and L. E. Marshall, Rockwood Psychological Services, Kingston, Ontario, Canada, and D. L. Burton, Smith College School for Social Work, Northampton, Massachusetts

Therapists have long held that the way in which psychological treatment is delivered is crucial if benefits are to be obtained (Sterba, 1934; Zetzel, 1956). Indeed some authors have claimed that the processes involved in treatment delivery are the vehicles of actual change with the procedures employed being no more than conveniences and having, at most, marginal effects (Frank, 1971; Frankl, 1978; Rogers, 1961). When behavior therapy emerged at the beginning of the 1960s (Eysenck, 1969; Eysenck & Rachman, 1965), advocates of this approach essentially declared the opposite; that is, they held that the implementation of clearly specified procedures designed to alter particular behaviors was both necessary and sufficient to generate desired changes (see Kazdin, 1978, for details of this history). The immediate progeny of these early behavioral notions, namely cognitive behavior therapy, likewise initially cleaved to this idea. Much of the motivation for the advocates of this view derived from a need to be sufficiently specific about what was employed to change behavior. This was consistent with the scientific background of these early behavioral, and cognitive behavioral therapists who demanded that treatment be specified in enough detail to allow independent replication by others. It was, and still is, easier to provide specific details of procedures than it is to describe the various aspects of treatment delivery. Thus it remains to this day, difficult to design treatment manuals that do not overemphasize procedures to the relative exclusion of the important, or as we hope to show, crucial treatment process features (Marshall, 2009).

While the introduction by behavior therapists of a rigorous scientific approach was a welcome advance, the neglect of therapeutic processes was an unfortunate by-product. It was not until Wilson and Evans (1976) drew attention to this neglect that cognitive behavior therapy (CBT) treatment providers began to show an interest in these issues. Since then there has been a proliferation of studies by therapists of all theoretical orientations focusing on the influence of treatment delivery processes.

In this chapter, we will provide a brief overview of the relevant aspects of the general clinical literature dealing with various Axis 1 and Axis 2 disorders other than those that are the focus of interventions with offenders. We will then consider what the evidence tells us about the treatment and group process factors associated with various, non-sexual offenders. Finally, we will give detailed attention to the emerging literature on the influence of treatment process issues, with a specific focus on group processes, with sexual offenders.

The features of the delivery of treatment with which we will be concerned are: (1) the style or characteristics of the therapist; (2) the therapeutic alliance between the therapist and client; and (3) the climate of the group. We include the latter because most programs for offenders are delivered in groups. It is important to note that the therapists' style, and the way the clients perceive the therapists' style (which are not always a match), appear to be the major determinants of both the therapeutic alliance and the group climate.

Non-offenders

There is now an extensive and detailed research literature on therapeutic processes involved in the treatment of most Axis 1 and Axis 2 disorders. What emerges from a reading of this literature is a consistent theme. If the appropriate features are targeted and an empirically sound approach to the delivery of treatment is adopted, then treatment will be effective; if not, then treatment is almost certain to either fail or generate weak effects. The following brief review will illustrate these points but first we need to note what constitutes meaningful effects. Sophisticated and respected researchers (Cohen, 1988; Rosnow & Rosenthal, 1988) have offered a framework for judging the meaning of observed treatment benefits in terms of what is called the 'effect size'. An effect size is, with a few statistical twists, the difference between the assessed outcome of a treated versus an untreated group of clients. An effect size (ES) of zero means treatment had no influence on the problems; an ES of 0.2 is considered small but meaningful; an ES of 0.5 is seen as moderate; while an ES of 0.8 or above is considered large. Nowadays treatment (usually a combination of psychotherapy and pharmacotherapy) for a variety of non-offending Axis 1 disorders is at or near the high range of effect sizes (see Marshall & McGuire, 2003).

Therapist features and group processes

Rogers (1957) was one of the first to identify what he believed were the essential characteristics of an effective therapist. He declared that if the therapist displayed warmth, genuineness, empathy, and unconditional regard for the client, then benefits would necessarily follow. These notions, however, simply reflected Rogers' keen clinical insights and although subsequent research by his students (Truax & Carkhuff, 1967) and by others (Orlinsky *et al.*, 1994; Orlinsky & Howard, 1986) has confirmed the importance of the first three features, it has been shown that unconditionally accepting clients is a mistake. Clients of all types, including offenders, not only need to be challenged, they desire it (Drapeau, 2005; Drapeau *et al.*, 2004; Miller & Sovereign, 1989). It is important to note, however, that these challenges need to be conducted in a supportive way (Levenson *et al.*, 2009; Levenson *et al.*, 2010; Marshall *et al.*, 2003a). The evidence clearly shows that with Axis 1 and Axis 2 disorders (Lieberman *et al.*, 1973), confrontational challenges have negative effects causing clients to drop out of treatment, remain in treatment but withdraw from effective participation, or to simply agree with the challenges while privately dismissing the relevance of treatment.

It is now clear that the range of therapist features having an influence on the attainment of treatment goals is quite extensive although from a broader perspective they all seem consistent with one another. Our review of the general clinical literature (Marshall *et al.*, 2003a) revealed convincing evidence of the role of therapists who display genuineness, warmth, empathy, respect, support, flexibility, encouragement and some degree of directiveness in effectively facilitating measurable client improvements. It is clear that most of these qualities are consistent with each other and often demonstrated, at least implicitly, at the same time; that is, it would seem all but impossible to be warm and empathic and not be respectful, supportive and encouraging. Thus it is the overall style of the therapist rather than particular characteristics that influences clients to fully engage in treatment and, as a result, derive benefits from it. This observation is derived from the results of various reviews and meta-analyses of the general clinical literature (Horvath, 2000; Martin *et al.*, 2000; Morgan *et al.*, 1982; Norcross, 2002; Orlinsky *et al.*, 1994; Schaap *et al.*, 1993). Indeed, Norcross (2002) showed that a positive therapeutic alliance explained 20 per cent to 30 per cent of treatment-induced changes whereas procedures accounted for just 15 per cent. The presence of these advantageous features not only facilitates beneficial changes, it also reduces drop-outs and non-compliance (Bennun *et al.*, 1986; Heppner & Clairborn, 1989; Horvath, 2000; Saunders, 1999).

Thus, when these therapist features are present, and the clients perceive them to be present, then the therapeutic alliance will be strong and it is this, rather than any specific therapist feature, that generates effectiveness. Interestingly, therapists and clients do not always agree on the presence of good therapist qualities (Bachelor, 1995; Free *et al.*, 1985). It turns out that it is the clients' view of the presence of these qualities, not the view of the therapist, that accurately predicts good outcome (Free *et al.*, 1985; Orlinsky *et al.*, 1994), suggesting that therapists should periodically determine whether or not clients perceive them as displaying the appropriate positive features.

Although the majority of studies in the general clinical literature on these issues have been focussed on individual treatment, there are studies examining effective group processes. In fact, some studies indicate that group treatment can be more effective than individual therapy (Bednar & Kaul, 1994; McRoberts *et al.*, 1988), and as a result, Yalom (1995) declared that 'it is time to direct our efforts toward a fuller understanding of the necessary conditions for effective (group) psychotherapy' (p. 47, word in parentheses added). Our earlier review of the evidence (Marshall & Burton, 2010) led us to conclude that a therapist holding the positive features described above is more likely to create the appropriately effective group climate than is a therapist without these qualities. In support of this idea, Karterud (1988) reported that among six programs he evaluated, the one that functioned most effectively had group leaders who were supportive, nonconfrontational, and encouraging. Group leaders displaying these characteristics are most likely to encourage clients to form cohesive relations with each other (Budman *et al.*, 1993) and the cohesiveness of a group is predictive of the amount of between-sessions work and the degree of active participation within sessions (Budman *et al.*, 1993). Braaten (1989) showed that cohesiveness also predicted beneficial changes.

Adult offenders

Non-sexual offenders

The most important findings concerning the effective features of treatment for adult offenders has come from a series of meta-analyses conducted by the Carleton University group of criminology researchers led by the late Don Andrews. In their studies Andrews and his colleagues integrated an extensive range of reports of treatment effectiveness within a series of meta-analyses (Andrews & Dowden, 1999; Andrews *et al.*, 1990; Dowden & Andrews, 2000; 2003; 2004; Dowden *et al.*, 2003; Hill *et al.*, 1991). The studies in these analyses involved treatment programs of various types (e.g. cognitive behavioral, relapse prevention, family interventions) addressing the needs of different types of offenders (e.g. adults, juveniles, males, females) having different problems (e.g. property offenders, violent offenders, sexual offenders) with the programs being run in different locations (e.g. prisons or community). Andrews and Bonta (2006) provided an integration of these and various other relevant studies, and it is largely from this edition of their book that we have drawn the following findings.

The first observation to be made from Andrews' work is that three principles account for the changes observed in effective correctional treatment programs. When all three of the principles are adhered to, treatment is very effective (ES = .28). These three principles are described as risk, need, and responsivity. The *risk principle* simply states that treatment resources should be directed at the highest risk group particularly when resources are limited. When there are sufficient resources the intensity and the extensive nature of treatment should be distributed according to risk level. Since, of the three, this principle has the least influence (ES = .10), we will set aside an in-depth consideration of it here and refer the interested reader to Andrews and Bonta's (2006) book.

The *needs principle* refers to the requirement that treatment should be directed at modifying those potentially changeable features of offenders that have been shown to predict reoffending. Such features are called 'criminogenic factors'. Andrews and Bonta (2006) report that the needs principle exerts a significant, although not remarkable, effect on reducing reoffense rates (ES = .19). Indeed the number of known criminogenic targets that are addressed in treatment is significantly related to the degree of reductions in recidivism. When non-criminogenic needs are targeted, the effects of treatment are reduced proportional to the number of such needs that are addressed. However it is important to note that some features of clients that appear to not be directly related to recidivism (i.e. are not directly criminogenic) may, nevertheless, be desirable targets of treatment. Dowden and Andrews (2003) specifically note this need. For example, both low self-esteem and empathy have been found to be unrelated to recidivism (at least in the majority of studies) and yet both play an important role in the skills training that is necessary to overcome an identified criminogenic feature (i.e. poor relationship skills). In addition, low self-esteem, as researchers (Baumeister, 1993; Miller & Rollnick, 2002) have shown, is an obstacle to treatment engagement and must, therefore, be addressed before criminogenic features can be targeted.

For the focus of the present chapter, it is the responsivity principle that is most relevant. The *responsivity principle* has two components: specific and general responsivity. Specific responsivity refers to the need to adjust treatment and its delivery to the unique features of each individual and in that sense it means much the same as the notion of 'flexibility' as this term is used in the general clinical literature. Adapting treatment to meet cultural needs, or adjusting treatment to each client's intellectual, educational and social status, are some of the ways of adhering to specific responsivity. While specific responsivity is obviously important, it has not received the same attention as has the general principle. In particular flexibility to a client's unique qualities appears most likely to be neglected the more rigorously therapists are required to adhere to a detailed manual.

The meaning attached to general responsivity has, unfortunately, varied across authors as well as over the various publications of Andrews and his colleagues. The most common, but we believe, mistaken interpretation has been to identify programs as meeting the requirements of general responsivity if they are described as cognitive behavioral (with or without relapse prevention elements). Since Andrews *et al.* (1990) found that cognitive behavioral (CBT) programs were the ones 'most likely to' reduce recidivism among offenders, they and others have assumed that choosing a CBT approach will meet the requirements of the general responsivity principle. There is a difference, however, between 'most likely to' and 'certain to' produce benefits.

Given that CBT programs for sexual offenders vary considerably in treatment targets and procedures (Burton & Smith-Darden, 2001; McGrath *et al.*, 2003; McGrath *et al.*, 2010) and that programs vary in demonstrated effectiveness (see details of the meta-analyses of Hanson *et al.*, 2002; and Lösel & Schmucker, 2005), it would seem unwise to equate the provision of CBT with the requirements of general responsivity. In fact, what this principle demands is that treatment should contain elements that maximize its possibility of being effective. Some CBT programs may meet these criteria but some clearly do not, and, more to the point, some other approaches to the treatment of offenders appear to be effective. For example, Multi-Systemic Therapy (MST) has been reported to produce significant reductions in recidivism among juvenile sexual offenders (Schaeffer &

Borduin, 2005) and the Duluth Model (Pence & Paymer, 1993) for treating perpetrators of domestic violence has also been shown to be effective (Babcock *et al.*, 2004). Interestingly, an examination of Babcock *et al.*'s (2004) report reveals that across the various Duluth model programs the magnitude of the treatment effects varied considerably; from around zero to ES = 1.0. When Fisher (2008) re-analyzed these results he found this variability could be explained by the degree of adherence to the treatment manual. Programs that slavishly conformed to the psycho-educational aspects of the manual produced negligible (and, in some cases, negative) effects whereas those that adopted a psychotherapeutic approach emphasizing good quality delivery generated substantial effect sizes.

The aim is, then, to select an approach that the evidence suggests will be most effective. Applying the general responsivity principle should provide an important part of a guide for this since Andrews and Bonta (2006) summarize evidence indicating that when this principle is appropriately adhered to it accounts for a significant amount of the treatment-induced benefits (ES = .23 compared with ES = .28 when all three principles are adhered to). Since the risk principle accounts for a very small part of the overall effects, it appears that when programs target criminogenic features (i.e., adhere to the needs principle) and meet general responsivity requirements, treatment of offenders is most likely to markedly reduce recidivism rates.

Finally, a closer examination of the data presented by Andrews and Bonta's (2006) review reveals that the most influential feature of the general responsivity principle concerns the way in which treatment is delivered. We (Marshall & Marshall, 2012) have provided a detailed analysis of this feature of responsivity and the evidence bearing on its crucial importance. Andrews and Bonta describe this delivery of treatment as involving what they call 'core correctional practices'. The features of these practices include 'relationship' and 'structuring' principles. The former principle identifies therapist characteristics such as empathy, warmth, respect, interest, enthusiasm and nonblaming communication, while the structuring principle covers several features but particularly effective reinforcement of prosocial attitudes and behaviors and appropriate disapproval of antisocial attitudes and behaviors. In addition structuring also includes modeling by the therapist of appropriate attitudes and behaviors. Throughout their discussion of these issues, Andrews and Bonta (2006) emphasize the importance of the utilization of motivational tactics aimed at engaging the offenders and winning their trust.

The combined effects of these core correctional practices (CCP) have been shown to be significant. Dowden and Andrews (2003), for example, found that when all aspects of CCP were met the effect size of treatment was impressive (ES= .39), when only one of these principles was present the effect size was lower but still meaningful (ES = .24), but when none of the CCP features was present the effect size was meaningless (ES = .04). Clearly the way in which treatment is delivered to offenders is essential to achieving the goal of reduced recidivism. Indeed when the appropriate criminogenic features are targeted and when treatment is delivered in the appropriate way (i.e., employing the CCP principles), treatment for offenders is highly effective (Andrews & Bonta, 2006). Unfortunately as Dowden and Andrews' (2004) study revealed, only 16 per cent of the 427 offender programs entering into their meta-analyses appropriately adhered to the CCP principles. If treatment for offenders is to maximally achieve the goal of reducing recidivism then the delivery of programs has to adhere to these core correctional practices.

Sexual offenders

Much of what we have discussed concerning the treatment of non-sexual offenders applies to sexual offenders. Indeed, Hanson *et al.* (2009) demonstrated that the principles of effective correctional treatment, as adumbrated by Andrews and Bonta (2006), applied equally well to sexual offender programs. They report that the risk principle exhibited a negligible influence on the results of sexual offender treatment, but that the other two principles, when properly applied, resulted in significant positive results. Although Hanson *et al.* did not directly examine the effects of the core correctional practices, they did show that the responsivity principle accounted for the greatest beneficial effects. As we have shown above, the effects of the responsivity principle are largely explained by the appropriate application of the CCPs. It therefore seems clear that it is the way in which treatment is delivered that predominantly explains the effects, or absence of effects, of sexual offender programs. This conclusion is strengthened by recent research showing that specific features of the therapist's style and behavior, as well as the therapist's ability to create the appropriate group climate, significantly influence the attainment of the desired goals of treatment with sexual offenders.

In two studies (Marshall *et al.*, 2003b; Marshall *et al.*, 2002) we demonstrated that among the various programs we examined, only those where therapists displayed empathy and warmth, and were rewarding (more accurately described as 'encouraging') and directive (more accurately described as 'guiding'), were treatment benefits attained. We also showed that a harsh confrontational style reduced any potential benefits that might otherwise have been derived from treatment. The effects of the four positive characteristics of the therapists' style of delivery were surprisingly strong; taken together these four features accounted for between 30 per cent and 60 per cent of the variance on an array of measures of treatment change. The reader will recall that with other Axis 1 and Axis 2 disorders, the therapists' style accounts for 20 per cent to 30 per cent of treatment induced changes (Norcross, 2002). Clearly the therapists' way of delivering treatment is more important when treating sexual offenders (and perhaps all types of offenders) than is true when treating people with other disorders. Perhaps this should not be a surprise given the general social repugnance with which sexual offenders are regarded and their understandable fear that divulging too much may prove to be seriously to their disadvantage. For this reason the first phase of our sexual offender program is focused entirely on winning the clients' trust, motivating them to participate, and engaging them in the process of treatment. Demanding full disclosures of their offenses at this early stage and strongly challenging any presumed dissimulations, which are all too common features of many sexual offender programs, seems ill-advised and contrary to the available evidence.

Drapeau's (2005; Drapeau *et al.*, 2004) examinations of the views of sexual offenders undergoing treatment revealed attitudes consistent with Marshall *et al.*'s findings. These offenders reported that they fully engaged with therapists whom they judged to be warm, empathic, caring, respectful, honest, noncritical and nonjudgmental; they counted the role of the therapist to be crucial to any benefits they derived from treatment, although they also noted that the use of procedures facilitated beneficial changes. This latter observation is consistent with Norcross' (2002) observation noted earlier, that while the therapeutic alliance was the most influential feature in the treatment of non-offenders, well chosen procedures accounted for 15 per cent of the changes. Given the findings of Andrews and his colleagues concerning the strong effects associated with the appropriate application of the needs principle (i.e., the requirement to target known criminogenic factors) it may well be that it is not simply the procedures that produce benefits but rather aiming treatment at the correct targets. It seems likely that a variety of procedures may produce the same benefits for each target of treatment. For example, we know that various types of behavioral techniques can all reduce deviant responding and increase appropriate arousal patterns (Marshall *et al.*, 2009) and no doubt the same is true for the other criminogenic features of sexual offenders.

In their studies of the group climate of sexual offender programs, Beech and his colleagues (Beech & Fordham, 1997; Beech & Hamilton-Giachritsis, 2005) have shown that two features of groups exert a profound influence on the attainment of treatment goals: group cohesiveness and group expressiveness. *Cohesiveness* refers to the degree to which group members work together, how much they support and respectfully challenge one another, and how effectively they bond with each other. *Expressiveness* indicates the comfort group participants feel to talk openly, offer their opinions, and participate in discussions, and particularly the degree to which they feel comfortable expressing their emotions. The latter observation is consistent with Pfäfflin *et al.*'s (2005) finding that it is only when emotional expressions occur in conjunction with an understanding of the issues that sexual offenders begin to change in the desired direction. Pfäfflin *et al.*'s findings are consistent with observations made in the treatment of a variety of Axis 1 disorders showing that emotional expressiveness during treatment significantly predicts treatment benefits (Cooley & LaJoy, 1980; Klein *et al.*, 1986; Orlinsky & Howard, 1986; Saunders, 1999). In a particularly relevant observation, Levenson *et al.* (2009) found that sexual offenders rated as very important, understanding their emotional needs and learning how to meet them in healthier ways. Subsequently, Levenson *et al.* (2010) showed that dealing with emotional issues was significantly predictive of clients' satisfaction with treatment.

Conclusions

Clearly the way in which treatment is delivered to adult offenders (both sexual and non-sexual) is crucial to maximizing benefits. Effective treatment delivery as defined above, keeps more offenders engaged, reduces drop-out rates, and enhances the benefits derived from programs. The same characteristics of the therapist, the quality of the therapeutic alliance, and the climate of group therapy, that enhance the effectiveness of programs for non-offenders with Axis 1 and Axis 2 disorders, appear directly relevant to the treatment of offenders including sexual offenders. In therapy programs for offenders the additional, although complementary, features of Andrews and Bonta's (2006) principles of effective correctional programs must also be met if treatment is to be effective. These principles, it should be noted, are equally relevant to both non-sexual and sexual offenders.

We now turn to a consideration of the literature relevant to these features of treatment with juvenile offenders.

Juvenile offenders

Young people with non-offending problems rarely come to clinics of their own volition; they are typically referred by someone else (Karver *et al.*, 2006). As a result, we would expect the therapist's approach to be even more important than with adults and this has been found to be the case (DiGiuseppe *et al.*, 1996; Shirk & Russell, 1996). More specifically Karver *et al.*'s (2006) meta-analysis of 49 treatment studies revealed that the therapist's style significantly predicted treatment benefits. They found that when therapists displayed empathy, warmth, genuineness, support and guidance, and were judged to be competent, treatment effects were maximized. In addition, the degree of active participation in treatment and emotional expressiveness by juvenile clients were also related to positive outcomes. It is noteworthy that positive affective expression by young people during treatment is elicited by the positive therapist behaviors listed above (Berg, 1999).

While these findings with non-offending youth are clearly relevant to dealing with juveniles who commit crimes, there is an additional study reporting treatment effects for abused youth (Eltz *et al.*, 2005) that seems particularly pertinent. This study is relevant because it is clear that a significant proportion of juvenile offenders have experienced trauma during their development (Briere, 1997; Loeber & Farrington, 1999; Wolpaw *et al.*, 2005) and so too have juvenile sexual offenders (Burton, 2000; 2003; McMakin *et al.*, 2002). Youngsters who sexually offend are also very likely to have been sexually abused themselves (Watkins & Bentovim, 1992). What Eltz and his colleagues (2005) found was that the treatment alliance was critically related to improvements among their traumatized youth. We know that traumatic symptoms interfere with treatment responsiveness in young people (Newman, 2002) and given the observed reluctance of all sexual offenders to engage effectively in treatment, it seems almost certain that the therapeutic alliance and the therapist's approach to treating these young people will be at least as, and likely more, critical than is true with adult offenders.

In terms of direct evidence, Edelman and Goldstein (1984) reported that delinquent youth responded far better to treatment with therapists they judged to be genuine. Richards and Sullivan (1996) found that juvenile offenders with whom the therapist developed a positive relationship were more likely to complete treatment and to benefit from it, than were delinquents who had a poor relationship with their therapist. Similarly, young offenders are more compliant with treatment requirements and, as a result, more responsive when their relationship with the therapist is strong (Langer, 1999).

In their report of an examination of the therapeutic alliance in the treatment of delinquent boys, Florsheim *et al.* (2000) note that a positive alliance was predictive of changes on the targets of treatment and lower post-discharge reoffending. When the strength of the alliance diminished so did engagement and treatment benefits were accordingly reduced. Diamond *et al.* (2006) made a similar observation in the treatment of substance abusing youth where the strength of the alliance was related to success while a poor alliance increased the rate of non-compliance and predicted the number of youngsters who dropped out of treatment. Interestingly, as we saw with adults, treatment studies with juveniles indicate that ratings of the alliance by therapists and clients typically disagree and it is only the latter that predict treatment effects (Bickman *et al.*, 2004; Diamond *et al.*, 2006; Florsheim *et al.*, 2000).

Turning now to therapist qualities in those who treat juvenile offenders, Alexander *et al.* (1976) found that the qualities described by Andrews and Bonta (2006) as relationship and structuring variables (i.e., their CCPs), were strongly predictive of beneficial outcomes. Alexander *et al.* concluded that it is the therapists' characteristics and style of delivery that makes the most significant contribution to treatment effects. Although as we (Marshall & Burton, 2010) noted, the literature on youth who committed non-sexual offenses is pertinent to considering the influence of treatment delivery factors on juvenile sexual offenders, there are some, but few, relevant studies directly involving this latter group. A number of authors have commented on the particularly strong resistance among juvenile sexual offenders (Jenkins, 1998; Print & O'Callaghan, 2004; Steen & Monnette, 1989) and as a result have recommended the adoption of a motivational approach such as that described by Miller and Rollnick (2002). In the literature on the treatment of adult offenders, a motivational style has been strongly encouraged (see Marshall *et al.*, 2011, for a review).

This motivational approach is contrary to the claim in both the adult sexual offender field (see, Salter, 1988; Wyre, 1989) and in the juvenile sexual offender literature (see Muster, 1992), that it is necessary for therapists to adopt a confrontational style (i.e. an aggressively challenging approach). In studies of the treatment of adult offenders it has been found that such a confrontational style markedly reduces the benefits derived from treatment (Beech & Fordham, 1997; Marshall *et al.*, 2003b), an observation that is echoed in the treatment of various non-offending Axis 1 disorders (DiClemente, 1991; Lieberman *et al.*, 1973).

Finally, Burton and Cerar (2005) have examined characteristics of adolescent sexual offenders that affected the therapeutic alliance. They noted that those young sexual offenders who were submissive, but who scored low on measures of emotional neglect, formed the strongest alliance with their therapists. Examining other forms of trauma such as sexual, physical, and emotional abuse, Burton and Cerar, surprisingly found no relationship between these factors and the alliance, nor did oppositional or unruly behaviors predict the quality of the alliance. Unfortunately Burton and Cerar did not report outcome data so we cannot be sure of the relationship between alliance scores and reduced recidivism.

Conclusions

It is a pity that more attention has not been given to examining therapeutic and group process variables in the treatment of juvenile offenders particularly now that treatment for these youngsters is well established both for non-sexual offenders (Altschuler, 1999; Dowden & Andrews, 2003; Lipsey & Wilson, 1999) and for juveniles who sexually offend (Burton *et al.*, 2006; Rich, 2003). We therefore encourage researchers working with juvenile offenders (both sexual and non-sexual) to focus more research on factors involved in the delivery of treatment to these youngsters. It seems already clear from the limited data available that these factors influence treatment effectiveness with adolescent offenders. This, therefore, represents a field of potential study that is likely to reward researchers and improve the quality and effectiveness of treatment for these troubled youth.

Overall summary

In considering all aspects of our review, we are persuaded that if the following elements are present in offender treatment then significant benefits will be derived:

1   An initial focus in treatment that is motivational and nonconfrontational, and is aimed exclusively at engaging the clients.
2   Targeting known criminogenic factors and minimizing targeting noncriminogenic factors.
3   Delivering treatment is a style consistent with the above research findings; that is, in a warm, empathic, respectful, nonconfrontational, encouraging way that takes into account each client's unique features, while offering some guidance when needed.
4   Creating a group climate that is cohesive and expressive.

It falls to those who conduct reviews or meta-analyses of offender (both sexual and non-sexual) treatment to examine this rather broad-based hypothesis. Our view is that we need to provide treatment for offenders using the same principles we would apply for non-offenders. Correctional and moral judgments inherent in the identification and referral process, when combined with the often disempowering rehabilitative history and methods of clinical work with offenders, serve to create a challenge to using what we have all been trained to use in any good treatment model.

The Rockwood Psychological Services' treatment program for sexual offenders, which is described in detail in our most recent book (Marshall *et al.*, 2011) adheres to these four principles. This program has been independently evaluated over a 8.5 year post-release period by two independent research assistants who were naive about sexual offender recidivism rates. These appraisals revealed a reoffense rate in 535 sexual offenders, who had pre-treatment scores across the full range of risk levels, of 5.6 per cent against an expected rate of 23.8 per cent. We believe these data support our approach and we further believe that the effectiveness of this approach is largely due to the way in which we deliver treatment. As we noted earlier, Dowden and Andrews (2004) lamented the fact that very few offender programs (only 16 per cent) included any concern about the style of delivery or the skills of the therapist, and our reading of the series of Safer Society surveys has led us to conclude that there is a similar lack of attention to these features of treatment delivery with sexual offenders. As a result we strongly encourage researchers to pay more attention to treatment delivery factors in their studies of sexual offender programs. Of course treatment providers should incorporate core clinical practice features into their programs for sexual offenders by ensuring that their therapists (by careful selection and training) have the desired qualities, and therapists should instil the appropriate features of a good, group therapeutic climate. We believe the future of sexual offender treatment, in so far as programs adhere to these crucial elements and address the appropriate targets, will reveal steadily increasing benefits so that one day we will be able to say with confidence that we are significantly contributing to the protection of the public while offering offenders a better life.

References

Alexander, J. F., Barton, C., Schivo, S., and Parson, D. V. (1976). Systems-behavioral intervention with families of delinquents: therapist characteristics, family behavior and outcome. *Journal of Consulting and Clinical Psychology, 44,* 656–664. DOI: 10.1037/0022- 006X.44.4.656.

Altschuler, D. M. (1999). Intermediate sanctions and community treatment for serious and violent juvenile offenders. In R. Loeber and D. P. Farrington (eds), *Serious and Violent Juvenile Offenders: Risk Factors and Successful Interventions* (pp. 367–385). Thousand Oaks, CA: Sage Publications.

Andrews, D. A. and Bonta, J. (2006). *The Psychology of Criminal Conduct* (4th edn). Cincinnati, OH: Anderson Publishing.

Andrews, D. A. and Dowden, C. (1999). A meta-analytic investigation into effective correctional intervention for female offenders. *Forum on Corrections Research, 11,* 18–21.

Andrews, D. A., Zinger, I., Hoge, R. D., Bonta, J., Gendreau, P., and Cullen, F. T. (1990). Does correctional treatment work? A psychologically informed meta-analysis. *Criminology, 28,* 369–404. DOI: 10.1177/1466802505053497.

Babcock, J. C., Green, C. E., and Robie, C. (2004). Does batterers' treatment work? A meta-analytic review of domestic violence treatment. *Clinical Psychology Review, 23,* 1023–1053. DOI: 10.1016/j.cpr.2002.07.001.

Bachelor, A. (1995). Clients' perception of the therapeutic alliance: a qualitative analysis. *Journal of Counseling Psychology, 42,* 323–327.

Baumeister, R. F. (1993). *Self-esteem: The Puzzle of Low Self-regard.* New York: Plenum.

Bednar, R. and Kaul, T. (1994). Experiential group research: can the canon fire? In A. E. Bergen and S. L. Garfield (eds), *Handbook of Psychotherapy and Behavior Change* (pp. 631–663). New York: John Wiley & Sons.

Beech, A. R. and Fordham, A. S. (1997). Therapeutic climate of sexual offender treatment programs. *Sexual Abuse: A Journal of Research and Treatment, 9,* 219–237. DOI: 10.1007/BF02675066

Beech, A. R. and Hamilton-Giachritsis, C. E. (2005). Relationship between therapeutic climate and treatment outcome in a group-based sexual offender program. *Sexual Abuse: A Journal of Research and Treatment, 17,* 127–140. DOI: 10.1007/s11194-005-4600-3.

Bennun, I., Hahlweg, K., Schindler, L., and Langlotz, M. (1986). Therapist's and client's perceptions in behaviour therapy: the development and cross-cultural analysis of an assessment instrument. *British Journal of Clinical Psychology, 27,* 145–150.

Berg, D. R. (1999). *An Examination of the Relationship between Process Variables and Outcome Indicators in the Therapeutic Use of Play with Children.* Unpublished doctoral dissertation, University of Illinois at Urbana-Champaign.

Bickman, L., de Andrade, A.., Lambert, E., Doucette, A., Sapyta, J., Boyd, A., Rumberger, D., Moore-Kurnot, J., McDonough, L., and Rauktis, M. (2004). Youth therapeutic alliance in intensive treatment settings. *The Journal of Behavioral Health Services and Research, 31,* 134–148. DOI: 10.1007/BF02287377.

Braaten, L. J. (1989). Predicting positive goal attainment and symptom reduction from early group climate dimensions. *International Journal of Group Psychotherapy, 39,* 377–387.

Briere, J. (1997). Etiology of posttraumatic states. In J. Briere (ed.), *Psychological Assessment of Adult Posttraumatic States* (pp. 1–23). Washington, DC: American Psychological Association.

Budman, S. H., Soldz, S., Demby, A., Davis, M., and Merry, J. (1993). What is cohesiveness? An empirical examination. *Small Group Research, 24,* 199–216. DOI: 10.1177/1046496493242003.

Burton, D. L. (2000). Were adolescent sexual offenders children with sexual behavioral problems? *Sexual Abuse: A Journal of Research and Treatment, 12,* 37–47. Doi: 10.1023/A:1009511804302.

Burton, D. L. (2003). Male adolescents: sexual victimization and subsequent sexual abuse. *Child and Adolescent Social Work Journal, 20,* 227–296. Doi: 10.1023/A:1024556909087.

Burton, D. L. and Cerar, K. (2005). *How Do the MACI and the Childhood Trauma Questionnaire Predict Youth Perception of the Helping Alliance after Controlling for Time in Treatment?* A workshop for the National Association for the Treatment of Sexual Abusers Conference in Salt Lake City, Utah, 17 November.

Burton, D. L. and Smith-Darden, J. (2001). *North American Survey of Sexual Abuser Treatment and Models: Summary Data 2000.* Brandon, VT: Safer Society Press.

Burton, D. L., Smith-Darden, J., and Frankel, S. J. (2006). Research on adolescent sexual abuser treatment programs. In H. E. Barbaree and W. L. Marshall (eds), *The Juvenile Sex Offender* (pp. 291–312). New York: Guilford Press.

Cohen, J. (1988). *Statistical Power Analysis for the Behavioural Sciences.* Hillsdale, NJ: Erlbaum.

Cooley, E. J. and LaJoy, R. (1980). Therapeutic relationship and improvements as perceived by clients and therapists. *Journal of Clinical Psychology, 36,* 562–570.

Diamond, G., Liddle, H., Wintersteen, M., Dennis, M., Godley, S., and Tims, F. (2006). Early therapeutic alliance as a predictor of treatment outcome for adolescent cannabis users in outpatient treatment. *The American Journal of Addiction, 15,* 26–33. DOI: 10.1080/10550490601003664.

DiClemente, C. C. (1991). Motivational interviewing and the stages of change. In W. R. Miller & S. Rollnick (eds), *Motivational Interviewing: Preparing People to Change Addictive Behavior* (pp. 191–202). New York: Guilford Press.

DiGiuseppe, R., Linscott, J., and Hilton, R. (1996). Developing the therapeutic alliance in child-adolescent psychotherapy. *Applied & Preventive Psychology, 5,* 85–100.

Dowden, C. and Andrews, D. A. (2000). Effective correctional treatment and violent recidivism: a meta-analysis. *Canadian Journal of Criminology, 42,* 449–476.

Dowden, C. and Andrews, D. A. (2003). Does family intervention work for delinquents? Results of a meta-analysis. *Canadian Journal of Criminology and Criminal Justice, 45,* 327–342.

Dowden, C. and Andrews, D. A. (2004). The importance of staff practice in delivering effective correctional treatment: a meta-analysis. *International Journal of Offender Therapy and Comparative Criminology, 48,* 203–214. DOI: 10.1177/0306624X03257765.

Dowden, C., Antonowicz, D., and Andrews, D. A. (2003). The effectiveness of relapse prevention with offenders: a meta-analysis. *International Journal of Offender Therapy and Comparative Criminology,* 47, 516–528. DOI: 10.1177/0306624X03253018.

Drapeau, M. (2005). Research on the processes involved in treating sexual offenders. *Sexual Abuse: A Journal of Research and Treatment, 17,* 117–125. DOI: 10.1177/107906320501700203.

Drapeau, M., Korner, C. A., Brunet, L., and Granger, L. (2004) Treatment at La Macaza Clinic: a qualitative study of the sexual offenders' perspective. *Canadian Journal of Criminology and Criminal Justice, 46,* 27–44.

Edelman, E. and Goldstein, A. (1984). Prescriptive relationship levels for juvenile delinquents in a psychotherapy analog. *Aggressive Behavior 10,* 269–278. DOI: 0.1002/1098-2337.

Eltz, M. J., Shirk, S. R., and Sarlin, N. (2005). Alliance formation and treatment outcome among maltreated adolescents. *Child Abuse & Neglect, 19,* 419–431.

Eysenck, H. J. (1969). *Behaviour Therapy and the Neuroses.* Oxford: Pergamon Press.

Eysenck, H. J. and Rachman, S. (1965). *The Causes and Cures of Neurosis.* London: Routledge and Kegan Paul.

Fisher, A. (2008). *Revisioning Male Violence: Men of Courage.* Paper presented at the First Provincial Conference on Male Sexual Victimization, Toronto, Canada.

Florsheim, P., Shotorbani, S., Guest-Warnick, G., Barret, T., and Hwang, W. (2000). Role of working alliance in the treatment of delinquent boys in community based programs. *Journal of Clinical Child Psychology, 29,* 94–107. DOI: 10.1207/S15374424jccp 2901_10.

Frank, J. D. (1971). Therapeutic factors in psychotherapy. *American Journal of Psychotherapy, 25,* 350–361.

Frankl, V. E. (1978). *The Unheard Cry for Meaning: Psychotherapy and Humanism.* New York: Simon & Schuster.

Free, N. K., Green, B. L., Grace, M. D., Chernus, L. A., and Whitman, R. M. (1985). Empathy and outcome in brief, focal dynamic therapy. *American Journal of Psychiatry, 142,* 917–921.

Hanson, R. K., Bourgon, G., Helmus, L., and Hodgson, S. (2009). The principles of effective correctional treatment also apply to sexual offenders: a meta-analysis. *Criminal Justice and Behavior, 36,* 865–981. DOI: 10.1177/0093854809338545.

Hanson, R. K., Gordon, A., Harris, A. J. R., Marques, J. K., Murphy, W., Quinsey, V. L., and Seto, M. C. (2002). First report of the collaborative outcome data project on the effectiveness of psychological treatment for sex offenders. *Sexual Abuse: A Journal of Research and Treatment, 14,* 167–192. DOI: 10.1023/A:1014624315814.

Heppner, P. P. and Clairborn, C. D. (1989). Social influence research in counseling: a review and critique. *Journal of Counseling Psychology, 36,* 365–387. DOI: 10.1037/0022-0167.36.3.365.

Hill, J., Andrews, D. A., and Hoge, R. D. (1991). Meta-analysis of treatment programs for young offenders: The effect of clinically relevant treatment on recidivism with controls for various methodological variables. *Canadian Journal of Program Evaluation, 6,* 97–109.

Horvath, A. O. (2000). The therapeutic relationship: from transference to alliance. *Journal of Counseling Psychology/In Session: Psychotherapy in Practice, 56,* 163–173.

Jenkins, A. (1998). Invitations to responsibility: engaging adolescents and young men who have sexually abused. In W. L. Marshall, Y. M. Fernandez, S. M. Hudson and T. Ward (eds), *Sourcebook of Treatment Programs for Sexual Offenders* (pp. 163–189). New York: Plenum Press.

Karterud, S. (1988). The influence of task definition, leadership and therapeutic style on inpatient group cultures. *International Journal of Therapeutic Communities, 9,* 231–247.

Karver, M. S., Handelsman, J. B., Fields, S., and Bickman, L. (2006). Meta-analysis of therapeutic relationship variables in youth and family therapy: the evidence for different relationship variables in the child and adolescent treatment outcome literature. *Clinical Psychology Review, 26,* 50–65. DOI: 10.1016/j.cpr.2005.09.001.

Kazdin, A. E. (1978). *History of Behavior Modification: Experimental Foundations of Contemporary Research.* Baltimore: University Park Press.

Klein, M. H., Mathieu-Coughlan, P., and Kiesler, D. (1986). The experiencing scales. In L. S. Greenberg and W. Pinsoff (eds), *The Psychotherapeutic Process: A Research Handbook* (pp. 21–71). New York: Guilford Press.

Langer, N. (1999). Culturally competent professionals in therapeutic alliances enhance patient compliance. *Journal of Health Care for the Poor and Underserved, 10,* 19–26.

Levenson, J. S., Macgowan, M. J., Morin, J. W., and Cotter, L. P. (2009). Perceptions of sex offenders about treatment: satisfaction and engagement in group therapy. *Sexual Abuse: A Journal of Research and Treatment, 21,* 35–36. DOI: 10.1177/1079063208326072.

Levenson, J. S., Prescott, D. S., and D'Amora, D. A. (2010). Sex offender treatment: consumer satisfaction and engagement in therapy. *International Journal of Offender Therapy and Comparative Criminology, 54,* 307–326. DOI: 10.1177/0306624X08328752.

Lieberman, M. A., Yalom, I. D., and Miles, M. K. (1973). *Encounter Groups: First Facts.* New York: Basic Books.

Lipsey, M. W. and Wilson, D. B. (1999). Effective intervention for serious juvenile offenders. In R. Loeber and D. P. Farrington (eds), *Serious & Violent Juvenile Offenders: Risk Factors and Successful Interventions* (pp. 313–345). Thousand Oaks, CA: Sage Publications.

Loeber, R. and Farrington, D. P. (1999). *Serious & Violent Juvenile Offenders: Risk Factors and Successful Interventions.* Thousand Oaks, CA: Sage Publications.

Lösel, F. and Schmucker, M. (2005). The effectiveness of treatment for sexual offenders: a comprehensive meta-analysis. *Journal of Experimental Criminology, 1,* 117–146. DOI: 10.1007/s11292-004-6466-7.

Marshall, W. L. (2009) Manualization: a blessing or a curse? *Journal of Sexual Aggression, 15,* 109–120. DOI: 10.1080/13552600902907320.

Marshall, W. L. and Burton, D. L. (2010). The importance of therapeutic processes in offender treatment. *Aggression and Violent Behavior: A Review Journal, 15,* 141–149. DOI: 10.1016/j.avb.2009.08.008.

Marshall, L. E. & Marshall, W. L. (2012). The risk/needs/responsivity model: The crucial features of general responsivity. In E. Bowen & S. Brown (Eds) Perspectives on evaluating criminal justice and corrections. (pp 29–45) Bingley, UK: Emerald Publising.

Marshall, W. L. and McGuire, J. (2003) Effect sizes in treatment of sexual offenders. *International Journal of Offender Therapy and Comparative Criminology, 46,* 653–663. DOI: 10.1177/0306624X03256663.

Marshall, W. L., Fernandez, Y. M., Serran, G. A., Mulloy, R., Thornton, D., Mann, R. E., and Anderson, D. (2003a). Process variables in the treatment of sexual offenders: a review of the relevant literature. *Aggression and Violent Behavior, 8,* 205–234. DOI: 10.1016/S1359-1789(01)00065-9.

Marshall, W. L., Marshall, L. E., Serran, G. A., and O'Brien, M. D. (2011). *Rehabilitating Sexual Offenders: A Strength-based Approach.* Washington, DC: American Psychological Association.

Marshall, W. L., O'Brien, M.D., and Marshall, L.E. (2009). Modifying sexual preferences. In A. R. Beech, L. A. Craig and K. D. Browne (eds) *Assessment and Treatment of Sexual Offenders: A Handbook* (pp. 311–327). Chichester, UK: John Wiley & Sons.

Marshall, W. L., Serran, G. A., Fernandez, Y. M., Mulloy, R., Mann, R. E., and Thornton, D. (2003b). Therapist characteristics in the treatment of sexual offenders: tentative data on their relationship with indices of behavior change. *Journal of Sexual Aggression, 9,* 25–30. DOI: 10.1080/355260031000137940.

Marshall, W. L., Serran, G. A., Moulden, H., Mulloy, R., Fernandez, Y. M., Mann, R. E., and Thornton, D. (2002). Therapist features in sexual offender treatment: their reliable identification and influence on behavior change. *Clinical Psychology and Psychotherapy, 9,* 395–405. DOI: 0.1002/cpp.335.

Martin, D. J., Garske, J. P., and Davis, M. K. (2000). Relation of the therapeutic alliance with outcome and other variables: a meta-analytic review. *Journal of Consulting and Clinical Psychology, 68,* 438–450. DOI: 10.1037/0022-006X.68.3.438.

McGrath, R. J., Cumming, G. F., and Buchard, B. L. (2003). *Current Practices and Trends in Sexual Abuser Management: Safer Society 2002 Nationwide Survey.* Brandon, VT: Safer Society Press.

McGrath, R. J., Cumming, G. R., Buchard, B. L., Zeoli, S., and Ellerby, L. (2010). *Current Practices and Emerging Trends in Sexual Abuser Management.* Brandon, VT: Safer Society Press.

McMakin, R. A., Leisen, M., Cusack, J. F., LaFratta, J., and Litwin, P. (2002). The relationship of trauma exposure to sex offending behavior among male juvenile offenders. *Journal of Child Sexual Abuse, 11,* 25–40. DOI: 10.1300/J070v11n02_02.

McRoberts, C., Burlingame, G. M., and Hoag, M. J. (1998). Comparative efficacy of individual and group psychotherapy: a meta-analytic perspective. *Group Dynamics: Theory, Research and Practice, 2,* 101–117. DOI: 10.1037/1089-2699.2.2.101.

Miller, W. R. and Rollnick, S. (2002). *Motivational Interviewing: Preparing People for Change* (2nd edn). New York: Guilford Publishing.

Miller, W. R. and Sovereign, R. G. (1989). The check-up: a model for early interventions in addictive behaviors. In T. Loberg, W. R. Miller, P. E. Nathan, and G. M. Marlatt (eds), *Addictive Behaviors: Prevention and Early Interventions* (pp. 219–231). Amsterdam: Swets & Zeitlinger.

Morgan, R., Luborsky, L., Crits-Christoph, P., Curtis, H., and Solomon, J. (1982). Predicting outcomes of psychotherapy by the Penn Helping Alliance Rating Method. *Archives of General Psychiatry, 39,* 397–402.

Muster, N. (1992). Treating the adolescent victim turned offender. *Adolescence, 27,* 441–450.

Newman, E. (2002). Assessment of PTSD and trauma exposure in adolescents. *Journal of Aggression, Maltreatment and Trauma, 6,* 59–77. DOI: 10.1300/J146v06n01_04.

Norcross, J. C. (2002). Empirically supported therapy relationships. In J. C. Norcross (ed.), *Psychotherapy Relationships that Work: Therapist Contributions and Responsiveness to Patient Needs* (pp. 1–10). New York: Oxford University Press.

Orlinsky, D. E. and Howard, K. I. (1986). Process and outcome in psychotherapy. In S. L. Garfield and A. E. Bergin (eds), *Handbook of Psychotherapy and Behavior Change* (3rd edn) (pp. 311–384). New York: John Wiley & Sons.

Orlinsky, D. E., Grawe, K., and Parks, B. K., (1994). Process and outcome in psychotherapy – noch einmal. In A. E. Garfield and S. L. Garfield (eds), *Handbook of Psychotherapy and Behavior Change* (4th edn) (pp. 270–376). New York: John Wiley & Sons.

Pence, E. and Paymer, M. (1993). *Education Groups for Men who Batter: The Duluth Model.* New York: Springer.

Pfäfflin, F., Böhmer, M., Cornehl, S., and Mergenthaler, F. (2005). What happens in therapy with sexual offenders? A model of process research. *Sexual Abuse: A Journal of Research and Treatment, 17,* 141–151. DOI: 10.1007/s11194-005-4601-2.

Print, B. and O'Callaghan, D. (2004). Essentials of an effective treatment programme for sexually abusive adolescents: offence specific treatments. In G. O'Reilly, W. L. Marshall, A. Carr, and R. Beckett (eds), *The Handbook of Clinical Interventions with Young People who Sexually Abuse* (pp. 237–274). New York: Psychology Press.

Rich, P. (2003). *Understanding Juvenile Sexual Offenders: Assessment, Treatment, and Rehabilitation.* New York: John Wiley & Sons.

Richards, I. and Sullivan, A. (1996). Psychotherapy for delinquents? *Adolescence 19,* 63–73. DOI: 10.1006/jado.1996.0006.

Rogers, C. R. (1957). The necessary and sufficient conditions of therapeutic personality change. *Journal of Consulting Psychology, 21,* 95–103. DOI: 10.1037/h0045357.

Rogers, C. R. (1961). *On Becoming a Person.* Boston: Houghton Mifflin.

Rosnow, R. L. and Rosenthal, R. (1988). Focused tests of significance and effect size estimation in counselling psychology. *Journal of Counseling Psychology, 35,* 203–208.

Salter, A. G. (1988). *Treating Child Sex Offenders and Victims: A Practical Guide.* Thousand Oaks, CA: Sage Publications.

Saunders, M. (1999). Clients' assessments of the affective environment of the psycho-therapy session: relationship to session quality and treatment effectiveness. *Journal of Clinical Psychology, 55,* 597–605. DOI: 10.1002/(SICI)1097-4679(199905)55:5<597.

Schaap, C., Bennun, I., Schindler, L., and Hoogduin, K. (1993). *The Therapeutic Relationship in Behavioural Psychotherapy.* Chichester, UK: John Wiley & Sons.

Schaeffer, C. M. and Borduin, C. M. (2005). Long-term follow-up to a randomized clinical trial of Multisystemic Therapy with serious and violent juvenile offenders. *Journal of Consulting and Clinical Psychology, 73,* 445–453. DOI:10.1037/0022-006X.73.3.445.

Shirk, S. and Russell, R. (1996) *Change Processes In Child Psychotherapy: Revitalizing Treatment And Research.* New York: Guilford Press.

Steen, C. and Monnette, B. (1989). *Treating Adolescent Sex Offenders in the Community.* Springfield, IL: Thomas Books.

Sterba, R. (1934). The fate of the ego in analytic therapy. *International Journal of Psychoanalysis. 15,* 117–126.

Truax, B. B. and Carkjuff, R. R. (1967). *Toward Effective Counseling and Psychotherapy.* Hawthorne, NY: Aldine.

Watkins, B. and Bentovim, A. (1992). The sexual abuse of male children and adolescents: a review of the current research. *Journal of Child Psychology and Psychiatry, 33,* 197–248. DOI: 10.1111/j.1469-7610.1992.tb00862.x.

Wilson, G. T. and Evans, I. M. (1976). Adult behavior therapy and the therapist-client relationship. In C. M. Franks and G. T. Wilson (eds), *Annual Review of Behavior Therapy* (vol. 4, pp. 771–792). New York: Burnner/Mazel.

Wolpaw, J. M., Ford, J. D. Newman, E., Davis, J. L., and Briere, J. (2005). Trauma symptom checklist for children. In T. Grisso, G. Vincent, and D. Segrave (eds), *Mental Health Screen and Assessment in Juvenile Justice.* New York: Guilford.

Wyre, R. (1989). Working with the paedophile. In M. Farrell (ed.), *Understanding the Paedophile* (pp. 17–23). London: ISTD/The Portman Clinic.

Yalom, I. D. (1995). *The Theory and Practice of Group Psychotherapy* (4th edn). New York: Basic Books.

Zetzel, E. (1956). Current concepts of transference. *International Journal of Psycho Analysis, 37,* 369–376.

9 Should group membership be considered for treatment to be effective?

Jo Thakker, University of Waikato, New Zealand

This chapter explores the question of whether the groups that offenders belong to need to be taken into consideration in order for treatment to be effective. For example, if an offender is Maori, is treatment likely to be more effective for that offender if it is tailored to the needs of Maori? And if an offender is religious, should treatment incorporate the offender's particular religious perspective? Along with an investigation into ethnic and religious groups, this chapter discusses the significance of group identification (defined below) in the context of group treatment.

The chapter begins by describing two pertinent rehabilitation models that direct and guide treatment for offenders. The chapter then examines the importance of group identification – using various examples – as a factor in offender therapy. Following this, the potential role of therapist stereotypes regarding group membership is explored in relation to group treatment. Finally, cultural factors as well as religion and spirituality are discussed in relation to treatment effectiveness before final summaries, conclusions, and areas for future treatment progression are suggested.

Given the paucity of literature available on the topic of group membership in relation to offender treatment, a very broad approach has been taken, including relevant research from the mental health field. Readers will also observe that studies of sexual offenders are more prominent in this chapter than studies of other offender groups. This is simply a reflection of the preponderance of literature associated with sexual offender treatment compared to other types of offence treatments. This is especially true in regard to the delivery of group treatment approaches. Furthermore, research from New Zealand (where the author is situated) will be used to highlight culture-based treatment approaches of key significance.

Key offending behavior rehabilitation models

In order to gain an understanding of the significance of the factors associated with group membership it is important to consider how such factors relate to overarching rehabilitation models. Perhaps the most relevant is the Risk Need Responsivity (RNR) model (Andrews & Bonta, 1998; 2003). As indicated by the name, the RNR model has three main components. The *risk* component refers to the level of risk that the offender poses and the requirement for treatment intensity to match risk level. The *need* component refers to treatment needs and the requirement that treatment should target those needs that are empirically linked with offending behavior. Thus, needs in this sense refer to dynamic risk factors which are essentially the key stable psychological factors theorized to contribute to offending. Finally, the *responsivity principle* refers to the treatment approach taken. This should be appropriate for the offender's particular characteristics (i.e. learning style, level of motivation, and personal qualities). In other words, this principle is concerned with enhancing the likelihood that treatment will bring about a positive response in the individual whom the intervention is targeted towards.

The RNR model has been very influential within the field of offender treatment generally and has 'constituted a revolution in the way that criminal conduct is managed in Canada, Britain, Europe, Australia, and New Zealand' (Ward *et al.*, 2008: 180). Perhaps the strongest aspect of the model is its practical application insofar as it provides a clear and comprehensive guide to the implementation of treatment. For example, it assists in prioritizing treatment needs and in deciding what sort of treatment is appropriate for a particular offender. In terms of this chapter, it is the responsivity principle that is most relevant. In other words, the primary concern of this chapter is with the aspects of group membership that are likely to impact on treatment responsivity.

Another relevant rehabilitation model is the Good Lives Model (GLM) developed by Ward and colleagues (e.g. Ward & Stewart, 2003; Ward & Gannon, 2006). The GLM has been used to explore the question of why sexual offenders find offending behavior rewarding. Put succinctly, towards the aim of addressing offenders' risk factors, the GLM examines the gap or need in the offender's life that offences appear to be filling and attempts to enable the offender to fill such gaps in more pro-social ways. The GLM centers on the idea that all human activity is aimed at obtaining particular human experiences or 'primary human goods'. When such needs are met in an individual, then it can be said that the individual has a 'good' life; that is, a life characterized by fundamental benefits such as sexual intimacy, friendship, physical health, autonomy, community connectedness, and creativity.

Ward distinguishes secondary goods from the more basic primary human goods that effectively meet needs. Here, secondary goods refer to ways and means of acquiring primary human goods. For example, if happiness is a primary human good then anything that is instrumental in enhancing one's happiness would be a secondary good. Drawing on work from a range of areas, including evolutionary theory, ethics, and anthropology, Ward and Stewart (2003) propose that there are at least 10 primary human goods. These are described as follows:

> Life (including healthy living and functioning), knowledge, excellence in play and work (including mastery experiences), excellence in agency (i.e., autonomy and self-directedness), inner peace (i.e., freedom from emotional turmoil and stress), friendship (including intimate, romantic and family

relationships), community, spirituality (in the broad sense of finding meaning and purpose in life), happiness, and creativity.

(Ward & Stewart, 2003: 356)

According to Ward (2002), offenders, like all human beings, need and value primary human goods and seek to acquire them. However, for a variety of reasons (e.g. inadequate internal skills or external resources) the way that they attempt to acquire them is problematic. For example, a sexual offender who finds it hard to socially engage with adults may seek to fulfill his need for intimacy by engaging in sexual activity with a child. Alternatively, a drug dealer who has experienced few opportunities for personal pro-social development may experience a sense of mastery in his ability to run a successful methamphetamine business. A GLM approach to treatment seeks to furnish individuals with the internal and external conditions necessary to implement and lead a good life which is both realistic and pro-social.

There are a number of aspects of the GLM relevant to this chapter. Perhaps most pertinent is the inherent human need to seek the primary human goods of community and spirituality as these are central to an individual's identity and his or her sense of belonging. In this chapter, then, offenders' various group memberships – which are likely to be associated with community and spirituality – and the possible effects of such membership on various aspects of treatment will be explored and discussed.

Treatment and group identification

One important aspect of group membership is the offender's sense of belonging to the group in the context of group therapy; referred to herein as *group identification*. This term is used in preference to the concepts of group climate and cohesion as these refer to more general group processes. Nonetheless, these concepts do inevitably overlap and interact with the concept of group identification. A key question is whether group identification is essential to effective group-based treatment. However, this specific issue is somewhat difficult to address given the lack of research specifically targeting this issue and so extrapolations must be made from other relevant literatures (e.g. general mental health or offender treatment group climate work).

Research examining general mental health indicates that group identification contributes to treatment efficacy (Fishbach *et al.*, 2011). This may be associated with the phenomenon of general in-group effects in which human beings naturally define themselves in terms of their identification and shared experiences with their in-group (e.g. Brewer, 2007; Sani *et al*, 2010). Thus, it may be hypothesized that group treatment is effective, at least in part, because it mimics a real world setting and utilizes an individual's tendency to identify with people who they see on a regular basis and with whom they have shared experiences.

Reimer and Mathieu (2006) explored the therapeutic factors that sexual offenders identified as being important in terms of the effectiveness of group therapy. They used the 12 therapeutic factors that were listed and described by Yalom (1995), namely: instillation of hope, guidance, catharsis, interpersonal learning (output), cohesion, self-understanding, interpersonal learning (input), altruism, existentialism, family re-enactment, identification, and universality. Results showed that cohesion – which was defined as: 'the group helps me because it is good to belong to a group of people that is together and cares about each person in the group' (Reimer & Mathieu, 2006: 61) – was ranked third out of the 12 items. Thus, group identification was viewed as highly important to the offenders who took part in the treatment. Similar findings have been reported by Levenson, Macgowan, Morin, and Cotter (2009) who found that a feeling of acceptance and a 'sense of belonging' within the group facilitated the development of generalizable relationship skills.

As already noted, the concept of group identification overlaps somewhat with cohesiveness and expressiveness (see Marshall *et al.*, Chapter 8). As explained by Marshall *et al.*, *cohesiveness* refers to the extent participants bond within the group and work together while *expressiveness* refers to the extent to which group members feel comfortable expressing and discussing their thoughts and feelings within the group setting. It may be hypothesized that group identification plays a key role in both cohesiveness and expressiveness. That is, if participants identify with the group then cohesiveness will be enhanced and they will be more expressive during sessions. Interestingly, research has found that high levels of cohesion within treatment groups contributes to a reduction in antisocial beliefs (Levenson *et al.*, 2010) and to general treatment gains (Beech & Hamilton-Giachritsis, 2005; Marshall & Burton, 2010).

Perusal of relevant literature shows that sexual offenders can often be overwhelmingly positive in their comments about group therapy. One study (by Garrett *et al.*, 2003), which is fairly representative of the general findings, reported that 93.7 per cent of the group members surveyed (total $N = 32$), described their experiences in group treatment as 'fairly positive' or 'extremely positive.' Furthermore, the study found that 90.6 per cent of offenders stated that they 'got on with other group members' 'reasonably well' or 'extremely well.' Thus, the idea that a strong sense of group identification could be therapeutic – either by itself or by its relationship with cohesiveness and expressiveness – and contribute to a reduction in sexual recidivism certainly has face validity. Arguably, if an offender feels that he belongs in the group then he will be more likely to participate and to express his thoughts and feelings; thus, responsivity, and thereby treatment efficacy would be enhanced.

Identification with offender groups

Another important question with regard to group identification is the extent to which offenders tend to identify with the particular group of offenders that they belong to, and whether, such identification impacts upon treatment. For example, in terms of the RNR model, identification with one's own offending group could represent a potential risk factor or need that should be targeted in therapy. For example, child sexual offenders may experience feelings of belonging to a group of individuals who commit similar crimes. Such identification might be particularly strong among those who communicate with, and send images to each other, such as users of child pornography websites. In fact, several researchers have proposed that identification with an offender group may be associated with particular offence-related cognitive distortions (e.g. Elliot & Beech, 2009; Taylor Quayle, 2003). Thus, offenders may form strong justificatory beliefs – a risk factor or need that should be targeted in therapy – that their behavior is normal because large numbers of other people are engaged in similar activities. Ward's (2009) extended mind theory of cognitive distortions in sexual offenders is relevant here. According to Ward, the extended mind theory posits that although the human mind has its seat in the brain and its neurological processes, 'cognitive systems ... extend into the physical and social world' (p. 253). Thus, interactions with others are seen as highly significant in terms of the development of one's attitudes and beliefs. More specifically, antisocial attitudes are seen as being embedded in a social network. As such, a therapist will need to adapt their communications and treatment styles (i.e. responsivity) with such individuals who identify highly with other antisocial individuals in order to ensure that clients do not disengage from treatment.

Research has shown that there is a strong connection between early antisocial behavior and on-going offending across the lifespan (Moffitt *et al.*, 2002). Thus, those who begin offending at a young age (and thereby, at the time that their sense of self is still developing) are more likely to continue offending into adulthood. Also, research has shown a strong connection between the presence of antisocial beliefs and recidivism (Thakker & Ward, 2011; Witte *et al.*, 2006) thus it may be reasoned that beliefs that conceptualize the self as an antisocial individual probably play an important role in antisocial behavior and represent a need to be targeted in treatment. It is also possible that these sorts of – what might be termed – career criminals, see themselves as belonging to the criminal fraternity and that, in this sense, their criminal behavior has become part of their personal identity. If this is the case then it is important to determine this in treatment so that an alternative sense of self can be established. For instance, if an offender identifies strongly with his or her offender group then ceasing offending may mean finding an alternative sense of identity and belonging and this, naturally, would be fundamental to the long term success of the intervention. This idea is consistent with the philosophy of the GLM which suggests that the success of offender treatment depends, at least in part, on providing the offender with an alternative sense of meaning and purpose. Further, there is a similarity here with the work of Maruna (e.g. Maruna & Roy, 2007) who discusses the importance of reinvention of the self in desistance from offending.

Thus, it is reasoned that some offenders may identify strongly with their general antisocial behavior or a particular type of crime. In such instances it would be important in treatment to assist the offender in developing an alternative sense of meaning, purpose, and belonging. The point here, which Ward has often emphasized, is that if an activity, which an offender has found rewarding, is removed then this activity needs to be replaced with something that is equally rewarding so that gains made in treatment will be more likely to be maintained over time.

Therapist's perceptions of offender groups

An offender's group identification may also impact upon therapy in other interesting ways. For example, therapists may respond to offenders differently depending on the offender group the offender belongs to. This of course is essentially an issue of stereotyping insofar as the group member may be perceived as necessarily having the characteristics that are generally ascribed to that group. According to the online Oxford English Dictionary a stereotype is 'a widely held but fixed and oversimplified image or idea of a particular type of person or thing' (Oxford English Dictionary, 2011). Stereotyping has been shown to be a natural human tendency that is probably related to the phenomenon described earlier, of defining oneself in terms of in-groups and out-groups (Brewer, 2007).

Collins and Nee (2010) explored this issue as part of a study of the various factors that influence the therapeutic process in the treatment of sexual offenders. They found that therapists tended to pigeonhole offenders depending on the type of sexual offence that had been committed. For example, one therapist expressed the view that rapists generally had problems with anger while sexual offenders held particular difficulties with social interaction. Furthermore, the study found that these sorts of classifications had an impact on the therapists' approach to treatment. For instance, one therapist suggested that while direct challenging was often constructive in working with rapists, a more subtle approach would be more effective in engaging with child sexual offenders.

This highlights the complexity of the issue of group membership in treatment. Not only is the *actual* group (of the individual) important, but also the therapists' perceptions of what constitutes that group. Although therapists are trained to avoid stereotyping in their work, given that it is a natural human tendency, it is probably impossible to eradicate it within a therapeutic context. However, one would imagine that trained therapists would be less likely to endorse and utilize offender stereotypes than lay people since they are able to interact with offenders and therefore gather real-life information about them, which is likely to challenge stereotypes. Indeed, this is consistent with research conducted by Sanghara and Wilson (2006) who found that individuals experienced in providing child sexual offender treatment were less likely to endorse negative stereotypes relating to child sexual offenders than those who had no or limited experience.

The issue of therapists' use of stereotypes obviously goes beyond the question of offender categories. Other stereotypes are also likely to be relevant, such as those that pertain to ethnicity, age, and religion. The literature in this area suggests that it is essential that therapists are aware of their use of stereotypes and make efforts to limit their impact on their clinical practice. In his discussion on working with clients from diverse cultural backgrounds, Baird (2005) emphasizes the importance of understanding one's own biases and prejudices and suggests that 'if one is to work with diverse clients, it is essential to be aware of personal biases and work to understand and overcome them' (p. 95). Thus, according to this view, self-awareness, especially of one's attitudes and beliefs in regard to those from diverse cultural backgrounds, is crucial to working effectively with those from such backgrounds.

It is understandable that therapists may have a tendency to perceive offenders as belonging to particular offender groups as research has found general differences between types of offenders. For example, research suggests that rapists and violent offenders have a tendency to have been intoxicated with alcohol at the time of the offence (Gudjonsson & Sigurdsson, 2000) and that child sexual offenders often have attachment difficulties (Marshall, 2010). However, it is important that these sorts of perceptions do not prevent the therapist from seeing the offender as an individual with unique motivations and needs.

Cultural factors in treatment

The discussion now turns to the issue of cultural factors in treatment. Given the limited literature available on this topic in the offender field, this section begins by examining relevant research from the mental health field.

Mental health

Within the mental health field, culture-sensitive treatment approaches have been used extensively due to a general understanding of the importance of culture in the manifestation of mental health difficulties. Evidence suggests that some disorders – culture-bound syndromes – occur only in certain populations while other more ubiquitous disorders may present differently in various cultural groups (Thakker & Ward, 1998). Thus, it makes sense to take an individual's cultural group into consideration in the delivery of psychological treatment. One particularly important difference between many Western and non-Western cultures is that the former tend to place a high value on individualism while the latter tend to emphasize the importance of the family (Aycicegi-Dinn & Caldwell-Harris, 2011; Le & Stockdale, 2005). For example, in many Asian cultures an individual's sense of identity is intimately connected with his or her family (Liu & Goto, 2007). In terms of the delivery of mental health treatment, this difference is crucial and pertinent because evidence indicates that the presence of social support plays an important role in people's recovery from mental illness (Hendryx *et al.*, 2009).

In discussing treatment approaches in the context of aboriginal people of North America, Green (2010) argues that consideration of cultural background is essential. In making her case, Green states that people's conceptualizations of health and wellbeing are embedded in cultural attitudes and beliefs and that therapy will be more effective if it is able to acknowledge and integrate culture-specific understandings. Green proposes that: 'At a minimum, health care providers of Aboriginal populations should identify the indigenous culture-specific concepts of care and disease, the attitudes toward health and healing, and the views regarding prevention and treatment' (2010: 33).

Duarté-Vélez, Bernal, and Bonilla (2010) presented a case study of a culture-sensitive approach to the treatment of depression in a Latino adolescent. The young man was treated with a cognitive behavioral intervention which was adapted to address his 'values, preferences, and context' (p. 895). While the intervention had a strong cultural focus, it also acknowledged the young man's gender identity, sexual orientation, and his religion. Thus, the treatment approach attempted to include the various groups that he identified with. Duarté-Vélez and colleagues found that the treatment was effective and they concluded that 'the therapist's expertise and skill in handling spiritual, family, and sexual minority issues … contributed to a positive outcome' (p. 904).

Offending behavior

As evidenced in the discussion that follows, in recent years, there has been increasing interest in the role of culture in the treatment of offenders. According to the RNR model this is an important responsivity issue as ideally treatment should be relevant and culturally appropriate. Also, according to the GLM, treatment should assist offenders in strengthening their sense of identity, connecting with their communities, and finding a sense of meaning and purpose; all of which are associated with offenders' cultural understandings.

Several programs in different parts of the world have begun to include culture-focused components. Many of these programs are designed to cater more directly to the needs of minority groups which are not always met by purely Western-based treatment approaches. Hackett (2000) suggests that failure to acknowledge the specific needs of minority groups in sexual offender treatment is a form of oppression. Accordingly, he states that 'it is important to use intervention strategies and methods that take into account abusers' own life experiences and are respectful of their individuality' (p. 4). He also proposes that it is 'not possible to counter the oppression of sexual abuse with responses which are in themselves oppressive' (p. 4).

Hackett's approach, which he terms *anti-oppressive practice,* involves incorporation of the offender's *cultural meanings* and acknowledgment of any experiences of oppression. However, this is conducted without allowing the offender to use such experiences as an excuse for his/her offending. The model also emphasizes the importance of therapist sensitivity to the offender's individuality and specific needs that arise from this. One of Hackett's key points is that sexual offending behavior may be associated with experiences of oppression and thus it is important not to continue to oppress during treatment because this would serve to minimize and counteract treatment gains.

A recent study (Cunningham *et al.*, 2010) examined the use of a culture-sensitive treatment approach for adolescent offenders. According to the authors, the approach was a response to the realization that the United States is becoming increasingly multi-cultural while treatment approaches have not kept pace with the increase in cultural diversity. Further, they propose that there is a need for more culturally appropriate treatment programs that can respond to the needs of various ethnic minorities. Cunningham and colleagues suggest that family-focused multisystemic therapy (MST) can be adapted to meet the treatment needs of adolescent delinquents and they provide some case examples which illustrate how this can work. Their case examples provide preliminary evidence to suggest therapist cultural sensitivity contributes to enhanced engagement with caregivers (this study specifically focused on therapists' interactions with primary caregivers).

Maori, the indigenous people of New Zealand are overrepresented in offender populations. While they comprise about 15 per cent of the general population they make up about 52 per cent of those who are in prison and about 30 per cent of individuals who are serving community-based sentences (Huriwai *et al.*, 2001). As noted by Huriwai and colleagues, during the 1980s, as there was a growing awareness of the limitations of Western models of treatment there was also an emerging interest in various facets of Maori culture. This led to the development of a number of Maori models of mental health such as Te Pounamu (e.g. Manna, 2001), which literally means 'the greenstone', and Te Whare Tapa Wha (e.g. Glover 2005), which translates as 'the four sided house'.

According to Glover (2005) the emergence of the Te Whare Tapa Wha model represents a paradigm shift according to Kuhn's (1962) model of paradigmatic changes. He makes this comment in order to emphasize the extent of influence that the model has had on understandings of mental health issues within Maori populations. While this may seem to be a rather grand claim, it is consistent with the views of other researchers. For example, Marie *et al.* (2004) state that the model 'has now been canonized within New Zealand public and social policy as the received view of Maori health' (p. 228). Te Whare Tapa Wha uses the image of a house to depict the four key elements of wellbeing, namely: te taha tinana (the physical body), te taha hinengaro (the psychological aspect), te taha wairua (the spiritual realm), and te taha whanau (the family and community). The image of the house is used to demonstrate the interaction and interdependence of all of these elements; for example, if one aspect is weak then the house itself is weakened.

While this model was initially utilized primarily in the mental health field it is now being used within correctional settings in New Zealand. For example, it has been integrated into treatment programs for offenders (such as group-based interventions for sexual offenders) and programs which are designed more specifically for Maori offenders (such as the Maori Therapeutic Program or MTP; New Zealand Department of Corrections, 2008).

Over the last decade there has been a move towards a more culture-inclusive approach to program delivery within correctional settings in New Zealand (New Zealand Department of Corrections, 2009a). Along with the inclusion of Maori models of wellbeing, attempts have been made to tailor Western-based treatment approaches, such as cognitive behavior therapy, to the needs of Maori offenders. For example, The New Zealand Department of Corrections states 'these programmes encourage participants to embrace values, motivations and social commitments derived from the traditional indigenous culture of the offender group' (2009a: 41).

One example of such a program in New Zealand is the Te Piriti Special Treatment Program for child sexual offenders. This program combines a cognitive behavioral approach with tikanga Maori (which translates as customs and traditions based on a Maori world view). The New Zealand Department of Corrections (2003) states that: 'The Te Piriti model works to produce a tikanga Maori context that enables a supportive environment within which to operate cognitive-behavioral based programmes' (p. 13). Interestingly, the Departmental 2003 evaluation (non-Maori N = 133 and Maori N = 68) of the Te Piriti program found that it was effective in reducing recidivism in both Maori and non-Maori sexual offenders. Thus, it was not only Maori who were found to benefit from the approach. This is important because it suggests that all sexual offenders may find the cultural content useful. There may be a number of reasons for this. For example, it is possible that non-Maori offenders benefit from involvement in discussions about the importance of family and of spirituality; both of which are prominent in the Maori cultural content. Also, non-Maori offenders may simply enjoy the cultural content as for many it may be their first experience of learning Maori concepts. This enjoyment may in turn facilitate their engagement in the program and cohesion in the group.

Along with the development of culture-sensitive programs, Maori Focus Units (MFUs) have also been developed in New Zealand in an attempt to create a therapeutic community within the prison setting. A recent evaluation (New Zealand Department of Corrections, 2009b) of the MFU reported that it contributed to the development of a stronger sense of cultural identity as evidenced by an increased motivation for taking part in cultural activities. Furthermore, there was evidence that participation in culture-based activities led to improvements in the quality of relationships with family members. The Department highlighted the significance of this finding with reference to the proposition that good relationships with family and a stable family environment serve to reduce the likelihood of reoffending. The Department also found that involvement in Maori-focused activities led to reductions in the presence of antisocial cognitions.

However, the long term outcomes pertaining to individuals who participated in the Maori Therapeutic Program (the key treatment program which is provided in the unit) at the MFU were less clear. For example, while there was evidence that program participants had learnt a range of useful skills, such as ways to regulate their emotions and manage their behavior, there was little evidence that these skills would necessarily be utilized in real-world situations.

The recidivism data that was collected did not yield statistically significant differences between those who participated in the MTP and/or the MFU and those who did not, although there was a slight reduction in reoffending. The researchers note however, that the lack of statistical significance may have been due to the relatively small sample size (MFU N = 122 and MTP N = 31). Also, they point out that a significant number of the offenders in the MFU would have been assessed as having a low risk of recidivism which would have made it more difficult to identify therapeutic effects.

During the last decade a treatment program has also been developed for Pacific Island offenders in New Zealand. Like Maori, Pacific Island people are over-represented in New Zealand prisons, making up 11 per cent of incarcerated individuals, compared to six per cent in the general population. Saili Matagi (translated as 'in search of winds'), which is a prison-based violence prevention program, combines Western cognitive behavioral therapy and 'Pacific values, beliefs and concepts that are familiar to Pacific offenders' (New Zealand Department of Corrections, 2005: 4). Although it appears that Saili Matagi has not yet been fully evaluated, preliminary research by the Department found that prison staff reported that individuals involved in the program demonstrated noticeable improvements in their behavior.[1]

The limited research that has been completed to date provides preliminary evidence that acknowledging an offender's cultural group and including culture-specific concepts in treatment has a range of benefits for the offender. This may, at least in part, be because doing so shows the offender that the therapist has some understanding of, and respect for, his or her background (although with regard to Te Piriti, this would not explain the benefits for non-Maori offenders). Thus, such an approach may simply facilitate engagement and rapport and enhance group identification and cohesion. Given the complexity of group treatment it seems likely that there are a range of important factors at work, such as the utilization of terminology and ideas that have more resonance for the offender.

However, despite these apparent positive effects of including a cultural component, the impact of such an approach on recidivism is less clear. While research indicates that the Te Piriti program reduces sexual reoffending, evaluations of other programs which target general offending have not shown a statistically significant reduction in recidivism rates. This is not to say that such approaches are not effective, rather that more research is needed in order to determine their true long term impact.

Religion

Mental health

While it appears that there has been very limited previous research on the inclusion of religious components in the treatment of offenders, there has been a reasonable amount of research on such components in the treatment of mental health problems. It has been suggested that given the prevalence of religiosity and the fact that many people use their faith in finding solutions to their personal problems, that it is not reasonable to ignore a client's religious beliefs in therapeutic settings (e.g. Weisman de Mamani *et al.*, 2010). Also, it has been suggested by some researchers (e.g. Powell *et al.*, 2003), that on-going involvement in religious institutions is associated with decreases in negative emotions and increases in positive emotions, perhaps because of religious rituals or the practice of prayer. Thus, giving consideration to an individual's religious affiliations may serve to strengthen a positive aspect of his or her life and allow him or her to feel accepted by the clinician.

According to Weisman de Mamani and colleagues (2010) evidence is generally supportive of the inclusion of religious components in mental health treatment.

Research has found that religious components in treatment lead to general improvements in mental health and wellbeing in both clinical (Longshore *et al.*, 2008; Mason *et al.*, 2009) and nonclinical (Rammohan *et al.*, 2002) populations. However, there is also some evidence that including religious ideas in treatment can be detrimental for individuals who are experiencing psychosis because it can lead to an increase in symptom severity (Siddle *et al.*, 2002; Weisman *et al.*, 2010).

Some studies have examined the efficacy of including a religious component in the treatment of specific mental health problems. For example, Shields and colleagues (Shields *et al.*, 2007) evaluated the inclusion of religion in substance abuse treatment programs and found that there was a 'weak to moderate relationship' between treatment efficacy and religiosity. This is an interesting and important area for research given the ubiquity of Alcoholics Anonymous (AA) groups which rely heavily on religion and spirituality in their Twelve Step approach. For instance a perusal of the twelve steps shows that seven of the steps make reference to God, a higher power, or religious activities such as prayer. Durrant and Thakker (2003) suggest that twelve step approaches 'are fairly clearly delineated cultural groups that have specific norms (e.g. the rejection of drinking), beliefs (that alcoholism is a disease; that alcoholics are powerless to control their drinking), and practices (abstinence, regular meetings, the use of rituals)' (p. 153). Thus, this is especially relevant to the present discussion given the reference to a cultural group.

Religiosity has also been explored in the eating disorders field (e.g. Richards *et al.*, 2007; Smith *et al.*, 2004; Spangler, 2010) and Spangler reports that 88 per cent of individuals diagnosed with an eating disorder expressed a belief in God. Spangler also highlights the positive correlation between 'spiritual wellbeing' and improvements in beliefs about body shape and eating in the research literature. Furthermore, she points out that in some cases attitudes and beliefs associated with disordered eating are intimately connected with an individual's religious and spiritual conceptualizations of the world. For example, Spangler describes a female client who initially viewed eating as unspiritual as it involved giving in to 'base' appetites. The treatment for this client, which was based on a mindfulness approach, included an acknowledgement of the client's conceptualization of her eating behavior, and then cognitive restructuring which focused on her tendency to see food as 'bad' and eating as indulgent. Thus, treatment targeted the moral and religious underpinnings of the woman's eating disorder.

Offending behavior

In 2003 the Department of Corrections in New Zealand opened a Faith-Based Unit (FBU) which was the first of its kind in a New Zealand prison. The unit, which was a joint enterprise between the Department and Prison Fellowship New Zealand (PFNZ) provided prisoners with the opportunity to live in a Christian-oriented prison community and to undertake programs which included religious teachings and various Christian practices (such as Bible study and prayer). As explained in a recent evaluation (New Zealand Department of Corrections, 2010), the development of the unit was based on the idea that exposure to Christian values and morals would lead to positive changes in individuals' beliefs, attitudes, and behaviors. According to the Department, the unit was modeled on similar units that had been developed in other countries, such as in Chile, the United States, and England, many of which reported significant reductions in re-incarceration rates following unit involvement.

The evaluation of the FBU in New Zealand took a qualitative and quantitative approach which involved gathering reconviction and re-imprisonment data (covering those who had spent at least six months at the FBU) and conducting interviews with unit inmates. While the data did not reveal statistically significant differences in reconviction and re-imprisonment rates between FBU prisoners and inmates from other units, small differences were trending in the direction of positive change. The evaluators also noted that the sample size was small ($n = 15$ offender interviews) and that the sample was not likely to be representative. With regard to the interviews, reports from FBU prisoners were overwhelmingly positive; they reported that they were treated with respect within the unit, that they experienced increases in self-esteem and self-worth, and that they felt supported in their decision to make pro-social life changes. The evaluation concluded that although the efficacy of this sort of intervention has not been established, 'it has the potential to be effective...' (p. 24).

A recent study (Laird *et al.*, 2011) explored the connection between religiosity and antisocial behavior in early adolescence (most participants were 12 or 13 years old). The study found that attendance at religious services and giving prominence to religion in one's daily life were associated with less antisocial behavior and greater self-control. However, the prominence factor (giving prominence to religion) was found to be more strongly associated with these variables (less antisocial behavior and greater self-control) than taking part in religious activities. While the authors do not offer a clear explanation for the finding, it is plausible that religious beliefs may offer a moral code which contradicts antisocial behavior. Furthermore, giving prominence to religion in one's daily life may be more strongly associated with adoption of a religious-based moral code than simply taking part in religious activities such as church-going. Laird and colleagues' findings are consistent with other research which has found a significant connection between a weakened sense of right and wrong and increases in offending behavior (e.g. McDermott & Nagin, 2001). If indeed such a connection exists then it is easy to see how religiosity could play an important role in offender treatment.

For example, one of the key components of motivational interviewing (as described by Miller *et al.*, 2004) is *developing discrepancy* which involves encouraging the offender to develop an awareness of inconsistencies between his or her current or previous behavior and his or her values and goals. Given that religious beliefs are often closely tied to values and goals it would be important, especially in encouraging behavior change, to include a discussion of the offender's religious beliefs in treatment.

This discussion overlaps with the issue of an offender's sense of belonging which was explored above. As mentioned therein, Ward's GLM proposes that spirituality is a basic human good. In other words, in order for a human being to be fulfilled and have a satisfying life, spiritual needs must be met. Note that spirituality here is broadly understood; while it may refer to religion, it may also refer more generally to a sense of meaning and purpose. According to Ward (e.g. Thakker & Ward, 2010; Ward *et al.*, 2009), in order for treatment to be successful it must focus on goals as well as risk identification. Thus, finding meaning in life is seen as a fundamental goal as it may provide an alternative to a life dominated by criminal activity. Also relevant here is the responsivity principle of the RNR model which requires that treatment should be consistent with an offender's individual characteristics. According to this view, responsivity would be enhanced if it accommodated the offender's religious beliefs.

As well as contributing a sense of meaning and purpose, involvement in religion can have a range of other benefits, such as providing a social support network (Powell *et al.*, 2003). This is important in offender rehabilitation as research has shown that the presence of support networks reduces an offender's risk of reoffending (e.g. Lodewijks *et al.*, 2010).

As shown by the research covered herein, religion and spirituality can be integrated into rehabilitation in a number of ways. It can take the form of a faith-based prison unit which is essentially a therapeutic community. Alternatively, it can be included as a treatment component which seeks to incorporate the individual's search for meaning in life. With regard to the former, there is some evidence that it may be helpful, however, the causal factors for any benefits are unclear. It may simply be the case that a faith-based unit provides a more pleasant environment within the prison because all of the inmates are making a particular effort to be more civil to one another. Thus, it may not be the faith per se that is important but rather the values that are associated with it.

Conclusion

The ideas covered in this chapter show that the issue of group membership and offender treatment is broad and diverse. Taken together, the research, although rather limited in many areas, suggests that the groups that an offender belongs to have important implications for treatment. Furthermore, therapists need to have some awareness of their tendency to stereotype offenders according to their offence type in order to minimize the impact of stereotyping on their clinical practice.

There is clearly a need for more research in many of these areas. In particular, there is a need for long term outcome studies of faith-based treatment units and culture-focused treatment. While the results of preliminary research have been encouraging it would be helpful to see long term recidivism data of those who have received treatment. Also, future research should aim to identify the particular aspects of these sorts of treatment approaches which are effective. For example, with regard to the Te Piriti Sexual Offender Treatment Program, it would be interesting to determine the factors in treatment that are contributing most to change in participants.

In conclusion, it is perhaps wise to heed the caution outlined by Marie (2010), who suggests, that in relation to Maori in New Zealand, it is problematic to see all Maori as holding the same overarching beliefs. As with any group of people, Maori ascribe to a multitude of world views, not just the traditional Maori world view. Thus, it is important when considering the groups that an offender may belong to, that his unique characteristics are acknowledged, and that he is not simply seen in relationship to his group affiliations. While group membership is important, it is only important insofar as it allows for a more complete understanding of the individual. If too much emphasis is placed on an offender's religion or cultural background there is a risk that the clinician will make assumptions based on stereotypes and generalizations which may overshadow the individual's unique needs.

The best way forward, perhaps, is to forge a clinical pathway that builds a picture of the unique individual that may be composed of various cultural, religious, and offence-related affiliations but which also incorporates the offender's unique manifestation of each of these aspects.

Notes

1   Note that this Departmental data and that from the Te Piriti and MFU evaluations has not been published elsewhere and has therefore not been scrutinised via the peer review process.

References

Andrews, D.A. and Bonta, J. (1998). *The Psychology of Criminal Conduct*. Cincinatti, OH: Anderson Publishing.

Andrews, D.A. and Bonta, J. (2003). *Psychology of Criminal Conduct* (3rd edn). Cincinatti, OH: Anderson Publishing.

Aycicegi-Dinn, A. and Caldwell-Harris, C.L. (2011). Individualism-collectivism among Americans, Turks, and Turkish immigrants to the U.S. *International Journal of Intercultural Relations*, 35, 9–16. DOI: 10.1016/j.ijintrel.2010.11.006.

Baird, B.N. (2005). *The Internship, Practicum, and Field Placement Handbook, Fourth Edition*. Upper Saddle River, NJ: Pearson Education Incorporated.

Beech, A.R. and Hamilton-Giachritsis, C.E. (2005). Relationship between therapeutic climate and treatment outcome in group-based sexual offender treatment programs. *Sexual Abuse: A Journal of Research and Treatment, 17*, 127–140. DOI: 10.1007/s11194-005-4600-3.

Brewer, M.B. (2007). The importance of being we: human nature and intergroup relations. *American Psychologist, 62*, 728–738. DOI: 10.1037/0003-066X.62.8.728.

Collins, S. and Nee, C. (2010). Factors influencing the process of change in sex offender interventions: therapists' experiences and perceptions. *Journal of Sexual Aggression, 16*, 311–331. DOI: 10.1080/13552600903497453.

Cunningham, P.B., Foster, S.L., and Warner, S.E. (2010). Culturally relevant family-based treatment for adolescent delinquency and substance abuse: understanding within-session process. *Journal of Clinical Psychology: In Session, 66*, 830–846. DOI:10.1002/jclp.20709.

Duarté-Vélez, Y., Bernal, G., and Bonilla, K. (2010). Culturally adapted cognitive-behavioral therapy: integrating sexual, spiritual, and family identities in an evidence-based treatment of a depressed Latino adolescent. *Journal of Clinical Psychology: In Session, 66*, 895–906. DOI: 10.1002/jclp.20710.

Durrant, R. and Thakker, J. (2003). *Substance Use and Abuse: Cultural and Historical Perspectives*. Thousand Oaks CA: Sage Publications.

Elliot, I.A. and Beech, A.R. (2009). Understanding online child pornography use: applying sex offense theory to internet offenders. *Aggression and Violent Behaviour, 14*, 180–193. DOI:10.1016/j.avb.2009.03.002.

Fishbach, A., Henderson, M.D., and Koo, M. (2011). Pursuing goals with others: group identification and motivation resulting from things left undone. *Journal of Experimental Psychology:* General, June. DOI: 10.1037/a0023907.

Garrett, T., Oliver, C., Wilcox, D.T., and Middleton, D. (2003). Who cares? The views of sexual offenders about the group treatment they receive. *Sexual Abuse: A Journal of Research and Treatment, 15*, 323–338. DOI: 10.1023/A:1025052212026.

Glover, M. (2005). Analysing smoking using Te Whare Tapa Wha. *New Zealand Journal of Psychology, 34*, 13–19.

Green, B.L. (2010). Culture is treatment: considering pedagogy in the care of aboriginal people. *Journal of Psychosocial Nursing, 48*, 27–34.

Gudjonsson, G.H. and Sigurdsson, J.F. (2000) Differences and similarities between violent offenders and sex offenders. *Child Abuse and Neglect, 24*, 363–372. DOI: 10.1016/S0145-2134(99)00150-7.

Hackett, S. (2000). Sexual aggression, diversity and the challenge of anti-oppressive practice. *The Journal of Sexual Aggression, 5*, 4–20. DOI: 10.1080/13552600008413292.

Hendryx, M., Green, C.A., and Perrin, N.A. (2009). Social support, activities, and recovery from serious mental illness: STARS study findings. *Journal of Behavioral Health Services & Research, 36*, 320–329. DOI: 10.1007/s11414-008-9151-1.

Huriwai, T., Robertson, P.J., Armstrong, D., Kingi, T.P., and Huata, P. (2001). Whanaungatanga – a process in the treatment of Maori with alcohol- and drug-use related problems. *Substance Use and Misuse, 36*, 1033–1051. DOI: 10.1081/JA-100104488.

Kuhn, T. (1962). *The Structure of Scientific Revolutions*. Chicago: The University of Chicago Press.

Laird, R.D., Marks, L.D., and Marrero, M.D. (2011). Religiosity, self-control, and antisocial behaviour: religiosity as a promotive and protective factor. *Journal of Applied Developmental Psychology, 32*, 78–85. DOI: 10.1016/j.appdev.2010.12.003.

Le, T.N. and Stockdale, G.D. (2005). Inidividualism, collectivism, and delinquency in Asian American adolescents. *Journal of Clinical Child and Adolescent Psychology, 34*, 681–691. DOI: 10.1207/s15374424jccp3404_10.

Levenson, J.S., Prescott, D.S., and D'Amora, D.A. (2010). Sex offender treatment: consumer satisfaction and engagement in therapy. *International Journal of Offender Therapy and Comparative Criminology, 54*, 307–326. DOI: 10.1177/0306624X08328752.

Levenson, J.S., Macgowan, M.J., Morin, J.W., and Cotter, L.P (2009). Perceptions of sex offenders about treatment: satisfaction and engagement in group therapy. *Sexual Abuse: A Journal of Research and Treatment, 21*, 35–56. DOI: 10.1177/1079063208326072.

Liu, F.F. and Goto, S.G. (2007). Self-construal, mental distress, and family relations: a mediated moderation analysis with Asian American adolescents. *Cultural Diversity and Ethnic Minority Psychology, 13*, 134–142. DOI: 10.1037/1099-9809.13.2.134.

Lodewijks, H.P., de Ruiter, C., and Doreleijers, T. A. (2010). The impact of protective factors in desistance from violent reoffending: a study in three samples of adolescent offenders. *Journal of Interpersonal Violence, 25,* 568–587. DOI: 10.1177/0886260509334403.

Longshore, D., Anglin, M.D., and Conner, B.T. (2008). Are religiosity and spirituality useful constructs in drug treatment research? *The Journal of Behavioural Health Services & Research, 36*, 177–188. DOI: 10.1007/s11414-008-9152-0.

Manna, L. (2001). Bi-culturalism in practice, 'Te Pounamu:' integration of a Maori model with traditional clinical assessment processes. *The Proceedings of the National Maori Graduates of Psychology Symposium.*

Marie, D. (2010). Maori and criminal offending: a critical appraisal. *The Australian and New Zealand Journal of Criminology, 43*, 282–300. DOI: 10.1375/acri.43.2.282.

Marie, D., Forsyth, D., and Miles, L.K. (2004). Categorical ethnicity and mental health literacy in New Zealand. *Ethnicity and Health, 9*, 225–252. DOI: 10.1080/135578504 2000250085.

Marshall, W.L. (2010). The role of attachments, intimacy, and loneliness in the etiology and maintenance of sexual offending. *Sexual and Relationship Therapy, 25*, 73–85. DOI:10.1080/14681990903550191.

Marshall, W.L. and Burton, D.L. (2010). The importance of group processes in offender treatment. *Aggression and Violent Behaviour, 15*, 141–149. DOI: 10.1016/j. avb.2009.08.008.

Maruna, S. and Roy, K. (2007). Amputation or reconstruction? Notes on the concept of 'knifing off' and desistance from crime. *Journal of Contemporary Criminal Justice, 23*, 104–124. DOI: 10.1177/1043986206298951.

Mason, S.J., Deane, F.P., Kelly, P.J., and Crowe, T.P. (2009). Do spirituality and religiosity help in the management of cravings in substance abuse treatment? *Substance Use and Misuse, 44*, 1926–1940. DOI:10.3109/10826080802486723.

McDermott, S. and Nagin, D.S. (2001). Same or different? Comparing offender groups and covariates over time. *Sociological Methods and Research, 29*, 282–318. DOI: 10.1177/0049124101029003002.

Miller, W.R., Yahne, C.E., Moyers, T.B., Martinez, J., and Pirritano, M. (2004). A randomized trial of method to help clinicians learn motivational interviewing. *Journal of Consulting and Clinical Psychology, 72*, 1050–1062. DOI: 10.1037/0022-006X.72.6.1050.

Moffitt, T.E., Caspi, A., Harrington, H., and Milne, B.J. (2002). Males on the life-course-persistent and adolescence-limited antisocial pathways: follow-up at age 26 years. *Development and Psychopathology, 14*, 179–207.

New Zealand Department of Corrections (2003). *Te Whakakotahitanga: An Evaluation of the Te Piriti Special Treatment Programme for Child Sex Offenders.* Retrieved from http://www.corrections.govt.nz/research (accessed 10 April 2012).

New Zealand Department of Corrections (2005). *Ministerial Review of Department of Corrections Saili Matagi (Pacific Violence Prevention Programme).* Retrieved from http://www.corrections.govt.nz/research (accessed 10 April 2012).

New Zealand Department of Corrections (2008). *Reducing Re-offending through Te Ao Maori.* Retrieved from http://www.corrections.govt.nz/news-and-publications/statutory-reports/maori-strategic-plan-2008-2013 (accessed 10 April 2012).

New Zealand Department of Corrections (2009a). *What works now? a review and Update of Research Evidence Relevant to Offender Rehabilitation Practices within the Department of Corrections.* Retrieved from http://www.corrections.govt.nz/research (accessed 10 April 2012).

New Zealand Department of Corrections (2009b). *Maori Focus Units and Maori Therapeutic Programmes: Evaluation Report.* Retrieved from http:// www.corrections. govt.nz/research (accessed 10 April 2012).

New Zealand Department of Corrections (2010). *Evaluation of the Faith Based Unit and Target Communities Programme.* Retrieved from http:// www.corrections.govt.nz/ research (accessed 10 April 2012).

Oxford English Dictionary (2011). Retrieved from oxforddictionaries.com (accessed 10 April 2012).

Powell, L.H., Shahabi, L., and Thoresen, C.E. (2003). Religion and spirituality: linkages to physical health. *American Psychologist, 58,* 36–52. DOI: 10.1037/0003-066X.58.1.36.

Rammohan, A., Rao, K., and Subbakrishna, D.K. (2002). Religious coping and psychological wellbeing in carers of relatives with schizophrenia. *Acta Psychiatrica Scandinavica, 105,* 356–362. DOI: 10.1034/j.1600-0447.2002.1o149.x.

Reimer, W.L. and Mathieu, T. (2006). Therapeutic factors in group treatment as perceived by sex offenders: a 'consumers' report.' *Journal of Offender Rehabilitation, 42,* 4, 59–73. DOI: 10.1300/J076v42n04_04.

Richards, P.S., Hardman, R.K., & Berrett, M.E. (2007). *Spiritual Approaches in the Treatment of Eating Disorders.* Washington DC, US: American Psychological Association.

Sani, F., Magrin, M.E., Scrignaro, M., and McCollum, R. (2010). In-group identification mediates the effects of subjective in-group status on mental health. *The British Psychological Journal of Social Psychology, 49,* 883–893. DOI: 10.1348/014466610X517414.

Sanghara, K.K., and Wilson, J.C. (2006). Stereotypes and attitudes about child sexual abusers: a comparison of experienced and inexperienced professionals in sex offender treatment. *Legal and Criminological Psychology, 11,* 229–244. DOI: 10.1348/135532505X68818.

Shields, J.J., Broome, K.M., Delany, P.J., Fletcher, B.W., and Flynn, P.M. (2007). Religion and substance abuse treatment: individual and program effects. *Journal for the Scientific Study of Religion, 46,* 355–371. DOI: 10.1111/j.1468-5906.2007.00363.x.

Siddle, R., Haddock, G., Tarrier, N., and Faragher, E.B. (2002). Religious delusions in patients admitted to hospital with schizophrenia. *Social Psychiatry and Psychiatric Epidemiology, 37,* 130–138. DOI: 10.1007/s001270200005.

Smith, M.H., Richards, P.S., and Maglio, C.J. (2004). Examining the relationship between religious orientation and eating disturbances. *Eating Disorders, 5,* 171–180. DOI: 10.1016/S1471-0153(03)00064-3.

Spangler, D.L. (2010). Heavenly bodies: religious issues in cognitive behavioural treatment of eating disorders. *Cognitive and Behavioral Practice, 17,* 358–370. DOI: 10.1016/j.cbpra.2009.05.004.

Taylor, M. and Quayle, E. (2003). *Child Pornography: An Internet Crime.* Hove, U.K: Brunner-Routledge.

Thakker, J. and Ward, T. (1998). Culture and classification: the cross-cultural application of the DSM-IV. *Clinical Psychology Review, 19,* 843–874. DOI: 10.1016/S0272-7358(97)00107-4.

Thakker, J. and Ward, T. (2010). Relapse prevention: a critique and proposed reconceptualization. *Behaviour Change, 27*, 154–175. DOI: 10.1375/bech.27.3.154.

Thakker, J. and Ward, T. (2011). An integrated theory of sexual reoffending. *Psychology, Crime, and Law*, 1–15. DOI:10.1080/13218719.2011.561765.

Ward, T. (2002). Good lives and the rehabilitation of offenders: promises and problems. *Aggression and Violent Behavior, 7*, 513–528. DOI: 10.1016/S1359-1789(01)00076-3.

Ward, T. (2009). The extended mind theory of cognitive distortions in sex offenders. *Journal of Sexual Aggression, 15*, 247–259. DOI: 10.1080/13552600903263087.

Ward, T. and Gannon, T.A. (2006). Rehabilitation, etiology, and self-regulation: the Good Lives Model of sexual offender treatment. *Aggression and Violent Behaviour, 11*, 77–94. DOI: 10.1016/j.avb.2005.06.001.

Ward, T. and Stewart, C.A. (2003). The treatment of sexual offenders: risk management and good lives. *Professional Psychology: Research and Practice, 34*, 353–360. DOI: 10.1037/0735-7028.34.4.353.

Ward, T., Collie, R.M., and Bourke, P. (2009). Models of offender rehabilitation: the good lives model and the risk-need-responsivity model. In R. Beech, L.A. Leam, and K.D. Browne (eds), *Assessment and Treatment of Sex Offenders*. Chichester, UK. Wiley-Blackwell.

Ward, T., Gannon, T.A., and Yates, P.M. (2008). The treatment of offenders: current practice and new developments with an emphasis on sex offenders. *International Review of Victimology, 15*, 179–204.

Weisman de Mamani, A.G., Tuchman, N., and Duarte, E.A. (2010). Incorporating religion/ spirituality into treatment for serious mental illness. *Cognitive and Behavioural Practice, 17*, 348–357. DOI: 10.1016/j.cbpra.2009.05.003.

Witte, T.D., Placido, C.D., Gu, D. and Wong, S.C.P. (2006). An investigation of the validity and reliability of the Criminal Sentiments Scale in a sample of treated sex offenders. *Sex Abuse, 18*, 249–258. DOI: 10.1177/107906320601800303.

Yalom, I.D. (1995). *The Theory and Practice of Group Therapy* (3rd edn). New York: Basic Books.

Index